Art & Craft of Writing Fiction

First Writer's Manual

Mendocino, California

victoriamixon.com

Published by La Favorita Press
PO Box 1203, Mendocino, CA 95460
lafavoritapress.com

ISBN 978-1-944227-00-5

Text set in Book Antiqua, by Monotype Staff, Microsoft Typography.
Titles and headings set in Poor Richard, by Keystone Type Foundry.

Manufactured in the United States of America

Art & Craft of Writing

Sign up to get your
free books on writing!

artandcraftofwriting.com/freebooks

"Mixon is brilliant.
These are the lessons
of a writing lifetime."
– Roz Morris, bestselling ghostwriter
and author of *Nail Your Novel*

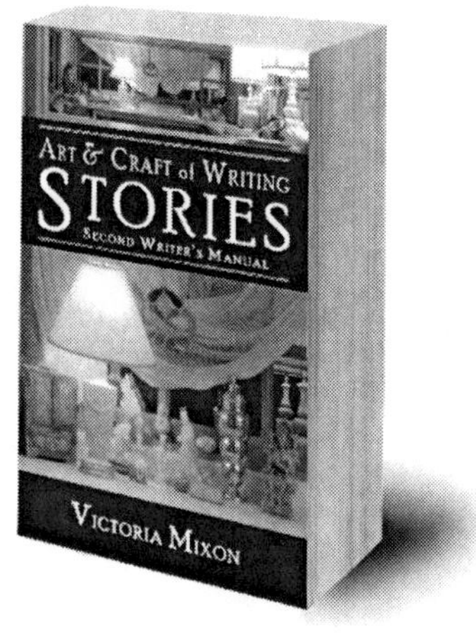

artandcraftofwriting.com

Acknowledgements

I am deeply grateful to every single one of my editing clients and blog and magazine readers for their honest, essential feedback and enthusiasm, which made this book first something to dream about, then something to wrassle with, then something real. I am especially grateful to my friends Carolyn Cassady, for her perfect grasp of proper grammar, Lucia Orth, for her support and encouragement, and Amy Bowman, for her humor and Yahtzee expertise. Above all else, I am eternally grateful to my husband, who did absolutely everything to create this book except write it—edit, format, publish, photograph the cat, everything—and my son, who kept me supplied throughout the writing with whipped cream and strawberries and always, every day, his extraordinary joy in living.

Table of Contents

INTRODUCTION

BOOK I: WRITING

PART 1: DEVELOPMENTAL ISSUES

Character is *Content*

Plot is *Context*

PART 2: LINE ISSUES

PROSE

SCENES ARE *SHOWING*

PART 3: COPY ISSUES

Book II: BEING A WRITER

Appendix

Introduction

Excavating the Bones of Storytelling

Why do human beings tell stories?

Seeking Hope

When did humans first begin telling stories?

And why do we continue?

Say it's 30,000 years ago. Say you're a member of a small tribe living out there on the surface of the planet without the benefit of fancy engineered stick-frame housing, electricity, interior plumbing, or 911. You lose members of the tribe fairly regularly to gangrene, food poisoning, hungry predators, and the occasional fatal illness masquerading as evil spirits. So you've got a lot on your mind.

Every night the dark comes back, and you're stuck inside your lonely little head out there, with nothing between you and excruciating death but the fire and a bunch of relatives you might not even like very much. What would you want?

A story.

A story about someone like you—a human being—who doesn't have to live this way. A story about this someone facing the same stuff you face so it's believable, but dressed up symbolically so it isn't so terrifying.

It's not a lion that's going to eat you, it's a wizard who's going to make you their slave. It's not your favorite aunt who got cold and stole your goatskin, it's a demon that's taken over her body. It's not your chief, your hero, who killed his wife in a fit of jealousy, it's some mysterious person who had more cunning, secret reasons for wanting her dead, and your chief is going to be very happy with you if you can prove it.

This someone just like you faces this scary symbolic stuff, goes through your terror, stretches their resources to the utmost, almost doesn't make it (as you're so deathly afraid you won't)—and, unexpectedly in the eleventh hour, *wins*!

Hurrah! Huzzah! The long, dark night is defeated, the fear is vanquished, and you're safe. *Forever*.

It's the same life, but it's different. They're overwhelming odds, but they're magically surmountable. You're the same scared person inside, but you're stronger, smarter, luckier, more attractive, and people like you. The ones who don't like you simply *misunderstand* you.

The world is sane, and your life makes sense.

For just an hour in the darkest part of your day, when you can't see beyond your tent and the lions are making dinner conversation back and forth over your head, you get to hide in this imaginary place.

This is why humans began telling stories. It's why we drew on the walls of caves, why we painted designs on our bodies.

"We can transcend the madness," we were saying.

And this is why we still tell them. Why we listen to them. Why we read, even cheap mass-market paperbacks—sometimes *especially* cheap mass-market paperbacks—desperate for anything to satisfy this eternal longing to know that everything, finally, ended okay. We made it through in one piece. It was all worth it, after all.

It might even have turned out that we were *cool.*

Finding Validation

But what about tragedies?

You don't get to the end of *Romeo and Juliet* and think, "What a relief, everything ended hunky-dory, just like I hoped it would!" Not while you're picking your way across the dead bodies, you don't.

You don't read Richardson's *Clarissa* and say, "Thank heavens that poor child was saved in time." She wasn't.

The ancient Greeks didn't get to the end of *Medea* and say to each other, "I knew those weren't *really* their children she fed to him." No. They were.

But a funny thing happens at the end of a tragedy. A funny and entirely pivotal thing: everybody dies—except the audience.

In fact, even the actors don't die. The fictional characters in the stories don't die. (Like zombies, fictional characters are always ready to be resurrected on a whim.) The publisher, producer, editor, agent, and guy stoking the fire around which we all huddle don't die. The author or storyteller *doesn't die.*

Everything turns out all right, in spite of death, destruction, and mayhem.

As Paul Bowles so accurately said, you are not I.

Readers *love* this.

Now, granted, it's harder to sell fiction these days in which the heroine and hero go down with the ship. *Titanic,* the movie, pretended to tell this story, but actually didn't. We're a spoiled race in a comfortable era. We don't do a lot of cowering by the tent while a lioness sports with one of our grandparents' bodies. We don't live under the constant taxation of armies rampaging back and forth across our little fields, trampling the crops we need to survive the winter and brutalizing our relatives in front of our eyes and kidnapping us into lifelong slavery. We don't even cope with the daily caution not to run out and catch the bubonic plague, like the Elizabethans who first brought *Romeo and Juliet* and their author their equivalent of blockbuster status.

We live a fairly pampered life, all things considered, so maybe we have less of a stomach for seeing everyone dead and dismembered in the end, leaving us to rejoice in our fully-memberedness. We *are* fully-membered. We have doctors and—just in case—lawyers. Dying of dismemberment isn't really one of our concerns.

And maybe what's going to keep us up all night turning those pages isn't whether or not Medea really cooked the kids, but whether or not she got a new lease on life after she recovered from empty-nest syndrome.

Maybe our idea of really scary obstacles *is* a bit tame by comparison.

You've got to expect a population to eat up the stories that give it a sense of comfort over its own very real nightmares. Lots of mass-market fiction characters lose sleep over their struggle for celebrity. To the average modern mass-market enthusiast, this seems like a very real concern indeed.

We writers ought to understand. *Emma Bovary, c'est moi.*

So tell me a story about someone who loses their job to the economy, loses their home to the real estate crash, has to cash in their 401k, winds up divorced, and now their teenagers hate them. How do they cope? And please don't just leave them there and call it a tragedy, because we're simply not that hardy anymore. We won't feel good enough, looking at our own kids later and saying to each other, "At least they're not skinheads."

Or tell me about creatures who feel just like me, facing troubles weirdly like mine, only with magical powers—people in the future, people in the past, people from other realities crossing the line into ours, easily-recognizable archetypes, anyone just like me *but one step removed.*

Tell me how they make it.

Or else tell me a story about someone beautiful, wealthy, sensitive, adored—an icon of my culture—who loses their best-beloved to cold-hearted evil and intrigue but finds even better love in the end.

It's not me, but it could be. And that's what matters.

It *could* be.

Creating Art

So, why are so many of us trying so hard to get ourselves on the speaking end of this deal?

The truth is that it's more comforting to be the audience than the speaker. It's simpler to listen than it is to invent. It's easier to read a story than it is to write it. This has always been the case.

Oddly, though, the *perception* of this has changed in the past century. And the change has accelerated with alarming speed most recently, as books are cranked out faster and faster, their publishers—desperate for unexpected blockbusters to pay their bills—snatching up lesser and lesser works with a greater and greater sense of panic, no longer editing, much less mentoring, so the clichés and plot holes and irregularities in voice go straight to press undetected.

All of this creates a composting heat for the extraordinary number of amateurs writing today, making it only too easy to read the publishers' hunger as an open invitation to gamble on the reading public's lack of discernment.

Nowadays we often get into storytelling, not for survival, but for notoriety.

Fame! Fortune!

It all looks so *simple*.

In this hyper-literate era, pretty much anyone can stick both arms into writing up to their armpits and squish it around like mud. We can mold it. We can recycle it. We can throw it at each other. And this is what many of us do.

Years ago, I went with a friend to an art show at UC Berkeley, the culmination of a year's worth of MFA student efforts. We walked through room after room of canvases and sculptures, photographs and installations, up stairs and down, pausing in doorways to look ahead and behind. When we came out the other end, my friend asked me what I thought.

"This might very well be the insides of these people's heads," I said. "But there are the insides of some people's heads I don't want to see."

Now, Jackson Pollock can get away with enormous canvases that look as though they've been driven like cars through a paintwash. Maya Ying Lin can design two surfaces of polished black granite to reflect the infinity of death into the faces of survivors. Charlie Chaplin can stick two forks in bread rolls and caper for an audience for a hundred years.

But many of today's aspiring writers don't want to do that. No, they don't. They want to create art about *themselves*.

Fortunately, the role of the professional artist is not to look in a mirror and, like some gruesome coroner, pull open their chest to admire the contents, then photograph it and offer it for sale. We all have squishy insides. We might be fascinated by our own, but we're not fascinated by each other's.

The role of the professional artist is to look outward, into life, and select more than one disparate real thing—a skull and a hollyhock, a child's toy and the notes of an octave, a dying woman and a piece of driftwood—and find in them the essential truth about life basic to them both. Georgia O'Keeffe, Pyotr Tchaikovsky, and Rebecca West found these real things, linked them in the essential, and gave them to the rest of us.

It's not easy. And not everybody who tries will hang in there long enough to get good at it. But for those who *do*—like our ancestors drawing on the walls of caves 30,000 years ago—even after their lives are long over, the movement of their lives continues on through ours.

This is the part of the artist that's worth knowing. This is the nature of art that remains.

Book I

WRITING

Chapter 1

Writing from the Internal World with Jane Bowles

The relationship between writer & work

Paul Bowles wrote *The Sheltering Sky* day by day, in bed in North Africa, using each day's experiences for his work. Although the plot rambles a bit, the writing's beautiful. (Well, of course, it's *Paul Bowles*.)

However, my favorite thing about Bowles is his wife, Jane.

Jane Bowles was also a writer. In fact, she was the writer who first inspired Paul to try his hand at fiction. He was originally a composer, a *protégé* of Aaron Copland, while she'd been writing since she was quite young. Her first completed work, now lost, was written entirely in French. (She was American, educated in Switzerland.) One of her most powerful works is a very brief puppet play.

Sadly for us, she wrote little and published even less, due in part to her tendency to lose manuscripts, one apparently left behind in a taxi and another blown out an open window in Mexico City.

I found Jane's work in a used bookstore on lower Polk Street in San Francisco in about 1994. I bought two volumes: *My Sister's*

Hand in Mine: The Collected Works of Jane Bowles and *A Little Original Sin: The Life and Work of Jane Bowles* by Millicent Dillon.

Those two books kept me absorbed for years.

Jane wrote in the most oddly un-literary style imaginable. There's the strong suggestion that she didn't, in fact, know how to write at all. (Paul castigated her for her sloppy pages, although she casually dismissed him.) Her sentences are often ungainly, her characters inexplicable, her choice of detail bizarre. Her plots aren't experimental, but they certainly give the impression she didn't know where they were going. Some authors can bumble along like that, and you never know. But with Jane. . .you know.

Her one novel, *Two Serious Ladies*, begins with a startling portrait of a highly unlikable character, Christina Goering, who at about thirteen years old bullies her sister's friend with her religious zeal. As a portrait, it's wonderful: exact and powerful, unflattering and still ringing almost unbearably true. The mania with which Christina demands that the other child cooperate in the "game" and the other child's unwilling cooperation are absolutely typical of children's interactions. Jane might have been describing a real event, except for one thing—the author's voice swings from understatement to exaggeration with precision, creating a portrait not only unbearably true, but hilarious.

And that's the end of that childhood story. The next thing we know, we're with the adult Christina, and the rest of that section of the book is about her, her friendships with the feckless lout Arnold and his wicked but charming father, her hostile companion Miss Gamelon who, ridiculously, becomes Arnold's "Bubbles," and her eventual abandonment of home and friends to seek an enlightenment that even she doesn't understand.

You'd think this would be enough story for one novel.

But, no. There's another serious lady. (There were originally three, but Paul convinced Jane that three was one too many.) Frieda Copperfield is a faintly-disguised self-portrait of Jane herself traveling in Central America with her fond, bemused, and distant husband, a sincere neurotic in his own right. (Jane and Paul had traveled in Central America for their honeymoon on the money she inherited when they married.) The events and descriptions are vividly authentic. They're also, in their different way, as hilariously idiosyncratic as those involving Christina.

Frieda is fussy and persnickety rather than bossy and overbearing, while expressing herself with childlike sincerity and a weird sort of profundity.

Frieda doesn't want to be in Panama, but she loves her husband, and this is where he wants to be. It takes her practically no time at all to find, in her fussy, weird way, something in Panama that speaks to her so profoundly that she becomes hopelessly addicted to it and, eventually, even chooses it over her husband – a brothel run by a no-nonsense British expatriate and peopled by Pacifica, the powerful and almost maternal prostitute, and her uncontrollable hangers-on. For some reason, this brothel feels to the easily-terrified Frieda like home.

Frieda, like Christina, lives in an internal world so bizarre that it's actually unintelligible from the outside. Yet its logic is magical to the woman who lives inside it.

Jane wrote often of this internal world, where what was strange to others felt natural and "sweet" to her. It forms the basis of her entire body of work, small as that is. Her characters are tormented, desperate, grasping – they fight for the words in their mouths, the gestures between themselves and others, the very thoughts in their own heads.

Every day you and I wake up wondering what the characters we are will do today. Humankind works so intently upon creating an external world of order and sense precisely *because* each of us lives alone in an internal world designed around logic peculiar to each of us individually. In this way, we're all in the closet. We can't ever join the living the way we long to—wholly and completely, with every fragment of guilt and shame healed. We know this about ourselves. And, just as importantly, we know it about each other.

Our common external world contains the stuff of fiction, the material we need in order to share the stories we tell. However, it's in the unique logic of the guilty, secretive, convoluted internal world that we find our essential links.

Chapter 2

Understanding Copy, Line, & Developmental Issues

The relationship between writer & world

Now, you should know that editors talk in terms of copy editing, line editing, and developmental editing. This is not an editors' secret handshake. This is because it takes that many distinctions to discuss in detail the intricacies of the art and craft of fiction. And if you want to learn to translate your daydreams into literature, you'll want to learn these terms, too:

Copy Editing

Copy editing refers to grammar and punctuation. (Sometimes both copy editing and line editing are referred to as copy editing, and sometimes both are referred to as line editing, but they are in fact two distinctly different things.) Copy editing is about written communication, so it's just following the rules. There is, honestly, very little of either art or craft to it. You simply have to learn the rules. They're different in the US, Britain, and other English-speaking countries.

Line Editing

Line editing refers to prose. It's about the craft of writing, and that means paragraph structure, sentence flow, word choice, and language-related techniques. That also means voice, style, readability, and forward movement. And in storytelling it means the difference between scenes and exposition. The only way to hone your skills is to stay away from crap and read great fiction.

Read it, read it, read it.

Train your mind to expect certain things in certain orders. Train your language to come out of you in simple and pleasing rhythms. Use short, declarative sentences interspersed with long, melodious ones.

When you edit, cut every single unnecessary word and be willing to rewrite anything and everything, whether it needs it or not. Take your time. Revise until it's just right. In this way, you know that you have written your story in exactly the words it takes and no others. That's craft.

Learn to recognize clichés.

Understand clarity.

Developmental Editing

Developmental editing refers to storytelling, both the art and the craft. This involves not just plot structure, but also character development and motivation, theme, premise, symbolism, tension, pacing, and the author's search for truth.

Truth?

Yes, truth.

That's the art of storytelling.

There are rules to developmental issues that, while not enforced through venerable documentation like grammar and punctuation guides, are enforced by readers who put down badly-imagined books and walk away.

And there are expectations that readers bring to fiction, which you really need to understand.

Readers read stories for two purposes:

1) to learn something they don't already know about survival
2) to be reassured that life is actually worth surviving

No matter what you write, no matter how you approach it, no matter what you expect to gain by it, you can never afford to forget these two expectations.

They are your reasons for what you do.

Part 1

Developmental Issues

Chapter 3

Bewitching Your Reader with Isak Dinesen

What is a story? characters in a plot

Isak Dinesen knew an enormous amount about the art of storytelling. She took as her sacred text *The Arabian Nights* and believed that everything we need to know about storytelling can be found among the thousand and one nights of that fourteenth-century Arabic manuscript. Her classic story "The Deluge at Norderney" ends at dawn after eighty pages of extraordinarily lush, complex, absorbing multiple narratives, a Rube Goldberg exercise in storytelling, on the French line – terribly unfair if you speak no French – "At that moment of her narration, Scheherazade saw morning arrive and, discreet, fell silent."

What did Dinesen see in *The Arabian Nights* that she saw nowhere else in the fiction available to her in her era, the first half of the twentieth century? Keep in mind that she was a native Dane, a highly educated aristocrat who spoke Danish, English, and French, as well as enough Kikuyu, Swahili, and Maa to act as doctor and judge for those living on her coffee plantation in the mountains of Kenya. The number of stories available to her was vast. And she *read* – read and analyzed and thought and talked about fiction with great eloquence and insight.

Dinesen said she began her writing career telling stories to her nieces in the evenings, making up the plots as she went along from the germ of a sentence given to her by one of the girls, all the way to a finale that wrapped the story like a Möbius strip back onto its original premise. In this way she taught herself how to create out of a seed of an idea, how to bring characters alive, how to plot, how to embellish, how to pace, how to give her characters' dilemmas meaning, and most of all how to keep an audience's attention. This was the pivotal element of *The Arabian Nights* in Dinesen's eyes—Shahrazad's very *life* depended upon her ability to keep her audience's attention.

Dinesen loved the cliffhanger element of each of the individual thousand and one nights. She loved that ending, "Morning arrived, and Shahrazad fell silent."

The thing we always hear in the publishing world is that there are two types of story: character-driven and plot-driven. But apparently nobody ever told this to Dinesen.

Dinesen's characters are mythical: the wonderful and cryptic Fanny and Eliza De Connick hold a feast for the ghost of their beloved dead brother; the strange child Jens claims his adoptive mother is the birth mother he can't possibly remember and turns out to be right; the mysterious and bewitching Pellegrina claims that she could not be accused of selling her soul to the Devil when she'd rather give it to him as a present.

At the same time Dinesen's plots are miracles: intricate, detailed, carrying an extraordinary sense of place and time (almost always in the past).

The universe Dinesen created was rich and profound, bigger than life and at the same time nearly microscopic. It seems impossible to keep a reader's attention through the labyrinths she forced on her characters. And yet she's hypnotic.

Her stories go on and on like fascinating dreams. Her characters tell stories. Their characters tell stories. The levels drop down and down, into the subterranean passages of the collective unconscious. By the time we come out the other end, we're changed. We've seen the other side of the world's tapestry.

If there is one thing we can learn from Dinesen, it is to go deep. The surface of a story—the simple progress of characters toward their fate, the bare bones of their dilemma—is only the beginning. We write our stories, and then write them again more honestly. Then write them again. And again.

Eventually, we find ourselves wandering the halls of the universe in the caverns inside us. Strange things live there, awkward creatures and inexplicable plot twists, actions and dialog both familiar and incomprehensible. We don't worry anymore about explaining this world to our reader. Just describing it is enough. We can look up to the light and see the reflections on the glass ceiling above, refractions upon the surface of the ocean. We are below the surface. We are under the wave.

Find out the truth about what's there. We're wading in the primeval sea, where the collective unconscious was born, and if we're very, very tough and very, very hardworking and very, very lucky, maybe we'll make it back into the world of light with fragments of it in our very own hands.

Then dawn comes. And, like Shahrazad, we fall silent.

Chapter 4

Storytelling

How to tell a story

Distinguishing Between Storytelling & Fiction

The only reason I know for writing fiction is to tell stories. And the only reason I know for telling stories is the same as that for telling jokes: to get to the punchline.

Once I had a client who was writing a brilliant story about a group of children trying to pry the truth about life out of a new baby. They asked the baby questions. They threatened and cajoled. They banged their heads with frustration. In the end, they had a food fight.

When I described my day to my twelve-year-old over dinner that night, he laughed himself off his chair. "They squirted mustard and ketchup all over the living room!" He loved it!

That was storytelling.

Those of us who have been writing fiction for a long time know how easy it is to get caught up in the act of writing, in the characterizations, structure, descriptions, dialog, polishing of language, and – that most hair-rending of all issues – whether or not it's *ever* okay to use words ending in -ly. We wrack our brains over this stuff. We read intensely for hours on end, taking notes, researching how the greats handled it. We lie awake nights and weep.

And yet the questions, "What happens in *Madame Bovary*? What's the point of *Moby Dick*? Why read about Scrooge?" have simple answers: "A woman who read too many romance novels became so deranged that she killed herself. A sea captain blew his entire life chasing a single whale. A man who hated to give learned from a couple of ghosts why it matters."

My client told the story of how a bunch of children made a mess.

Only someone as highly-educated as John Gardner is going to explain that *Moby Dick*'s nearly 1,000 pages of nineteenth-century technical authority is brilliantly established by its brief first sentence. Only Flannery O'Connor is going to point out that *Madame Bovary* contains some of the most exemplary descriptive passages in the English language (although it was written in French). And only I am going to go out on a limb here and suggest that, if you can't learn from ghosts, you can't learn from anybody.

The basic act of fiction is the art of telling a story. We can—and will—spend far more hours and energy on the craft of *writing* fiction than we do on creating the story itself, but the reason for writing a story remains the same: to tell it.

This is true for all the arts. The basic act of creativity is saying something worth saying. If we're painters, we say it on a canvas. If we're dancers, we say it through movement. If we're sculptors, we say it in stone. If we're musicians, we say it with melody. And if we're storytellers, we say it in so many words.

However, if we have nothing to say, it doesn't matter how good we are at our medium. We have created nothing.

Whatever else we do, whatever other skills we learn, however many years we spend bent over our desks, we must never lose sight of the purpose behind writing fiction.

We're here to tell a story.

Writing What You Know

Nobody wants to write fiction about what they know. I mean, if we were interested in what we already know, we wouldn't waste so much time making up *fiction*, now would we?

Besides, we keep hearing that literary fiction is dead, fiction for the sake of beautiful fiction is dead, the only thing selling these days is genre. Thriller. Mystery. Fantasy. Science Fiction. Historical. Romance.

But nobody lives that way!

Then again, we wouldn't be writing fiction if we were in love with journalism, either. Hey, everyone, let's do some research! *There's* a conversation-stopper.

I was at a party once with friends who lived in a big converted house full of little artsy apartments. I was working with abused children at the local Battered Women's Shelter at the time, and I got in an argument with a neighbor who had what I considered less-than-accurate views on the subject. The argument grew heated. I held my ground. I cited statistics. She finally conceded, but grudgingly and with bad grace. The next day I got a call from my friend, who told me she'd chastised her neighbor on my behalf, saying, "For crying out loud, you acted as though Victoria made those statistics up!"

"I did," I said. "But I was still right."

This is why I write fiction. I *like* making stuff up.

So does this mean that we should all write stories we know nothing about, just get in there and say whatever we feel like saying, crank up the fictional volume, really let it fly? Should we flout that old fuddy-duddy control freak who sputters, "Write what you know, you hooligans! Write what you *know*!"?

Sorry. No.

There is no question that a really good writer—someone who's earned the title—writes about what they know. It's inevitable. That knowledge is the source of all telling detail.

But how do we know about our chosen genres? How do we know about murder investigations, future quantum physics, witches' zombie covens, seventeenth-century Southeast Asia, sky-diving over K-2, and love that never falters, fades, or succumbs to child custody disputes?

Two ways.

The first is that ever-horrible sucker of the creative soul: research. If you hear screams, they're from me. But if we're interested in it enough to write about it, we'd better be interested enough to learn about it. Otherwise, we'd better write about something else.

The second is human nature. We're human. We haven't lived in a closet all our lives. This means we have two resources at our disposal, resources so fundamental and all-encompassing that, although great fiction has been written without research, no great fiction ever has been written without these both: personal knowledge of daily human life, and personal knowledge of the people we know.

Of course, I'm not suggesting that we go out and concoct the perfect plan to murder the one we hate most in the world, however good this idea might sound in passing. I am not suggesting that we spend our evenings in mad scientist laboratories in our walk-in closets investigating alchemy, or experiment with belladonna, or adopt a Thai beggar, or fling ourselves off a Himalayan peak. (Go ahead, fall in love, it really is great—But be prepared for the therapy bills if you want it to last.)

I am, however, suggesting that, if we resurrect Captain Nemo and give him a unicorn buddy and set them investigating the murder of innocent Wiccan Tibetan athletes who love each other with a timeless love, we imbue them all with the mannerisms, foibles, blind spots, nervous ticks, conversational oddities, and overriding passions with which we're most familiar.

Make them spill their coffee. Give them clothes they forget to mend. Put pebbles in their shoes, telemarketers on their phones, glitches in their Internet connections. Let them have bad breath in the morning. Let them screw up. Let them get lost. Let them fight.

Let them lose.

And, whatever else we do, we must pretend to hide their greatest lifelong shame while scribbling it all over the sky for the other characters to see. Give them not only pride, but humility, not only confidence, but despair. Make their lives suck in *exactly* the way life so often sucks for us.

We must write what we know.

Pushing Your Reader Off the Rainbow

Raymond Carver studied under John Gardner and said later that Gardner had absolutely no use for shock endings. Gardner felt it was dishonest to deliberately withhold information from the reader. Why? What possible good could it do? It's not like writing is a practical joke.

The writer who turns their work into a trick or a gimmick doesn't know what writing is. Writing is not about fooling our reader.

Writing is about sharing everything we have.

Writing is an art form that communicates directly, by way of the lingual brain through which we process direct thought, between the writer and the reader. Writing is as close as we can get to sitting at the kitchen table with our reader, taking their hands, and saying in the utter nakedness of our soul, "This is how life is for me."

Is that the moment to yank their chair out from under them?

Once, a friend told me the story of a man who raised his little child to jump off a table into his arms. Week after week, the child jumped off the table into his father's arms, until one day the father stepped aside and let the child fall to the floor.

"That'll teach you never to trust anyone," he said.

Do you want that idiot to be you?

Our work as a writer is to create a world our reader can believe in. We go into it the way we'd step into thin air, blindly, in unavoidably two-dimensional faith.

There is nothing between us and this new world but a page. At first, the page looks like all this new world is: two dimensions, two colors, black and white. Nothing else. Just us and this painful, simple truth.

We have nothing yet in which to believe.

Then slowly and methodically, carefully and with the most single-minded attention, we open ourselves up to this world and begin to take notes. Why do we want to be here? Why would our reader? There's something in this world that means everything to us, and it's our job to find it and write down everything we possibly can about it.

We write. We're writers.

This world must be visible. It needs specific light and dark, scenes, sights, and objects with shapes and sizes and colors. It must be audible. It needs sounds and silence, voices and a lack of voices. It must be tangible, with textures and temperatures, tastes and smells, bodily experiences and the absence of them. It must be a real place. We are here to record that real place.

And while we're learning everything we can about this world, we look for the characters who own it. We watch them from a distance, paying attention to their physical bodies, their ages, their mannerisms, the sounds of their voices. We see how they interact with each other, what words they choose and do not choose. We ask ourselves, "Why say that? Why not say the other thing?" And we listen for the answers. We note down their body language, their tics and gestures, how they move around each other and through their environment, whether or not they touch, if they do how they do it, if they don't why. We keep asking ourselves, "Why? Why this? Why here? Why now?"

We can introduce ourselves to them, but we don't try to make ourselves part of their story. We're not. We're the writers.

We pile up scenes on paper and in our minds, watching these characters living in their world. We begin to see the links between the scenes and realize that certain scenes, when put together in a certain order, create certain episodes. *Aha!* we think. *That's very interesting!*

We play around a little. What if the scenes really go in this other order, maybe not that scene but another one, and they end in a scene we haven't seen yet—what episode does that create?

Oh, yes. That episode tells more about this world. That episode clarifies so much.

The episodes begin to pile up and bear resemblances to each other. We realize that they're following a trajectory. Some episodes that we figured out later happened before the first episodes we figured out, but that's all right. The trajectory is beginning to make sense. We see the base of the rainbow. We see where it's going.

There's the first disaster! We can tell because it hurts, but it hurts in a kind of subtle, complex way. There's the second disaster! That one hurts more—it changes things. There's the third disaster! That one's a double-header, and it wreaks real havoc.

Our characters are damaged now. But they're undaunted. They're made of tough stuff.

We're at the peak of the rainbow, and we can see in all directions. *Of course.* This is where it was all leading. With their personalities, in this world, under these circumstances, with that series of disasters behind them—where else could they have wound up?

We stop awhile, sit down, dangle our legs, and ask ourselves in all seriousness, "Where else could they have wound up?"

As though it were a holograph of the whole, we move into that possibility. What's there?

Then we spend some time thinking about rewriting the entire thing.

This is the work of creating a novel. It's complex, it's exhausting, and it takes a *really* long time. If you're in a hurry, I wouldn't bother to start. We're not going to fly through becoming writers any more than we're going to fly through becoming high-divers. At least a failed writer doesn't wind up in the hospital.

Because after we've explored this entire new world, climbed the rainbow with our characters, taken in the view, made sure that we've looked under every rock and turned over every leaf, written it down, written it down, written it down—we still have more to do. We must get our characters back to earth. It's going to take everything we have and know and believe. These are their lives we hold in our hands.

And while our characters are surviving or not surviving whatever we have to do to them, our reader is falling off the rainbow into space, taken there by the naked insight into what means everything to us.

We don't push our reader off the rainbow by driving a story into them like a car. We do it by leading them to an extraordinary, vivid, real view and then leaving them standing out there—on the thin air of faith.

Character is *Content*

Chapter 5

Telling the Truth with Emily Brontë

Stories are about human beings

Wuthering Heights' story of the remorseless Catherine and uncontrollable Heathcliff bears all the marks of a particularly rancid 1970s category romance. An impetuous, selfish young woman falls in love with a brooding, vicious man who finally admits that he loves her back. There is no sweet, shy heroine to save them. They destroy their own lives and the lives around them with their violent shenanigans. That's all.

No wonder her contemporaries rolled their eyes in horror.

And yet Emily Brontë was one of the greatest of the greats. With a single novel, she made literary history.

Brontë managed a feat the rest of us can only dream of—she told the appalling story of an unsympathetic couple in such a classical manner that readers elevate her characters to the status of archetypes and her conflict to the realm of Greek tragedy.

How did she do it?

The story of *Wuthering Heights* is told through an unusual structure: a frame-within-a-frame-within-a-frame. That is, the narrator—so unimportant that his own name and life mean nothing to the reader at all—relates the story *as told to him* by a servant, who has grown up with Catherine and Heathcliff and personally supervised them through their tumultuous drama. By all accounts, this structure should remove the reader so thoroughly from the action that it becomes hardly more than a summary. Even the double first-person narrative voice can't overcome the fact that the reader never actually gets inside the head of either Catherine or Heathcliff, never feels their feelings, never thinks their thoughts, never follows the logic of their internal conclusions to the rationale that would make their highly idiosyncratic behavior even the slightest bit justified.

Nobody should be able to identify with these people.

And yet we do. In spite of the amazing unlikelihood than any of the millions of readers who've loved *Wuthering Heights* in the century-and-a-half since it was first published ever destroyed either themselves or their families through the reckless narcissism of their combined self-love and self-loathing in such a spectacular and memorable way—we identify. Something in Catherine and Heathcliff lives on in us.

What the double distance of Brontë's complex structure does is allow her to show her characters externally in the most intense terms she could possibly imagine. Catherine taunts, mocks, slaps, and raves. Heathcliff kidnaps people, locks them up, beats, torments, and kills. They're monsters! But they're removed so effectively from the reader that they become theater, in exactly the same way that Greek tragedians were able to tear out their own eyes, marry their own parents, even—horribly—feed each other their own children and still bring their audiences back for more.

At the same time, Brontë loads her characters with almost unbearable internal conflict, a devouring obsession with each other that reveals her wonderful, agonizing insight into the depths of human nature.

Deep in the infantile recesses of the subconscious, Catherine and Heathcliff's passion for each other *is* how we love a single partner throughout life. We *do* confuse our beloveds over the years in our own minds with ourselves, with our own hopes and fears, our own desires and phobias, our own wants, our own selfish concerns, our very identities. But Brontë doesn't tell us what Catherine thinks about this. She makes Catherine *say* it.

And Catherine and Heathcliff's acting-out of their confusion is unpredictable, tormented, and, inevitably, disastrous. Heathcliff finally admits that he loves Catherine—he's rising from his knees, embracing her—and she grabs his hair and yanks him back down. This *is* how we feel at the height of emotion, after decades of sharing a heart with only one other person. We *do* want to both keep them and reject them, to pull them to us and punish them for abandoning us, to cling to them no matter what it does to them, just to control them, to finally control them. Brontë doesn't tell us this is what Catherine wants. She makes her *do* it.

In all its complexity, ambiguity, hunger, and heartbreak—this *is* what it's like to love.

Emily Brontë never loved a man other than her brother and father. She didn't flout authority, taunt her siblings, insult, pull hair, kick, or laugh at others' misery. She didn't gamble, trespass, maliciously betray love, force anyone to marry, or hang anybody's lap dog. She didn't know anyone who did. She lived a quiet life in the cold stone house where she grew up, baking, cleaning, writing secret poetry about an imaginary country, trying to avoid having to teach school for a living, and periodically firing her father's gun for him when he became too blind to shoot holes in the church tower outside his bedroom window for himself.

She didn't want to *theorize* about how it would feel to love and hate the man in her dreams, the archetype who visited her late at night in her tiny room as she bent with a candle over her portable lap desk. She didn't want to *wonder* what it might be like if that man were real.

She wanted to *know*.

And through her meticulous, specific portraits of the impossibly-conflicted characters she pictured, she did.

She gave that to all of us.

Chapter 6

Delving into the Mythic Life

How to create character

Creating the Look of a Character

There are only so many auburn-tressed, emerald-eyed, white-skinned, spunky/seductive/mysterious temptresses in the world. And, unfortunately, all of them have already made it into print.

You know who's there with them? The curvaceous, giggly blondes and the sultry, sloe-eyed brunettes. They fell in love with and married all of the strapping/hunky Ken dolls with chiseled jaws and molded abs a long time ago, and now they spend their Saturday nights as a gang down at Cyrano's throwing back the shots and swapping house keys.

Their children, I'm afraid, are in rehab.

So who's left to populate our stories? Faceless characters in the land of Godot, sitting on invisible furniture in empty space and trading banal conversation to prove they're real?

No, that's the kids *before* rehab.

I'm afraid there's only one type of character left for stories being written these days, and there's only one place to find them.

They're real people out there living their lives in the real world.

Yes, I know we're not writing realistic stories about real people. We're writing fantasy about dragons and fairies and haunts. We're writing about aliens without space suits colonizing New York City under the guise of celebrities. We're writing about beautiful people seducing each other with just that light touch of brutality that makes them charming in bed. We're writing terrifying thrillers with authentic weaponry and technical covert-operations expertise. We're writing about post-apocalyptic cowboys who never get out of the saddle, not even to do their business, who can spin a sharp-shooter on one finger while simultaneously lighting a cigarette on a horse's hoof (provided, of course, that the horse is cooperative). I know.

But we *still* have to create real people.

I am so sorry. Really, I am. I have created my share of ideal women and men to live out the adventures I imagined and solve the riddles I posed for them. I have given them lovely faces, thrilling voices (thank you, F. Scott Fitzgerald, for the thirty-six mentions of Daisy's low, thrilling voice in less than two hundred pages), and insightful commentary. I didn't always mention it, but you know every one of them had perfect skin.

Then I had to go back and scrap them all. I saw them at Cyrano's.

Here's what I did after that: I took a notebook and pen and started hanging out at sidewalk cafés. I lived in downtown San Francisco at the time, a half-a-block into the notoriously scary Tenderloin neighborhood below Nob Hill, in what I affectionately called Nob Valley.

I spent hours on the weekends in my own neighborhood and on my lunch hour near my job South of Market (before it was gentrified, when it was still the place no one went unless they were looking for a newspaper plastered to a chain link fence).

I was absolutely *surrounded* by material.

So I wrote. I didn't make anything up. I just wrote. Long, detailed descriptions of everyone I saw. Most of those turned out to be the homeless who wandered by, because, frankly, the homeless can be pretty amazing.

There was the emaciated, bug-eyed woman in a dirty tennis dress scuffing along, muttering, her reddened heels sticking out the backs of her broken tennis shoes, looking as though she'd been freeze-dried. There was the gaunt old man in a drooping grey forty-year-old suit, with one black infected toe sticking horribly out of a hole in his shoe, who stood up suddenly on the bus and deliberately let his pants fall off. There was the woman in the bright yellow, baggy clown britches and enormous green and purple leather boots, her face spotted with acne and her hair curled almost too perfectly in Marlo Thomas rolls to her shoulders. There was the wreck of a young man with a once-classical fine-boned face who dragged himself up the steps of the bus and croaked with what appeared to be the last of his strength, "Y'goin—y'goin—y'goin to Chinatown?"

Now, I can hear you cry, "But I'm not writing about the homeless!" Of course not. Okay, you in the back, you are. But nobody else is. That's not the point. The point is that writing about real, living, startlingly interesting-looking people trains us to notice and note down the unique characteristics of *everybody*.

I started doing it at bars. This was harder, because people in bars have a tendency to hit on anyone with a notebook who looks like they might be A Writer—a tip for those of you still on the prowl. But I managed. I saw archetypes (and, in reading these, please keep in mind I've been out of the bar scene for years).

There was the young man with short hair dyed flaming yellow and orange with dark roots, who accessorized his look with black-rimmed Buddy Holly glasses. There was the woman with pancake white on her face, straightened black hair, fire-engine lipstick, and scrolling Egyptian eyeliner. There was the chrome-plated couple with rainbow hair and studded dog collars and permanent hip disdain. There was the shaved-bald bartender with the baggy, day-glo T-shirt whose world-weary correctness didn't involve actual words.

The plethora of piercings and tattoos was staggering. And each unique instance of each particular character type had a mole here, a zit there, a pair of especially large or small front teeth, a squint in one eye or the other, a misshapen nostril or ear or finger or lip, a bruise or band-aid, a way of jerking the head or picking a tooth or coughing into a fist that made them different from all of the other instances of their type around them.

What I realized is that, even when we try to blend in with the crowd, we can't stop one crucial, inescapable fact from slipping through the disguise: we're real people. We live our lives out here in the real world.

Once I learned this, I started taking real risks. I started describing my friends. Not right in front of them — not when they were looking, anyway — but late at night after I'd been with them, back in my apartment. I noted their uniforms, the clothes and hairstyles they used to make themselves look like each other, all in meticulous, scientific detail.

Then I noted the crucial, inescapable facts of their personalities that slipped through — the body parts that twitched, the nervous picking at themselves, the coughing and sneezing and hiccupping and winking. It was all there, just waiting to be noticed and noted.

We're really such transparent creatures. We live inside these bodies bearing almost grotesque resemblances to our parents, doing our best to disappear in our crowd, doing our best to be a cliché of something we admire.

And yet our humanity inevitably slips through.

Creating a Name for a Character

Uriah Heap. Oliver Twist. Herbert Pocket. Pip.

Guess who was really good with names.

Naming is a serious issue in the creation of character, and I will tell you why: because John and Susan Smith could be absolutely anybody. I'm sorry, they could. And every character must be unique.

I happen to know an editor who wants to see a name on every character, however fleeting. But Lorrie Moore's breakout story, "People Like That Are the Only People Here," is about the Mother, the Doctor, and the Baby. Characters don't *have* to have names. There are no Names Police.

I, personally, have suffered terribly over the incredible significance of character names. In my early writing days, I was so struck by option paralysis that I sincerely wanted everyone to be called the Woman, the Man, the Guy with the Hat. I wrote stories of deep, poignant significance in which the characters could only be identified by their looks:

> "It wasn't like that," said the man with the bent nose.
>
> "How would you know?" The woman with the long earlobes toyed with a pocket knife.

> "He's lying," said the man with two pigtails.
>
> "The truth would be a lie for him," answered the woman with the fingernails with no moons.

I wrote a whole novel about characters with completely fantasial names like Miff and Gumbo, until someone said, "Are they aliens?"

Then I buckled a bit and started letting characters have real names, but only names I would consider for my own children—lovely, melodious, slightly unusual names that reminded me of people I'd loved in passing (or wished I'd known) years before. It was *great* when they did completely banal things.

> Theodore Isaac Peter blocked the door with his tennis shoe. Isabella Louisa, outraged, knocked him into the wall with her umbrella, while Anna Mathilda Magdalena Rebecca looked the other way and picked her nose.

But even then I couldn't bring myself to give my characters last names. It just seemed too. . .portentous.

Then one winter my husband and I spent the coldest months face-to-face in rocking chairs on either side of our woodstove—partly because we had no money for heating, and partly because he'd just installed wireless Internet so we *could*—and I laughed so hard over Horace Walpole's *The Castle of Otranto* that I felt compelled to write my own faux-twelfth-century Gothic comedy.

I mean, *Otranto*'s got everything. Drama. Passion. Terror. Death threats. Thwarted romance. Thwarted death threats. Threatening romance. Denied birthright and forgotten history and secret catacombs and one *heck* of a hilarious ghost giant. Plus someone gets squished by a gigantic helmet.

It took about six weeks to write a first draft of my own, and in order to make it authentic I looked up Medieval English names.

And I stumbled on the motherlode! AEleueua, Aunphelice, Aylyetta, AElfuini, AEdilualch—that's just the A's.

But, wait. There's more. I looked up surnames, too. Smalbyhind, Aydrunken, the cryptic Latethewaterga (Let the Water Go).

Those were people who knew the real significance of *names*.

The thing is that, as with everything else in fiction, it does our reader no good for us to include details that do not in any way illuminate our characters. Rebecca West put a character into *The Fountain Overflows* who poisons her husband to death and serves prison time for it, while her daughter and unbelievably hapless sister move in with the protagonist's family. Ditzy, delicate, floppy Aunt Lily would lose her head if it weren't screwed on. But her murderous, remorseless sister is Queenie.

Of course, *I* probably would have named them AEglyuu and Mogg. But I also probably would have tried to work a squishing by gigantic helmet in there somewhere.

We writers collect names. Whenever we hear or see one that strikes us as interesting or poignant or particularly telling, we jot it down. We read baby name books. We browse bookstores for author names. Once I interviewed a local sheriff's deputy for a murder mystery and nearly died when I heard his name, Sheriff Schnitzius (pronounced *Snitches*). He said he has a cousin who's a detective in Oakland. Is that rich or what? A friend was telling me the other day that she was reading *The Time Traveler's Wife,* by Audrey Niffenegger, and I said I don't think a person with a name like that should have to write books to go along with it—the name is enough.

We list the names we collect alphabetically. I know this sounds trivial, but it's a fact that if we give more than one main character names beginning with the same letter, it slows the reader down sorting them out and wakes them from, as John Gardner described it, the *fictional dream*. I keep a list scribbled on a sheet of paper by my elbow when I'm writing a first draft to make sure I don't accidentally name a new character something too similar to somebody already up and about. And if I do, I go back later and change one of them.

Anne of Green Gables was absolutely right when she insisted that not only every person but every object in the world must know what it's called. How can our characters reveal their true selves if nobody knows their true names?

Creating Action for a Character

I recently began reading Syd Field's canonical work, *Screenplay*. And what an eye-opener it is!

I decided to study screenwriting specifically for plot. What's a movie if not a plot, right? Even *Down by Law* has a plot (although action-wise it makes *The Bridges of Madison County* look like *Rambo*).

I'm five chapters and fifty-five pages into the book, and you wouldn't believe what Field—one of the stars of the screenwriting world—has been talking about this whole time.

Yep. Character.

Field has a list of things that comprise character:

personality
point of view
attitude

behavior
identification
revelation

He splits character into:

interior (what has happened to the character before the story)

exterior (what happens to the character during the story)

He discusses:

content
context

He focuses first and foremost on what the character *needs*.

So what's *your* character? Are you an introvert or an extrovert? Do you spend most of your time swimming through legions of voluble extended family and friends, or alone in a closet with a hamster in a cage? Do you need validation? respect? comfort? distance? mystery? understanding? to be recognized for the hard-bitten/tender-hearted/expert/misunderstood/adored/dingbat character you know in your heart you really are? to be ignored?

We are who we are—that's fine. Our characters are who they are, too. And if that was all there was to it, the conversation would end here.

But if we want to create fiction about a character, it's not enough for them to just be who they are. We have to delve into the business of how they show it.

F. Scott Fitzgerald taught us that action is character. How do we show who our characters are through their actions?

What actions express personality?

Being an introvert is one thing, but when we take an introverted character and put them on a page, we have to come up with actions that show how that person *expresses* their introversion. Go ahead, show them sitting at the kitchen table chewing a toothpick and staring at their hand for two hours.

Good thing this isn't a movie. We just wrote *Down By Law II*.

Now start over again. Show the character doing something slightly more interesting to express their introversion. Maybe the phone rings, and they go through a whole physical expression of their indecision about answering it—jumping away from it, leaning toward it, touching it, pulling back from it, putting it in a drawer, taking it out again, opening the window and setting the phone on the windowsill and then sitting down, looking the other way, whistling and picking their teeth and nudging the phone ever-so-casually with one foot to see if they can "accidentally" knock it out.

What actions express point-of-view?

Dialog, of course, is the natural conduit. But body language does it, too. How does our character act while they're talking about something they fervently believe in? How do they move in response to someone who fervently disagrees? Point-of-view has to do with the distinctions between characters, so it's our characters' interactions that give us the best stage on which to express it.

But maybe we have a character who has a hard time even holding a point-of-view. Maybe they waffle between the points-of-view of those around them. This character needs either to be liked by everybody or to not be held responsible for anything. So we have to come up with actions that show that character's difficulty with point-of-view. Every time someone around them expresses an opinion, the character agrees. Insert them into an argument between two or more people with really strong opposing points-of-view and see what hits the fan.

Crispin Glover does a hilarious job of portraying this character in *Back to the Future*, yanked back and forth between his future boss' bullying and his future son's demands that he stand up to the bullying.

What actions express attitude?

Mannerisms work well. Everyone needs to blend in with their tribe, and we do this through mannerisms and choices: choices of food, clothing, habitat, vocabulary, vocation or lack thereof, religion or lack thereof, manners or lack thereof.

A character who chooses to dress in a tuxedo for dinner and then feeds the dogs from the table is showing us, through their actions, what attitudes they have toward the formal habits of Western culture, the owning of pets, the owning of food, the dinner in front of them at that moment.

If we give this character some mannerisms, such as a nervous shrug of one shoulder whenever someone comes in the room or the habit of scratching the top of their head before they speak, we're showing this character's attitudes toward both their boundaries and their intellectual abilities.

Jim Hutton created the quintessential film Ellery Queen with these mannerisms for the 1970s television show.

What actions inspire the reader to identify with a character?

Every culture has its own ideal character, and the closer we get to this character the more likely our reader is to identify. This doesn't mean perfection. Nobody's interested in reading about perfect people, because nobody can identify with being perfect.

But we need to identify with *someone.*

In American culture, we like someone who's desperate to get something (the old American self-starter mentality), is willing to fight over it (American rebellion against authority), has personal quirks that make them appear maverick (American individualism), and at the same time suffers bouts of indecision or questioning themself (we like to think it's lonely at the top). All of these traits are inherent to the national 'character' we Americans are taught as schoolchildren to admire and aspire to—the kind of people who'd attack our own government because, gosh darn it, we're just too smart *not* to. I know! Let's dress up like oppressed people of another race, sneak out at night, and throw someone else's expensive cargo in the bay. Boy, howdy, that'll teach 'em to try to govern us!

We in America are raised to identify with this type of character. We *loved* Han Solo.

And what about revelation? What actions are going to lead our reader to this?

If we study character arc, we find it's a slippery little devil that very often evades the writer searching for it. But we all need change in our lives—our brains aren't built for coma. And a revelation doesn't have to be life-altering. In fact, if it's true to reality it's generally not even permanent.

Maybe we have a character so cripplingly dependent upon others' opinions that they can't act in any way *except* in rebellion and submission, wildly out of control, yet still under the illusion their choices and behavior aren't really damaging, just, well, a little hard to understand.

At the very end of our story, this character finally has an epiphany—"Aha! I've been out of control! But now I see that I can take control of my life without either rebelling or submitting, I just have to make a choice and follow through on it." And for the first time, this character smiles a truly sincere smile (*Muriel's Wedding*).

When a character moves from one fundamental perspective on their needs to another, the reader learns something about themself in the process, something about the flexibility of our perception of need, something about being human.

This is revelation.

And, for my money, the next story—the story about what happens when that revelation doesn't stick—is where it gets really interesting.

Most importantly, though, what actions express the needs *of a character?*

Because need is the basis of all character. Stories happen because people need things. Those needs are rooted in survival.

Maybe our character needs to dominate. Maybe they're a bookshop clerk. Not much to dominate there, but you know humans are very inventive critters, we'll find a way to pursue our needs no matter what our circumstances. So this character shows their need to dominate in the way they act all day: handling books, sorting them, shelving them, carting them around, working with customers, listening or not listening to them, instructing them, helping them or not helping them, leading them, pushing them, shoving them, throwing them out when the character decides it's time.

In *High Fidelity,* Jack Black's character has a fantastic scene in which he throws a customer out of the store for asking for Stevie Wonder's "I Just Called to Say I Love You," infuriated that anyone would listen to such a thing, much less buy it for someone they loved.

You'll notice that every single aspect of character has, at its base, some form of need. Needs come out in actions. Action is character.

Actions the reader doesn't see are *internal* character. Actions the reader does see are *external* character.

And this is why Field categorizes everything that happens to the character before the story as internal: because those are actions we don't show. (If we're using flashback rather than backstory, that's part of the story, so those actions are externalized for the reader.)

What happens to the character and what the character makes happen during the course of our story are the externalized expressions of the interior with which the character arrives at our doorstep. It's our job to externalize this internal character, to turn it into a stream of actions for the reader to follow.

That's our story.

I hope you love working with this character. I mean, really *love* it. Because the actions that you, the writer, choose to take or not take in researching, pondering, delving into, and then locating the right words for the characters and their actions are what separate the amateur writer from the professional. The amount of activity you're willing to get involved in to bring characters to light is an indicator of your own character as a writer.

Even off the page—action is character.

Creating the Character in a Character

So, I read the transcript of the five-day story conference that spawned *Raiders of the Lost Ark*. Guess what it's all about?

Indiana Jones.

I find this simply fascinating. I don't mind telling you that, so far as I remember, *Raiders* of all stories is *nothing* if not plot-driven. What purpose could it possibly have served these three major forces of Hollywood to sit around for five days ignoring plot and instead talking at length about just this one guy?

That's how important character is.

Far too much aspiring fiction is about characters without much going on inside. Then their aspiring creators wonder why that fiction doesn't live.

We've talked about noticing the clues we all give, all day long every day, that there are real human beings living inside our personas, the things that set us apart from each other. These clues all come from someplace inside, and unless we, the writers, know where that place is, we won't be able to construct a really gripping story in which those clues get to appear.

Another word for this is motivation. Ever wonder why agents and editors and fiction teachers are so fond of that word: **motivation**? This is why. People are, basically, nothing more than walking bundles of *want*.

So we ask ourselves, "What do I really want? Deep down inside? Past the part about chocolate and cheese puffs and reruns of *No, Honestly!*?"

If we go deep enough, we get to where we all live, which is that we need to be loved and accepted. Sometimes we'll take just being accepted. So there's our common ground at the core of all character.

So we float a tiny bit higher and ask ourselves, "In the pursuit of love and acceptance, what do I need?" And there we get the key to our own characters: our motivation in life.

Lots of the time what I, personally, want is to be right. Heck, yes! In my extended family while I was growing up, we argued a lot, and whoever was right got a lot of (admittedly grudging) admiration from the rest. This became extremely important to me, as it did to all of us.

Lots of the time what I also want is to be seen as good-hearted. There was plenty of competition for attention in my immediate family, and the one job nobody seemed much into was service. It's not really much of a job. But I learned early on that if I appointed myself the guardian of my baby sister and reported on her every desire to my mother the instant it was expressed, I garnered some nice little pats on the head. That was great! So I grew up highly invested in those little pats.

H'm—I wonder if these are motivations that would form a good foundation for a character who devotes themself wholeheartedly to a particular art form and then pursues it, willy-nilly, for a long time with little or no reward before branching into similar, more monetary fields, finding in this art form a parallel to their deepest moral standards and eventually achieving a hilarious level of satisfaction in discoursing upon it voluminously to an invisible, mostly-silent audience.

Every now and then maybe a nice little pat?

We don't have anyone to mine for character motivation but ourselves. We don't really know anybody else deeply enough. So we'd better make it worth our while.

1) If we have a protagonist who's a journalist who stumbles on the story of the century but can't report it because to do so would be to endanger international relations and, coincidentally, prove their own most adamant opinion false—we must be able to pinpoint for ourselves what needs it fulfills in that character to a) be a journalist, b) respect international relations, and c) hold the opinion that they don't want proven wrong.

2) If we have a protagonist who's already married and still looking for love in all the wrong places, who winds up caught between the spouse they don't want anymore, the children to whom they have a responsibility, the job they desperately need to keep, and the love that gives them reason to live—we must know what needs it fulfills in that character to a) be married, b) look for love in the wrong places, c) stay with that spouse, d) not want that spouse, e) take responsibility for the children, f) keep that job, and g) attach themself to the beloved who turns their life inside-out.

3) If we have a protagonist who's a hardboiled world-weary pro on the far end of an under-appreciated career who has to choose between the principles that guided that career and the realities they never realized were forming it—we must understand exactly what needs it fulfills in them to a) be hardboiled and world-weary, b) stick with an under-appreciated career to the bitter end, c) hold the principles they do, d) have been blind to the realities around them up until now.

We can't just assume that because it makes sense to us it will make sense to our reader. They didn't live our childhoods—neither, for that matter, did our characters. We must dig into this stuff, even when it feels like digging splinters out of our hearts.

Especially then.

Who taught these characters to value the things they do? When? Why? What's in it for them? How is valuing those things worth everything they have to go through in order to keep valuing them no matter what you throw at them? (We already know we're going to throw everything we've got.)

And *what would happen* to them if they changed their minds, abandoned their values, wandered out of the novel and left the rest of us hanging empty-handed?

Now that's a story!

Plot is *Context*

Chapter 7

Finding a Story to Tell with Edgar Allan Poe

Stories are about human beings in trouble

Edgar Allan Poe has gone down in history for writing the most morbid, depressing, horrifying stories of his day. With *great* tension.

Poe knew trouble—boy, howdy, did he. Abandoned as a small child when his mother died, although his grandmother was still around and even had a long relationship with him when he was an adult, he was adopted and raised by a Richmond philanthropist and her husband. He returned to Baltimore as an adult, met up with his grandmother and aunt, and fell in love with his cousin Virginia, with whom he had an apparently happy twelve years before he lost her to general delicacy.

In the meantime, his adoptive mother died, and his wealthy adoptive father disowned him.

Poe wrote passionate poetry to a whole slew of women after the loss of Virginia, worked like a fiend to turn around the fortunes of more than one failing magazine, and published stories and poetry right and left. But he remained broke. It has only been since his mysterious death—presumed but never proven due to alcoholism—that he's become recognized as one of the great literary innovators of the nineteenth century, credited with the single-handed invention of the entire Western murder mystery genre.

What can we learn from Poe?

Where to find stories.

Sometimes I hear from aspiring writers asking for a plot. As in: "I want to write. Please give me something to write about."

On the one hand, I find this odd because the whole point of writing fiction, when you boil it down, is to tell a story. If we don't have a story to tell, why write?

On the other hand, it makes complete sense to want to write without having anything to write about, given that fiction is not just storytelling, it's a craft, and all craft takes practice. It's like my son's response when I told him that our doctors practice medicine: "No, they don't. It's their job."

We writers write because we love to write. This is the bottom line. But does this mean we always have something in mind to write about? *Nah.*

Sure, we can find aspiring writers who metaphorically spit on the shoes of anyone calling themself a writer who dares ask for a story idea to write about. But if we love to write, we feel good when we're writing, we have writing muscles itching to be exercised, then, for heaven's sake, we don't sit around unable to write just because we're temporarily devoid of ideas. That's like piously refusing to bicycle because our bike's in the shop.

Flannery O'Connor said that anyone who's survived childhood has enough stories to last a lifetime, and this is true *if* we hope to write mostly about childhood. It's a fact that most first-time authors go through a childlike period when the story that feels most right to tell is one with a child (or someone very nearly like a child) for a protagonist. I think this is because the first-time author feels a child's real sense of both wonder and intimidation about the whole world of literature. They're right to view their work through that lens. They haven't grown up as writers yet.

But there are only so many childhood stories that any given person wants to read (or write, for that matter). Naiveté and innocence are all well and good, but readers want a protagonist with guts.

1) So we start with an ordinary premise—we're going to the grocery store, or we're washing the dog, or we're having the same old fight with our partner—and we ask ourselves, "What could go really, really wrong?"

What if my chair flew over backward and I hit my head, and suddenly I understood calculus as a formula for personal relationships, even though I hate everyone? What if my teenager got pregnant while I was running for vice-president of the country? What if I were invited to visit an old school friend who turned out to live in the most ungodly depressing mansion with a dying sister, and, through one thing and another, we accidentally buried his sister alive?

We start our story with a sentence announcing what's going wrong, and extrapolate from there.

2) We look around wherever we are and ask ourselves: "What if *x* did *y*, and that caused *z* to go wrong?"

We take *z* as our jumping-off point and think of more and more things that could continue to go wrong.

3). We think of one or two (or three or four) really interesting people we've met and wish we knew better. Mix a couple of their traits, ponder long and deeply about their characters and why we're drawn to them, and then imagine the one thing they would most not want to happen to them.

Extrapolate.

Personally, I love this part of writing, the brainstorming, no-holds-barred, words-through-a-goose part. Proust could go on and on and on for pages about the instant right before he fell asleep. Apparently, a lot happened to him.

And you'll notice something obvious about these ideas—they're all about things going wrong. That's right: fiction is about bad news. A man concocts the perfect murder, successfully hides the body in his basement wall, but mistakenly buries a live and extremely annoyed cat along with it, and then invites the police downstairs. Jane Eyre is raised by a mean old monster so that she has to leave home and fend for herself at a young age, only to be pursued by a man who can't possibly have good intentions, and when it turns out he does it also turns out he's got a wife he's hiding from her. Moll Flanders goes from marriage to marriage, from prison to exile and back again, bouncing off the extremes of her life like a ping-pong ball, until it turns out she's managed to accidentally marry her own son.

Not only is the news bad, but it keeps getting *worse*.

Remember why? Because we want to read about how people cope. That's why books about helpless victims fail. Poor old *Clarissa*—what a loser she was. And she wouldn't make it into print today.

No, what we want are fighters. Chronic failures, maybe, but ones who never know when they're beat. We want to see someone fall off a high dive into deep water when they can't swim and then go up and down, up and down, thrashing all the way, until either they sink (tragedy) or even better they teach themselves *through thrashing* how to swim.

We want to read about how people suffer, struggle, go down for the count, and in the final moment pull it together and somehow survive.

You can call it *schadenfreude*. But really—it's life.

Chapter 8

Plotting Your Way Out of a Paper Bag

How to plot

Plotting & Pantsing

Every now and then I read about the random great writer who says, "I don't plot. I never know where my story's going until I get there." It's like a religious visitation. They make it sound so *mystical*.

So we sit down to write our little one-inch snapshot à la Anne Lamott, and we're chugging along watching these characters come to life and wander around and get in arguments and make clever remarks and slap each other in the face with kid gloves.

And we think, *This is the best movie ever!*

Wow, the Blithering Phase is fun!

I once spent a couple of months in a little coffee shack on a mountainside overlooking the ocean in Hawaii. (I was outside Captain Cook, but I told everyone I was in Kealakekua because it sounds better.) Every morning I got up, stretched, went out my bedroom door onto my miniscule lanai, downstairs over the little creek in the living room and into the open-air kitchen, then back with my coffee to my lanai to sit at a borrowed manual typewriter and write all day. I had the ocean far below my feet and a gorgeous carved ivory statue my landlady had brought back from Bali on the lanai rail for inspiration.

And I wrote. . .and wrote. . .and wrote.

Years later I did the same thing on the buses and sidewalks of San Francisco.

Even more years later I did it on a yellow legal pad with a child and toy skeleton on my lap.

And you know what? It was *fabulous.* I wish all writing were the Blithering Phase!

But none of that produced a marketable novel.

When I interviewed Carolyn Cassady about her life with Neal Cassady and Jack Kerouac, I was asked by a reader to find out whether or not Jack really wrote *On the Road* on that single scroll.

Jack apparently found the roll of taped-together pages in the apartment of a friend and typed the first draft of *On the Road* on it, including real names and details. He sent it to Allen Ginsberg, who sent it to the literary agent Sterling Lord, and Lord spent the next four years trying to find a publisher. In the meantime, Jack installed himself in the attic of Carolyn and Neal's house in San Francisco and continued to work on *On the Road,* writing new scenes to be inserted. Years later, after Lord found Viking Press, the legendary editor Malcolm Cowley came out to San Francisco, and he and Jack spent a month editing before they sent *On the Road* to press.

How utterly and totally disillusioning: even *Jack Kerouac* did not produce his one-scroll magnum opus writing by the seat of his pants.

Jane Bowles, on the other hand, struggled so hard to write her extraordinary work in just one draft that it took her all day sometimes to cough up a single sentence. By the end of her life, she could no longer write at all because she'd had a stroke at the age of forty, and perfect first-draft sentences were no longer within her grasp.

The thing about "pantsing," or writing by the seat of our pants, is that it's essential brainstorming, splendid for surprise twists and unexpected character development, and, besides, great gosh-darn fun. But it is only half of the job.

The other half is keeping the reader interested.

It's just like life. Childhood is a wonderful time of experimentation and discovery, when everything is brilliant and startling, and the intuitive leaps of logic are completely beyond the ability of any plodding old boring adult. But children can't connect the dots that keep life moving forward. As far as a child is concerned, life could end either when they fall off their beloved bike or when Great-grandpa doesn't wake up one morning—either way, they're equally devastated. It's only in retrospect, from an adult perspective, that they understand the difference in significance.

Children are narcissists. They're only interested in themselves. They don't need to understand epiphany. It's all they can do to understand toilets.

Writers, conveniently enough, are also narcissists. This is how we access the subconscious, the essential links between real things that lie at the core of our art.

However, adults must be more than narcissists—we must be able to take into account the needs of others, the difference between falling off a bike and losing a loved one, the interplay of *cause-&-effect,* the balance of all things that leads to epiphany.

Writers, if we're any good, must also be adults. This is how we *share* our subconscious with our reader.

Far too many canonical works on the craft of writing leave this important element dangling in the wind, as if it were just a side path on the road to literary heaven. Anne Lamott, for all her humor, tells the aspiring writer that when we're done we'll just know. Ray Bradbury describes plot as the footsteps our characters leave in the sand.

What the heck, guys? Can you be the *tiniest bit* more specific?

Here's the truth: plotting and pantsing are two different activities. They occur in different parts of the brain. And no great literary work ever got written without extensive use of both.

We can pants the plot of a story. We sit down with an idea and some characters and a dilemma for a Hook and jot them down. Then we ask ourselves, "What is the worst possible nightmare that could come out of this dilemma?" We jot that down: that's our Climax. Then we ask ourselves, "What conflicts of increasing anguish can we inflict upon these characters on their way to their nightmare?" (Three's a good number.) We jot them down: that's our Development. They're going to involve a certain amount of Backstory, which we jot down elsewhere. Then we ask ourselves, "What would make these characters think their troubles are over without having to face their nightmare?" We jot that down: that's our Faux Resolution.

Finally, if we're still in the mood, we ask ourselves, "What might we do with these poor saps after we've fed them to the wolves?" We don't jot it down, though: that's only a tentative (tentative!) Resolution. It will continue to change and grow throughout the writing of the story.

When we arrange them, we arrange them in this sequence:

HOOK

Backstory

DEVELOPMENT (Conflicts)

Faux Resolution

CLIMAX

Resolution

We take our time! We can go on with this for months. Some writers go on with it for *years*. This is not dry technique. No.

This is brainstorming on the *deepest* level.

We're reaching into the bottom of our subconscious to pull out completely wild and unexpected things to do to perfectly innocent characters who, in all likelihood, do not deserve it by half. We probably don't even know how to get from one idea to the other. We just have an instinct about the logic running behind the lives of these people. And we know what feeling we want our reader to walk away with at the end.

These are our notes—masses and masses of notes (sometimes whole scenes arranged experimentally into episodes) that we'll have to try to keep organized to some extent, so when we reach the point of writing into our story a certain character, a certain scene, a certain plot point, we don't spend a year agonizing over writer's block or Writer Attention Deficit Disorder (WADD).

We just read through our notes—all over the board—and pick and choose only those most exciting and vivid details we want to include in the scenes of the overall idea we're developing. The more staggered the dates on our sets of notes for any given topic, the greater the variety of details we'll have. And the greater the variety of details, the more layers. And the more layers, ah, the more depth, the more fascination, the more intrigue, the more thrilling the fiction.

HOOK

Ellen, who likes to call herself Disraeli, has a problem.

Right after her first heady date with Beatrice the bird-hating but brilliant child psychologist, Disraeli's beloved pet crippled osprey Poo-Poo comes down deathly ill.

Backstory

Everything Disraeli understands about the meaning of life comes from her love for Poo-Poo. The worst thing that could happen to her would be to lose Poo-Poo. But Disraeli is also a young woman with hopes and desires and hormones like anybody else, and when her hormones instruct her to fall in love with Beatrice, she does.

DEVELOPMENT

1st Conflict:

The regular vet can't help. Poo-Poo is interesting as all get-out, but he won't let the vet get near him.

2nd Conflict:

The wildlife vet can't help. Poo-Poo doesn't respond to treatment. Sometimes wild animals just get sick and die, especially in captivity.

3rd Conflict:

The zoo can't help. Although Poo-Poo would probably do better in a larger environment, their waiting list goes on for years.

Faux Resolution:

Only Beatrice, who suspects out of her expertise as a deeply intuitive child psychologist that Poo-Poo is suffering from emotional problems, can help. And

Beatrice has fallen in love with Disraeli and can't bear to see her suffer.

CLIMAX

But when Beatrice finally agrees to help Poo-Poo, Poo-Poo attacks her and puts her in the hospital, and while Beatrice is recovering Poo-Poo suffers a deadly setback.

Resolution:

Disraeli has to cope. Will she connect with Poo-Poo on a level she never understood before she fell in love with Beatrice? Will she resolve Poo-Poo's loss of his will to live? Or will she face Poo-Poo's inevitable death and discover the rest of her life?

I don't personally know. I'm just entertaining myself with the name Poo-Poo.

We must know the very last thing our protagonist would ever want to cope with, because how they cope with this at the Climax is what our reader most wants to read. We brainstorm the connections between the events we're putting our characters through and develop the *cause-&-effect* that leads our reader through the logic of our story. Everything that happens after the Hook is an effect caused by what's already happened.

We play in the subconscious, mess around with our hands in our brains, pulling on the events to find out what obscure links lie between any two given elements.

What leads Disraeli to the regular vet? (Poo-Poo's illness.) What leads her to the wildlife vet? (Probably the regular vet.) What leads her to the zoo? (Probably something the wildlife vet said, such as, "Captive birds do tend to die.") And what leads her to seek a solution in Beatrice? (Maybe this reminds her of something Beatrice has said about the captivity of childhood.)

If we find that we're satisfied by this brainstorming, that when it comes down to it we don't really feel like writing this story after all, we don't worry. It was good work. It taught us how to think like a writer. We will take that new skill with us into our next story.

Cause-&-effect.

We've got to be grown-ups to understand how it keeps a reader hooked.

But creating the weird, wild, and lovely elements of our story, the characters, their exteriors and interiors and actions, their dialog and communications, the world they navigate, and especially unexpected insight into the issues they confront—we've got to have a child's eye for life to capture all of that.

Plotting to Handel's *Largo*

I play the piano to avoid writing. I write to avoid playing the piano. It's pretty much a scientific demonstration of inertia in action, but it does have the benefit of keeping me busy.

The thing about Handel's *Largo* is that, even if you play some insanely simplified version of it (as I do), and you spend most of that time playing it either too fast, too slow, too quietly, too loudly, melodramatically, perkily, broodingly, or with that touch of poignant cynicism Dylan Thomas would have used if he hadn't had his finger stuck in a bottle—it still works.

So one day when I was hiding from analyzing my plot deficiencies, I analyzed Handel's *Largo* instead, in order to learn what he did right:

introduction
1st drama
quiet
2nd drama

quiet
3rd drama
lovely sense of resolution and peace
all holy hell breaking loose

Seems simple, doesn't it?

But you see here something fascinating, akin to the principle of the three-legged stool—human beings like things that come in threes. Twos are nice, they're the classic romance, but they're polarized, and eventually something's got to give or there's no punchline. Fours are too stable. Even in bridge, someone's got to play the dummy or the game gets dull (and bridge is not exactly an uncomplicated game). Fives are asking for trouble, and the higher we go the more trouble we're asking for. One, as Three Dog Night pointed out a long time ago, just isn't worth it.

Threes, however, have the inherent complexity plus quixotically-concrete stability of a pyramid. They *look* unstable. A three-legged stool *seems* like it would dump you without preamble. In my mind, all three-legged stools are surrounded by a bevy of concerned characters, pointing and shaking their heads. And yet. . .there are the pyramids.

Over and over I fingered that melody while I thought about this. One, two, three, pause, *slam*.

It works!

And so I acquired a real, usable skeleton on which to hang any plot. Yank the reader's nose-ring to get their attention and introduce the main characters. Then put those characters through three hoops of increasing difficulty. Give them a little time in between to catch their breath and blow their noses, but don't let them wander off. Keep them jumping. After the last hoop—*voila*!—give them their reward. They did it! They survived! *Halleluiah!*

Now comes Handel's great effect. *They're not done yet.* Because the one thing readers want more than anything, the reason they follow any story in the first place, is catastrophe.

Readers want to know, "When all else fails and I am confronted with impossible disaster, how do I survive? And why is it worth the effort?"

We have to give them that.

The best method is to get them really well-acquainted with our characters through a series of increasingly disturbing conflicts in a good solid trio until the reader subconsciously feels an emotional investment in the characters and what's going to happen to them next. Then take a breath and just sock it to them.

"You want Climax? I'll give you Climax." Plow them under. This is the point readers are after all along, bizarre as it may seem.

The reader *wants* to see Jane Eyre come back to the burnt-out shell of Thornfield. They're *dying* for the fake spy of Havana to be confronted with his own diagrams of the insides of vacuum cleaners. They would sell a *kidney* to find out what Ahab's going to do with that homicidal whale when he finally gets his hands on it.

Listening to and reading stories is not an activity that human beings take lightly.

No.

This activity is about life itself.

Sylvia Plath liked the epigram, "Get your hero up in a tree and throw stones at them." Are we going to knock them out? Destroy them? Rub the reader's nose in the fact that life really is bigger and meaner than we are—that life is, in fact, the ultimate bully on the block?

Or are we going to give our characters an escape route, something simple but perfect, something we cleverly planted clues to in the very early pages of our story, where the reader knew we would never have any use for it and therefore must be employing it simply for local color?

What are we going to reveal about our understanding of life to our reader through the juxtaposition of that essential clue and its final revelation? Are our characters going to survive their Climax or not?

Well, that's your business. You're the writer. I'm just over here at the piano.

Pouring Your Story into Dramatic Paradigm

Syd Field has this wonderful thing he calls the *dramatic paradigm*. It's a little diagram of a three-act play, which is the standard structure for screenplays in general.

The three acts consist of—are you ready?

Act I: Setup (ending in the first plot point)
Act II: Confrontation (ending in the last plot point)
Act III: Resolution

Now, these are concepts we've seen before. Gustav Freytag used them when he designed his plot pyramid:

Exposition
Rising Action
Climax
Falling Action
Denouement

Oddly, Freytag called hook "exposition," development or confrontation "climax," and climax "falling action," causing no end of confusion. But it's still the same structure.

Think about the Shakespearean five-act play:

Act I: Introduction
Act II: Development

Act III: Conflict

Act IV: Climax

Act V: Denouement

What names have we given them?

HOOK

(with Backstory)

DEVELOPMENT

(three Conflicts)

CLIMAX

(with a Faux Resolution but with or without a final Resolution)

Are you getting the rhythm?

1) Call it setup, exposition, introduction, hook, or whatever we like, we must deal with first things first

The first thing the reader wants to know about our story is *who* it's about and *why* they're upset.

It's a given that they're upset. Stories are about when things go wrong. To whom does this story happen? And what is the first thing that goes wrong? What's the first domino to fall?

> "Guess what I happened today, honey! Everything went just the way I planned."
>
> "Well, guess what happened to *me*. When I got out while the car was idling to put Rover in the back in her new carrier case, I accidentally locked the car keys inside."

2) Call it a plot point, rising action, or development, the next thing we must deal with is why our story doesn't end there

What is it about these characters and their dilemma that draws the reader in? What turns the reader into our ally? What makes the reader think, "Oh, no! That could have been *me*"?

> "Oh, honey! Well, it's all over now. Let me get you some chocolate bunnies and a foot rub."
>
> "Not by a long shot. I had to break the kitchen window to get in the house and find the second set of keys."

3) Call it confrontation, climax, or conflict, the middle of our story must make the reader want to pull out their hair

Every time the reader thinks we've rescued our characters, what keeps them turning the pages? How do we prevent them from saying, "Well, that's that. All done reading"? What are they hanging in there waiting to find out?

> "Well, we'll fix it in the morning. Thank goodness you didn't kick in the door."
>
> "It gets worse. I made it outside just in time to see Rover break out of her carrier and jump, trailing a rope of slobber and that awful chew toy, into the driver's seat."

Keep in mind the secret—I call it the Faux Resolution—which is misleading the reader into believing we've solved our problems. It's extremely important:

> "She slobbered all over everything? Are we going to have to replace the *car*?"

"No, it's okay, because I remembered to put down a fresh garbage bag on the driver's seat before I loaded her into the back."

"Thank goodness for that! Well, all's well that ends well."

4) Call it resolution, falling action, or climax, our story must finally come to a head.

Why did we start telling this story in the first place? What's our *whole point*?

"Tomorrow I'll fix the window—"

"—but that's when she knocked the gearshift into drive and drove the car into the—oh. Ahem. You already saw the swimming pool?"

5) And call it denouement or resolution, we must decide when to stop

It can't go on indefinitely. Even Balzac's *Human Comedy* and Proust's *Remembrance of Things Past* end eventually. There's a kicker to our point, something that's going to throw our reader off the rainbow:

"*What*? Did you get Rover out in time?"

"Are you kidding me? Who do you think that is in the shower?"

Plotting by Domino Theory

The most important elements of three-act structure are the plot points at the ends of Acts I and II. Syd Field describes these two all-important points as the events or actions that "spin" the story around. They're like our canines: only two of them, evenly spaced, but they hold our entire dental structure together.

Stories need to become more complex as they go along, as we get the reader used to the tension and they start thinking about being finished. We have to keep yanking them back in. We can think of the three dramatic upheavals in Handel's *Largo* in terms of the Acts, what I like to call three "Conflicts" of increasing tension.

Act I has a Hook plus Conflict #1, culminating in the first plot point that alters the characters' trajectory.

Act II has two Conflicts (raise the ante!): pivotal Conflict #2 halfway through the story, the fulcrum that alters a beginning into an ending, plus devastating Conflict #3, culminating in the second plot point that alters the characters' trajectory yet again.

Act III starts out deceptively—the reader thinks that last plot point leads to a solution, that it finally shows the characters how to get out of this mess alive. But no!

While Act III begins with the Faux Resolution, it's really organized around the impossible disaster, the final catastrophe, the Climax that says, like the Grim Reaper, "*Nobody* gets out alive."

Whether or not we make room for a final Resolution—whether we choose comedy or tragedy—is just a question of how close we put the Climax to the very end. Either the Grim Reaper is right, or we've got time to show how they're wrong.

Whatever throws the reader off the rainbow ends our story.

Act I

So here we are, chugging along down the track. We start out with a main character, a protagonist, and their need to not knock over their dominoes, and we throw a problem at them to upset them. Our Hook is our first domino going down.

Oh, no! Don't knock over that first domino! *Too late.* So now things are falling in some particular direction.

Then about a quarter (absolutely no more than a third) of the way through our story we come to a place where the dominoes are a little further apart, and it looks as though that last one's going to go down without quite touching the one after it. *Whew!* Thank goodness we got through that. And by the skin of our teeth. But wait. . .no! no! The falling domino's just caught the edge of the next one, and now the reader realizes that little extra space was there because the row of dominoes went *around a corner*!

Canine.

Act II

So now our trajectory has altered, we're headed in a different direction, and the dominoes are falling faster than ever. The reader's rushing to keep up with them. It's just one minor disaster and recovery after another, and everywhere the reader looks things are going wrong. We're right in the middle of our story, and the dominoes come to another corner, almost stop, go around it—and suddenly there are *two* rows of dominoes! We have just passed the fulcrum.

This story is no longer moving away from the beginning, it is now moving toward the ending.

But the two rows have a beauty of symmetry that's becoming visible, and that is their glory and their heartbreak. We're about three-quarters (absolutely no less than two-thirds) of the way through our story. The dominoes run into each other, knock each other explosively down, and stop. They're done. That trajectory went someplace our characters did not expect *at all*.

Canine.

Act III

The rest of the line remains upright, undaunted, ready for another day. The reader is ready to weep with relief. Yes, there was damage, yes, there was trauma, yes, we suffered. But the rest of the line is safe. And it's always possible to rebuild. . .

Except that the story is still moving forward, and its new trajectory takes our characters out of two dimensions into three. The table that the dominoes stand on is not a table, it's a board balanced on a single foot, and now that the dominoes all stand on one side, there's no help for it. It's tipping. . .it's tipping. . .grab your neighbor, there it *goes*!

All the dominoes on the floor at once, a completely surprising and yet inevitable Climax. The reader has been so focused upon the falling of individual dominoes that they never even considered the deeper significance of the greater situation. The entire game is destroyed. There's no rebuilding now.

This story is O.V.E.R.

And it might very well be. That's the writer's decision. We can walk away and leave the reader standing over the pile of dominoes sobbing into a handkerchief, cursing the day they were born, wondering if it's too late to move to a cave in Tibet and shave their head.

Or we can take pity and shine one little ray of sunshine through a high window so they can see: life is not dominoes. They're standing in a room crying over a pile of spilt toys.

There's actually a whole other world going on out there.

Being Sort of Unique

Agents and publishers see tons of queries. Literally. Even as we move into the world of electronic communication, the paper that still goes in and out of their offices in any given year could sink a ship. And an awful lot of what they get is either inappropriate for their lists, unprofessional, or simply crazy. They get numbed. Glassy-eyed. Comatose.

So when they say that they're looking for something fresh and new, what they mean is they're looking for something to snap them out of their trance.

Does this mean we have to rack our brains for some totally unique and original plot structure, something that's never been thought of before? Ever? In the history of literature?

Wow. *Good luck.*

The truth is there are only two types of plot in the world: the **relationship** and the **quest**. People together (suffering). People alone (suffering). Both struggling against the odds to get something they desperately – even if unconsciously – need.

Now, the British moderns of the post-WWI era did their darnedest. Virginia Woolf wrote "Kew Gardens" and "The Mark on the Wall," among other stories, to find out whether or not you could write a story about nothing at all. And it turns out that, if you can write prose the way Woolf could, the answer is yes.

But it's still a qualified yes. Both of those stories are, in fact, miniature quests. In "Kew Gardens" the quester happens to be a snail. And in "The Mark on the Wall" the quester refuses to get out of her chair all afternoon, even to satisfy her hunger to know what's happened to her parlor wall, conducting her entire quest inside her own mind while sitting among her comfy parlor cushions.

There is a plot, however vague, in both stories: an event, a Hook, sparks the quest; an on-going observation of the world Develops around the quester; Conflicts occur, however brief and ethereal; and a Climax is reached, however existential. Woolf did without Resolution. We can, too, if we design our Climax properly. However, as Woolf discovered, any structure less than this is boring, and readers won't bother to read it.

In "Kew Gardens" the Climax is the author's commentary on the afternoon passing, as life passes, simply rounding out the quest with the inevitable result of all quests. And in "The Mark on the Wall" Woolf's husband Leonard walks into the room and picks a climbing snail off the wallpaper.

As a side note, it does make you wonder about Woolf's fascination with snails.

We can work our poor sincere authorial hearts to shreds seeking that one brilliant plot structure that no one has ever thought of before, and we will still be lying there on our deathbeds, clutching the sheets, gasping, "I—think—I—got—it—"

Relationship. Or *quest*.

Pick one or both. Then construct a really gripping, amazing, satisfying series of Conflicts with a wonderful Faux Resolution to run from Hook (why should the reader care?) through Development (who's going to help these poor people?) to Climax (nobody! oh, no!).

The fresh and new that agents and publishers talk about are the scenes and methods of interweaving them. Of those there are an infinite supply.

By all means, we must take the time (lots more than seems necessary) as we bend our efforts toward coming up with those unique and original scenes and intriguing ways to interweave them. We create characters that only we could create, out of telling details that only we would ever notice, with motivations that nobody else could disentangle from their overwhelming internal conflicts.

So that we make our reader believe our story with all their heart—as though the *believing itself* were unique.

Practicing Literary Jujitsu

I put off writing this one off for awhile. It's such a vast, complex, and tricky plotting technique.

But it's so *fabulous.*

Douglas Adams has this great gimmick in his *Hitchhiker's Guide to the Galaxy* series: the ultimate torture is a box that the victim is put into that destroys their mind. Everyone who goes in comes out a gibbering idiot, completely and permanently mind-jellied. Everyone. It's terrifying.

So along comes egomaniacal leader Zaphod Beeblebrox, and the bad guys get their hands on him, and they're going to put him in the box, and the tension is mounting, and you know it's going to destroy him. . .and what's going to happen to the story once Zaphod is mind-jelly? The end! And so of course something has to happen before they succeed. There has to be some wild rescue, probably time travel. Because they can't turn *Zaphod* into mind-jelly—

But they win.

They put him in the box. Lock the door. He can't escape. They turn on the brain-mushing machine.

And when he comes back out again. . .he's fine!

What happened?

Well, we don't find out right then. But it perfectly serves the purposes of the plot at that point, in which Zaphod must survive the torture chamber and wow and amaze everyone so that they can go on to their next adventure, begrudgingly following this ultimate narcissist.

However, at the very end of the book, Adams reveals that the torture chamber is a box in which you are exposed to the entire universe in all its infinite glory—and you're shown yourself in it, infinitely trivial and infinitely useless. Which utterly destroys your sense of self-worth, along with your will to live.

The only thing is that Adams has long since told us the universe in which they do this to Zaphod just happened to be expressly designed for Zaphod, in a complicated über-plot in which someone needs to manipulate Zaphod in a particular way. So when he's put into the box what he sees is the entire universe in all its infinite glory—and he's the most important thing in it!

So of course he comes out cockier and more megalomaniacal than ever.

Adams plants the clue early on. We just don't understand the significance until he points it out at the end.

Henry James did the same thing in "The Turn of the Screw," in which he set up all the conditions for his terrible finale as essential elements of the plot: the unswerving focus on death, the apparently evil ghosts, the governess' overbearing control-freak self-involvement, along with her single-minded determination to sacrifice everything to the fantasy of herself as the children's savior. So when she finally sees the ghost herself and yanks the boy into her arms to "protect" him, we're scared out of our wits over whether the ghost is going to get them both—and James flips this around on us in the very last word, when the governess accidentally kills the boy *herself.* And I mean, he gets us to the Very. Last. Word.

Sheer mastery.

The whole point of telling a story is the ending. We're trying to tell the reader something about surviving life. We're saying, "If you stick your finger into a light socket, you will get electrocuted."

And readers appreciate this. They would like very much to know what happens if you stick your finger in a light socket, without having to try it themselves. They strongly suspect that they would get electrocuted, but they can't help being a teeny bit curious about it—what if they didn't? And if they did, what would it be like? I mean, that's pretty exciting! Transcending electrocution!

So we tell them, "Once upon a time, there was this finger, and there was this light socket. And the finger was really curious about the light socket and thought it might be pretty great to get into it. Of course, the finger's worst nightmare was that it would *hurt like nothing ever hurt before*. But that finger was powerfully, almost insanely motivated to believe that the light socket might actually be the best experience ever! So the finger set out to get into that light socket. And it encountered obstacles. Obstacle after obstacle, conflict, melodrama, failure, triumph. It overcame them all, one by one. Eventually the finger faced the light socket. This was its shining hour. Glory in a haze all around. And the finger inserted itself with infinite care and innocent hope into the light socket. And guess what? *Electrocution!*"

We build this Climax by building the elements of it into the story itself. We make sure that the reader knows: common sense says this megalomaniac is the leader and therefore must survive; if the governess is actually willing to sacrifice everything for her savior fantasy, that makes her dangerous; this finger is the protagonist and must *not* be electrocuted.

Then we set about carefully building the reader's expectation that this time the leader or the governess' ability to sacrifice or the finger itself is going to fail!

Oh, *no*!

Then we do something sneaky. We set up an opposite expectation. This megalomaniac is a jerk; this governess, narcissistic as she is, *loves* these children; this finger is incredibly creative and has such innocent hopes for what might happen when it gets into that light socket!

Now the reader kind of *wants* things to turn out the opposite of what common sense dictates.

We keep the reader focused on the tension between these two expectations. The megalomaniac can't escape the ultimate torture; the governess can't save the children; the finger can't get to the light socket. We've got the reader between a rock and a hard place. They know what they think the *point* of the story is, but they also know what they *want*.

As long as we keep the reader firmly involved in our obstacles — the attack on the megalomaniac's ego, the governess' failure to save the children, the difficulty the finger has getting to that light socket — we've distracted them from what anyone in their right mind would want, which is that *none of this succeed*.

Are you *mad*?

And then in our Climax, when the whole thing turns out the way common sense predicted, after all — the torture chamber can't possibly work on this particular megalomaniac, the governess is a bigger threat than the ghosts, the light socket is. . .well, a light socket — the reader realizes in a flash: I've been duped! How did I miss what I knew all along?

The megalomaniac is the ultimate megalomaniac, the governess is dangerously insane, the light socket is. . .well, a light socket.

But the reader hasn't been duped. No. We put the clue in the Hook. If Zaphod's one ultimate strength is his ego, the switcheroo Climax must be due to his ego (certainly not in spite of it). If the governess' one overriding characteristic is that she's a fantasizing control freak, the Climax must be due to her control issues. If the finger's one unavoidable quality is its innocence, that Climax must be due to that innocence.

What startles the wits out of the reader and gives them a whirl for their money is the fiercely-conflicting opposite expectations. But what really ejects them through the ceiling is that we gave them the vital clue *in the beginning*.

Adams was so good at this kind of thing that he layered it all the way through his novels. Not only did he practice jujitsu on us over Zaphod coming out of the box, he went on to practice jujitsu over the whole universe made entirely in Zaphod's image. We find out about this after Zaphod survives what turns out to not be torture, but we're so caught up in the barrage of excitement that we don't stop to put two and two together.

"Hey, wait a minute. If this universe was made in Zaphod's image, that means that torture box couldn't possibly have hurt him—" We just keep rolling along, playing ball with Adams because it's so fun, until Adams points at the grand Climactic moment back over our shoulders and yells, "*Ta-dah!*" We already knew!

D'oh. We knew it all along.

Chapter 9

Hooking Them in the Jaw

Hook

Starting with Famous Last Words

I was once in a writer's workshop at the Community of Writers at Squaw Valley that focused entirely on finding the beginnings of our novels. That's all we did. Each of us read our first chapter, and then the teacher asked us, "What's the first exciting thing that happens in your story?" So we turned to that part of the manuscript and read *that*.

I wish I could remember the name of the writer who taught that workshop, because he made a brilliant point about the Hook without having to spell it out for us.

When Lucia Orth read to us the first most exciting thing that happens in her novel, the inauguration of Philippine dictator Ferdinand Marcos, she got as far as the playing of Handel's *Messiah* and we gave her a standing ovation. That debut novel went on to be published in 2008 as *Baby Jesus Pawn Shop,* garnering accolades from Kirkus Reviews, Publisher's Weekly, and NPR and being nominated for the top national American literary awards of 2008.

Of course, I'm not suggesting that Orth's fine writing and extraordinary vision hinge entirely upon the applause she received from a roomful of unpublished hopefuls early in the writing of her novel.

I'm just saying that the first exciting thing is where the action is.

I was at the Mendocino Coast Writers Conference a few years ago when a woman asked if, instead of the first scene, she could read her favorite. That scene turned out to be halfway through her novel, a gripping moment involving all of the main characters when they're first brought into contact with each other through the tragedy that powers the plot. I said that her favorite scene ought to be her first.

She was surprised to hear that you can do that.

I am here to say: "You can do that."

This is why writers invented backstory.

Backstory is everything the reader needs to know about what has happened to our characters *before* our story becomes interesting. It's not that we're going to leave all that out—although the more we can imply and the less we have to pontificate, the better—but stories are not chronological histories. Even historical novels don't start at the beginning. (I mean, what would that be? *Bang!*)

Every writer has to pick a point at which the plot heats up, where we toss the reader into the cooking pot like a lobster with its claws rubber-banded.

You think we have to respect our reader's feelings, slide them onto the dinner plate, break it to them gently so they don't feel the pain?

Nah. Readers like being boiled alive! It makes them feel frisky. That's why so many languages have a pluperfect.

We start with the premise. If our story is about the tyranny of a remorseless psychotic, we start with a scene demonstrating something subtle about that remorseless psychosis. If our story is about love, we start with the ignition. If our story is about crime, we start with something criminal.

We fill in the backstory in chapter two or three, while the characters are taking a breather. That's where it belongs, just like the editorials in a newspaper. Otherwise, we've got nothing to put there, and the reader is going to object to all those blank pages.

However, before we pick that first scene, we remember one thing: not only must we start with the first *exciting* thing that happens (and never before), but that Hook must also be the *crucial* scene that ties into the final scene, the Climax, the premise that's going to lead to the whole point, the one scene that shows how the ending is inevitable because—given the personalities of our characters, the mazes in which they're destined run, and including every event that happens to them between the first and last pages—nothing else could reasonably result from that original genesis. Our initial scene must contain the essence of all that follows.

I like to imagine the protagonist's famous last words. If the character's a scoundrel, the first thing they say is, "I never get caught." Then I show how they never do—until that Climactic scene. If the character's a wallflower due for volcanic passion, they say, "I was going to be one of those shut-ins with a yappy little dog and an expertise in tatting." And if it's a drama about a husband and wife arguing over a pool game, one of them says, "Watch this."

Believe you me, those are some famous last words.

Pulling Out the Crook-Neck Cane

Imagine our reader on a vaudeville stage. They're out there singing and dancing across the hallowed, dusty boards, waving their little straw boater, *clickety-clickety-clack*, ululating for all they're worth. They're paying attention to their own life, entertaining their own audience.

We are not a part of this picture.

No. It's our job to extend the crook-neck cane from the wings, hook them, and yank them willy-nilly out of *their* world into *ours*.

There was a time when we could do this gradually. We could assume they weren't tap-dancing when we met them, they weren't in front of an audience—they weren't even ululating. They were settling down in their comfortable old armchair, putting up their feet, and ready to sink luxuriously into our fictional landscape all of their own free will. We could spend entire pages discussing our protagonist's ancestry before we got around to so much as mentioning why we needed the reader's undivided attention.

We could be Maria Dermout.

Unfortunately that time is past, and we live in the present, as does our reader. They are this very minute carting around enough technology to start their own small government, and we are saddled with the responsibility of hacking through that technology like an adventurer through the underbrush of the Amazonian headwaters, waving flags, yelling through bullhorns, and setting off flares. If we've got a cannon, we'd better fire it.

And all in the first sentence.

How do we do it?

The first thing to do is be succinct. A good, clean, straightforward approach. That's what we want:

> There was something wrong with the figures backlit in the doorway.

I skidded to a stop at the corner of Pico and Alvarado.

Suzette hadn't meant to set Mr. Innagoddadavida's forehead on fire.

The last thing we want is to be vague, rambling, or cliché:

Harold would have given me the shirt off his back if I'd been there, but I was still walking up the driveway, and the dog that was chewing on the paper under the bushes was making noises I thought sounded like either mosquitoes or a helicopter, which I knew about because my aunt Nougat was a helicopter pilot when I was six, or was it seven, anyway I was wondering what I should do about writing to her, although all of this has nothing to do with my story.

When you stack firewood, you must be aware that damp wood will foster bugs and, under the worst circumstances, grow mushrooms, and this is why you might have to ladder it, because it's important for airflow, and sometimes you can ruin a whole cord of wood that way, I think.

Mercy was born on a small island on Lake Washington in Seattle forty years earlier to Lummi Indians who spent most of their time down on Second Street before Seattle became famous, and she lived with them until she was thirteen.

Specifics are good! Details are essential. We just have to be sure they're the significant, telling ones that apply to this particular story we're about to tell.

I had a client once with an extraordinary first chapter—a complete short story setting up wonderful inescapable tension between what the protagonist needs to do and what he *does*. An agent had told this writer that his novel had no Hook.

"You've got a Hook, all right," I said. "And it's *fabulous*. Your novel just isn't the story this particular Hook leads into."

Readers imprint on the first characters they meet in exactly the way ducklings imprint when they hatch out of eggs. Think of readers as ducklings. If we spend the first chapter describing a situation or character that never appears again, we have just sent our reader waddling cheerfully off into the bushes in search of the wrong narrative. And it's going to take us twice as much work to run after them, waving our hands over our heads, and herd them back to where we started in order to point out the *real* protagonist with their *real* dilemma, the *real* concerns we expect the reader to harbor in their breast.

The biggest obstacle to starting a story in the correct place is the writer's natural tendency to do some writing—flex authorial muscles—before launching into the intended plot.

I once started a novel with a long, involved description of a begonia hanging in a pot outside the window over my desk. I waxed quite lyrical on the subject, pointing out how it was a metaphor for immediacy, while my story was set in the past, and eventually (I promised) I would get around to telling that story if the reader was only patient enough.

I showed it to a friend.

"That's nice," she said, bemused. "Why the begonia?"

Of course, there was no reason. It was just something to rest my eyes on while I thought about how to start my great novel.

We must always be aware that, in this day and age, there are literally tens of thousands of aspiring writers *exactly like us*—with our skills, our experience level, our taste, our type of insight, our very ages—scrambling desperately, just as we are, to be seen and heard. There are more than ever in history. There are more than there were when I wrote my begonia Hook in 1992.

We must keep this in mind when we're choosing our words. We might desperately want to write, with Dostoyevsky, "My protagonist was one of the children of an important man, a pillar of our community, whom we all came to know as the star of a particularly dreadful criminal trial (as we still remember him today) because of the way he died many years ago, which I will tell you all about at the correct moment." And we might be right to do so.

But we're competing for our reader's attention with the author who writes, "Alyosha didn't kill his father. He just found out which of his brothers did."

Chapter 10

Running Them Like Rats in a Maze

Development

Causing Effects

What's the worst thing we can do to a story, from our reader's point of view?

Make it meaningless.

But what gives a story meaning? The attractiveness of the characters? The reader's sympathy with their joys and sorrows? The thrill of the plot points? The mystery of what's behind the big secret of the plotline?

No. *Causes*. And their *effects*.

Human beings are interested in stories because they teach us about life. What happens when we do something? We get into hot water!

Yes.

And what do we do about that? And is it worth it?

> Alice O'Flummery wants to get married sky-diving. It's taken her seven years to talk her beloved, Mark Stick, into it, but now finally he's agreed, and they're doing it. They're jumping out of a plane holding hands.

Unbeknownst to Alice and Mark, though, the pilot is in love with Mark's ex, Beany, and Beany doesn't *want* Mark to marry Alice. Beany wants Mark miserable. For all eternity. And spares no words on the subject.

So the pilot, who will do anything for Beany, has secretly severed the pulls that activate Alice's parachute.

But! Unbeknownst to the *pilot*, Mark is a paranoid fanatic whose worst fear is that Beany, whom he knows hates him, will somehow manage to ruin his big day. So he's planning to hold onto Alice for all he's worth, even if that means entangling their parachutes and taking them both down in a bundle of arms and legs and flapping silk. He'd rather die alongside Alice than risk surviving her.

But Alice knows about Mark's paranoia, so she's using a specially-designed parachute that *should* survive entangling. It just hasn't ever been tested.

So, just as Alice and Mark leap out of the plane and the pilot veers off, a meteor comes out of the sky and smashes the airplane to smithereens. The End.

What?

Here we've got all of these causes set up: Beany's divorce from Mark causes her to hate him, which causes her to need to destroy his new wedding ceremony, which causes the pilot who loves her to sever Alice's pulls in order to cause Alice's parachute to fail, while also causing Mark to suspect foul play, causing him to become paranoid and plan to hang onto Alice for dear life, which paranoia causes Alice to get wise and buy a specially-designed parachute. . .and suddenly there's a meteor? Why? Where did the whole point of this story *go*?

Well, I don't know. I just suddenly lost interest in my protagonists and felt like writing about the pilot instead.

Writers, don't do this to yourself. Because even if *we* neglect cause-&-effect, our reader lives life strictly according to its dictates, and if we *cause* the reader to lose their investment in our story, the *effect* will be them chucking our book over their shoulder and walking away.

The stronger the cause-&-effect in a story, the more powerfully our reader becomes invested in its outcome:

> Eaggins is desperate to be the first person to secretly live an entire month in the Anasazi settlement, House of Many Windows, at Mesa Verde National Park, which desperation is caused by his intense sense of his Pueblo ancestry and personal creed of rebellion against the oppression of federal law.
>
> This goal causes him to study rock-climbing. His rock-climbing lessons introduce him to Biff, the legendary Mesa Verde ranger with a nearly endless knowledge of the Anasazi and a heart of absolute gold, so long as nobody messes with his precious ruins.
>
> This meeting causes Eaggins to pump Biff for not only his knowledge—which Eaggins finds fascinating—but the measures Biff takes to ensure that nobody trespasses on the ruins.
>
> This intense interest causes Biff to fall in love with Eaggins. Which causes Eaggins to question his hostility toward park rangers. Which throws Eaggins into an identity crisis, causing him to act strangely. Which causes Biff to question how well he really knows Eaggins. Which causes Biff to question his own

understanding of character, including his attachment to all he holds dear.

Which causes Biff to take a long-overdue sabbatical to get his head together.

Which gives Eaggins the perfect opening to achieve his original goal, fueled by his despair over the loss of Biff.

Which leads Eaggins to trespass on the House of Many Windows at midnight that night under a full moon, unconscious of the fact that Biff's self-questioning has led him to his favorite place in the world, which—according to the story as we've told it—is exactly the same place at exactly the same time. . .

Do you see how the strands weave tighter and tighter around the characters, locking them inevitably into the forward motion of their story? Every time something causes an effect, it strengthens the inevitability of the Climax. Every time a character comes to a crossroads, A or B, the factors that force their choice become more vivid and inescapable. And every time that character starts down one road rather than another, the cause-&-effect of their choice rolls that road up behind them.

Not only must our characters get to their Climax as though towed by a rope, *they must burn their bridges behind them as they go.*

So we keep this in mind as we craft our story—"and then they'll do this, which causes that, which leads to this other thing, which can, obviously, only cause *that.*" We're stringing the reader along, giving our characters opportunities to save themselves, while preventing that by the forces we're creating, which act upon the characters. And the reader can see all this perfectly clearly if they just understand the principle of cause-&-effect.

Why is Eaggins so desperate to flout authority over the Anasazi ruins? It must be absolutely fundamental to his character. *Why* does Biff decide to go up to House of Many Windows on that full moon? It must be the inevitable result of everything he is.

There is only one way each of these characters can possibly react to every situation that we, with our vicious authorial agenda, impose upon them. And every time they react, it feeds the fire that drives them relentlessly toward their doom.

We're cruel, we writers. We leave no loose threads, no exit plans, no possibility of rescue. This causes our reader to follow dutifully along, helpless to our every whim.

Pacing

There's a myth in the world of the literate that we read fiction to relax.

This is a lie. We sleep to relax. We get massages to relax. We lie in hammocks under trees on sunny days eating chocolate to relax.

We read to have the wits startled out of us.

Say we're in a bookstore, browsing the fiction aisles, and we see a couple of books whose covers or titles get our attention, and we flip them both open to the first page:

How to Bake Your Own Head, A Novel

> Mackie had studied the fine art of baking since he was young, and he knew everything there was to know about flaky pastry, tart fruit combinations, and how to

french-braid a danish. He even knew how to get pastry dough to thin and separate without ice water. He was that good.

We join Mackie on a typical April morning at his new bakery, where the dawn light has just begun to reach the tops of the trees across the street. The delivery van drives up close to the sidewalk, and a young woman with dark hair pulled back in a ponytail climbs out the driver's door, opens the back, and shuffles through the day's orders, searching for Mackie's. When she finds it, she smiles.

The Idiot's Guide to Baking, and Other Culinary Adventures

Footsteps sounded on the brick patio, and the front door of the bakery swung open.

"Where do you want these?"

Herb yanked his head out of the oven.

"Here looks good." Diamond Jane dropped the milk crates on the far end of the counter with a jolt that shook the walls.

"Dammit, Jane! There goes my chiffon cake."

As much as I love pastry and am interested in the first title, I'm going to pass over the slow start and go straight for the thrill. What's with Diamond Jane? Why can't she set things down normally? And why does Herb have his head in the oven? What *else* just happened in that crash?

We force our reader to ask themself questions. They keep reading to find the answers.

One other thing you may or may not have noticed about that fast opening: it starts with a conversation. Dialog, among its other virtues, is one way to catapult a reader smack into the middle of an on-going scene. Does the reader want to be led into the story gently, given the visual clues, shown around, made to feel comfortable before we introduce them to our characters?

Heck, no. They want to wake up on the operating table to the doctor saying that things might not be going as planned. Hey! Is that their *liver* that just went by?

Readers like to be roughed up. They like to be jerked out of their chairs, thrown around, dragged by the hair, and flung out of windows. They like to have their heads yanked back and forth so fast they can't keep track of who's doing what and then be drop-kicked off the deck into shark-infested waters.

Why do they like this? I have no idea. They must have inferiority complexes.

A good way to do this to our reader is to start with conversation. An even better way is to start with specific action. Cut off the anesthesia. Show them their liver.

However. The corresponding way to lose our reader's interest is to start *every* scene the same way. We humans have adrenaline responses. That's exciting. We also have protection against adrenaline, so if too much adrenaline gets administered too fast for too long we stop paying attention. That's boring.

I'm not done with Syd Field yet, but I've been sidelined by Donald Maass. Maass, if you don't know, is an independent literary agent and the author of several books on the craft of fiction. Maass says that we need tension on *every single page.*

Now, there's a difference between using tension properly and trying to inject tension gratuitously into scenes that are not inherently tense. The best way to lose a reader's interest is to use too little tension. The next best way is to misunderstand what tension is.

Tension is not pretending that something ordinary like tooth-brushing is of devastating import to our characters. Tension is keeping our reader addicted.

So we pace ourselves. We are always very aware of which scenes carry the greatest weight in our plot, and we make sure our reader is wide awake for them. We administer digitalis, if necessary. Then we bookend those scenes with neighboring scenes that carry secondary weight, and use more subtle tension in those to let our reader breathe. (Don't bother to include scenes that carry no weight at all.)

We don't let the reader go to sleep. That's indistinguishable, from the writer's perspective, from putting down the book and wandering away. But we give them a break. Let their pulse rate slow a little. Let them wipe their brows.

They've got to have oxygen, after all. How else are they going to cling to the chandelier in the next scene, when we toss them their kidneys?

Shoving Your Reader Around

I just spent an afternoon working with one of my clients who reels stories off the top of his head like he's reading them off a ticker-tape. When we went back through what he'd just written, we could see where he'd instinctively packed every page with tension—not just one type of tension, but two or even three types to a page, layers upon layers, so that the reader is skimmed over the scenes, bounce, bounce, bounce, ricocheting sparks of light in all directions as they go.

It's *fantastic.*

Almost every single piece of dialog—almost every single line—is in conflict with the preceding piece of dialog. Those people can't even say hello without arguing. And it's great!

Every line counts toward confusion, curiosity, and tension. Only toward the end of the story do characters begin occasionally cooperating with each other in words, and only then in carefully-timed moments that break up the pattern of tension to increase the contrast.

The protagonist goes through a baffling experience on page one and spends the rest of the story trying to find someone to either solve or at least corroborate what has happened to them, to the extent that they begin questioning their own perceptions. The internal conflict becomes as baffling as the external event. Is this character nuts or not? Only toward the end does the character begin to make decisions about what they're willing to believe, moving the plot relentlessly forward.

The rare lines of exposition keep the reader in a state of constant curiosity. What's going on here? Why does this happen? What's that about? Where is it all leading? Like the dialog and action, the exposition starts feeding us little bits of the answer toward the end, but only enough to justify upping the ante even more as we get closer to the Climax. Never once does the writer let the reader turn their head away. Only at the very last moment do we learn how things are going to turn out. Surprise!

I have a theory about addiction, which I developed when I worked with the victims of domestic violence many years ago at a Battered Women's Shelter. We saw these people come in—grown adults, plenty old enough to know better, having put up with all kinds of ungodly treatment and, even worse, stood by passively while their children suffered all kinds of ungodly treatment as well—and we had to ask ourselves: *Why? What's in it for them? What keeps them hooked?*

I learned about the Hearts & Flowers phase of battering, when the batterer returns after an abusive incident contrite, full of anguish and promises, focused on nothing but winning back the favor they've so aggressively alienated (often, in fact, bearing heart-shaped boxes of candy and flowers).

Awww, the victim thinks. *They didn't really mean it. It was an accident. A justified reaction to external pressures. An anomaly.*

So they take the batterer back. Until it happens again.

Then they take the batterer back. Until it happens again. And again. And again.

And the more often they take the batterer back, the more confused they become, and the needier their confusion makes them feel. The needier they feel, the more willing they are to take the batterer back, and the more abuse they're willing to take after they do.

And the more abuse they take, the more anguished the apologies and promises, and the more confused they are about what. . .just. . .happened. . .

Until they're hooked like a fish on the line, and nothing can stop them from pursuing this person with every ounce of the life force in their poor, knocked-around hearts—the one person on earth they should be fleeing with wings on their heels.

Push them away, pull them back, push them away, pull them back. It becomes a rhythm in the deepest, darkest, most inaccessible regions of the heart.

The human psyche craves this rhythm.

Now, far be it from me to suggest we set out to do our reader bodily harm. This is why I love literature. Performance and three-dimensional art are too immediate. Literature is words, nothing but words, just little black marks on a page, and they can do a thousand things, but the one thing they can't do is get to anyone physically. Readers and writers enjoy their shared adventures from the tops of our ivory towers.

No, what I suggest is that we learn from the human craving for rhythm: in particular, the push/pull rhythm of the longing for fulfillment.

Push the reader away—shock them, startle them, confuse them, intrigue them.

Pull them forward—relieve their anxiety, answer a question, give them a glimpse of resolution, show them a fantasy world, make them laugh.

As soon as they get close, push them away.

Pull them forward again.

Push them away.

Pull them forward.

Et cetera. Et cetera. Et cetera.

We don't wait for them to let us know, "Getting kind of tired of being pushed away here. I'm about to give up and leave."

Or, worse yet, "Getting bored with being pulled in. Falling asleep here."

We catch them by surprise every time, right *before* they expect it:

> Xavier backed through the swinging doors into the barrel of a gun.
>
> *That's the last time I carry two trays at once.*
>
> "Take off your shoes and throw them in the corner."
>
> That gun had to have the longest, blackest, most serious barrel ever built. Xavier had seen plenty of pictures of guns, and none of them had ever looked like that.
>
> Solemn brown eyes stared out of the ski mask behind it.
>
> *Aunt Penelope! No wonder we couldn't find Uncle Manfred after the honeymoon!*

"Now your socks." The gun wavered, and the woman's finger trembled on the trigger, pointed straight at Xavier's head.

Please, Uncle Manfred, if you ever loved me, save me from this maniac you called a wife.

Xavier pulled his socks off and threw them after his shoes. As they flew through the air, something small and shiny fell out and rang on the stone kitchen floor. The woman bent to pick it up. The gun jerked, her finger twitched, and a shot fired, so loud that five minutes later—after the dust had settled—the crystal glasses on the shelves were still faintly chiming.

Meeting Across the River

Lucia Orth once quoted Oscar Hijuelos as saying that sometimes we need to write a transition to find our next scene, even if we're planning to throw that transition away.

Syd Field points out that the best place to start a scene is at the end, where all the excitement is.

Remember that readers like to get roughed up.

When I was about eleven or twelve I thought it would be absolutely grand if someone wrote the story of my life. I'd be taller, and my bullying older siblings would be—I don't know—in a zoo somewhere. But other than that it would be basically the truth. All about *me*.

How would you like to watch an eleven-year-old eat breakfast exactly the same way day after day? Watch her walk in and out of her house over and over again as she goes about her daily business? Listen to her bicker with her little sister about the *same stupid dolls* unfailingly every afternoon? See her mother roll her eyes at the same predictable objection to cleaning the table before supper every single night? Brush her teeth? Blow her nose? Trip over her shoelaces? *Constantly*?

Now, the truth is that my life at the age of eleven and twelve was actually rather riveting. I lived in a two-hundred-year-old hacienda in rural Ecuador without plumbing or electricity, one of a family of six. I got up before dawn every morning and walked a mile down a dirt road between adobe walls to a Spanish-language convent school in a miniscule mountain village and came home at lunch time to schoolwork from the Calvert School of Correspondence in Baltimore. I spent my afternoons playing alone in unending fields peopled by quiet Ecuadorian peasants plowing with mules and oxen under a fathomless blue sky. Lines of eucalyptus in the distance marked the foot of the snow-covered cone of Chimborazo, the highest mountain on the equator, which dominated our view. Sometimes I was woken at night by the rumbling of Sangai, the live volcano nearby.

There's plenty of material there to write about. More, quite honestly, than I can handle. But a live-blog of my daily activities would not be part of it.

The thing is that we can't possibly tell the entire story of everything our characters do from the first significant event to the grand finale. That would take as long to read as it would to live, and our reader has a life of their own. They spend a massive amount of time walking in and out of rooms, opening and closing doors, arriving and leaving, going to bed and getting back up again. It's all *periphery stuff*!

Transitions are that periphery stuff, all the things our characters have to do to get themselves between those few essential moments in which the elements of our plot occur. Transitions weaken fiction and distract the reader from the actual story. A huge part of first-draft revision is simply going through and removing every single instance of, "He went over and opened the door. She got up and left the room. He took off his clothes and went to bed. She put on her jacket and sat down."

Say we've got a scene in a crappy little apartment in urban New Jersey. Our characters need to get from the apartment to New York City where they're going to rip someone off, and they need to do it in a state of acute anxiety. They're both bit players, they've screwed up in the past, and this is their one chance to either be incredibly cool or suffer the consequences. One of them is a bumbler, but the other's got a more level head and knows that their only chance of pulling this off is to keep their mouths shut and their eyes open.

What do you say we put them in a ratty old car and drive them over there talking the whole way about how nervous they are, arguing about how to handle it, and remembering how they've bungled jobs like this before?

If the main scenes are in the apartment and city, this scene in the car is a transition. The reader doesn't learn anything about the story that keeps them focused intently on the upcoming scene that's going to determine their fates. In fact, it diffuses the clarity of the scenes on either side, in taking reader attention upon itself.

So let's try this instead: we'll put the characters in the apartment where they're getting ready for the gig, and the level-headed one spends the whole time admonishing the bumbler on how to behave, chiding and instructing, all but tucking their shirt in for them, then comments briefly at the end upon a rather poignant fantasy of how they'll use the money they're going to steal to win back a girl.

Then we cut straight to the scene in the city and show them blowing it.

If, like Bruce Springsteen when he wrote "The Heist," we're very good and know *exactly* what we're doing, we can even leave out the scene in the city.

Chapter 11

Lulling Them into a Dream, Then Whacking an Epiphany Out of Them

Climax

Faux Resolution: Tuning a Harp on a Cloud

One thing I never hear anyone talk about is the extraordinary moment between Development and Climax.

Suppose we structure our story without that timeless moment. We throw our character at one Conflict after another, *bing! bang! boom!* We've got them by the collar and are shaking them upside-down off a bridge over a speeding locomotive. Utterly thrilling stuff.

We know our Climax is even bigger and better than that. We can't wait to spring it on them.

We leap straight from the last Conflict to the Climax. At some point, we simply let go of the character's collar, and there they go—smashing and crashing from the heights to the depths, into the arms of their worst imaginable nightmare. That ought to give our reader a run for their money!

Or does it?

Sure, it's probably exciting, alarming even, a good, hefty jolt to get their blood up. But is it absolutely the very best bang they can get for their buck?

Not yet.

First we must prepare the ground.

Think about horror movies. Well, don't think about them too hard (I hate horror movies), but think about how the action scenes are constructed. Ominous music, dark shadows, no dialog, slow-motion tip-toeing down a long, long hall in silence. . .the protagonist gets to the door at the end, they touch it, and it swings open with an eerie creak, the frying pan is raised high over their head, and inside—there's nothing! The room's empty! What a relief. They're just dropping the frying pan and turning away when. . .*bam!*

This is how you learn to levitate.

This is also the response we want out of our reader at the Climax.

We raise the hair off their head with our last Conflict (not the Climax), drag them around and wrassle them in our teeth like a terrier. Fake them out that this is the grand finale. Really let 'em have it.

Then we drop them and keel over. Let the heavens open and the angels tune their harps—the lovely sound of golden strings against the clouds.

The reader's thinking, *We did it! We beat the monsters! We survived the trauma! We climbed* Chimborazo*!*

Wow, do they feel good now.

We want them to feel good. We want them to feel *great*. All of that rattling down the Spanish Stairs in a Mini Cooper, beaning their heads on the ceiling of the car, clutching the door handles, the dashboard, and the other characters in their anxiety, and then suddenly smooth, delicious sailing straight ahead to the harmonies of an angelic choir.

They are *so* not expecting our Climax now!

Climax: Walking on Water with a Pen

Flannery O'Connor, in some of her essays on craft, wrote about the evolution of a story. She explicated in detail a particular story, "Good Country People," describing how she casually wrote the protagonist's false leg into the plot only to see how it came up again and again until, as she said, it began to take on meaning from the different situations in which it appeared. Then she went back and structured the Climax to reflect what she felt was the whole point, which is that attachment to false support is crippling.

It was her understanding of symbolism that showed her how to end in a surprising but inevitable way. It's a fabulous story.

What happens is this: we explore our fictional world until we've uncovered the bones of a good, solid plot, with a Hook, Conflict Development of increasing tension, a Faux Resolution, and a Climax to blow the lid off a pressure-cooker. We work out each individual Conflict with its own hook, development, and climax that leads inevitably to the next hook.

This is the thrilling part of writing a novel—the part where we're soaring on waxed wings. We have to keep pumping up again and again to stay in the air, we have no idea where we're going or what we're going to do when we get there, but our heart's in our mouth over the unbelievable view.

This is also what's frequently mistaken for writing the first draft. It's usually not. If we do it sequentially rather than in sketches, it's usually just writing a whole lot of exposition that will have to be turned into scenes later. And if we do it as part of a word-churning project like NaNoWriMo, we wind up with as many words of brainstorming as we intend for our final novel.

But unless we force ourselves to brainstorm really, really slowly by writing each scene in full detail, this part isn't the actual writing.

The thing is that it's *excruciatingly* difficult to plan a novel really, really slowly so that we can write each scene sequentially in full detail at the same time. It's like running a snow-plow while stopping to examine each snowflake with a magnifying glass. Chances are almost certain that our snow-plow's going to wind up in a lake and we'll wear ourselves out and eventually break our own hearts trying to get it back out again.

Writers who regularly attempt to plot and write at the same time are the ones who end up drunks.

So we mull our story over for a long time, we think it all out, we make sure that every plot point is necessary. Every scene has a hook, development, and climax, every incident causes the next effect, every single twist teaches the reader something they don't already know about life.

Then we sit down and write our scenes (or re-write, if we've done our planning in 72,000 words), entertaining ourselves mightily as we go.

This part's luxurious. This is the long, slow, steady joy of writing fiction.

In every scene, we strive to include telling details – not just things that anyone might notice, such as the character being medium-height, but something that only we might see, such as that their nose has a jog in the middle. Not just a red carpet, but a feathery pattern with a spot near the doorway worn down to weave. Not just a coffee cup, but a china cup of milky 1930s green with a white chip in the rim above the handle.

Flannery O'Connor quoted a friend who said that every character description takes three strokes to make it three-dimension. Even the rooms our characters walk into get their strokes.

Characters pick things up as they talk, put them down, notice things in hallways as they pass through, lean on things they maybe shouldn't. Their world is full of three-dimensional objects—not just things anyone might notice, like chairs, but small carved figures, flowered baking bowls, hats with broken crowns, pink gardening gloves, square drinking glasses, dismantled fingernail clippers. Things that have been *used.*

And as we go along writing our scenes, coming up with these trivial details that don't need to be planned because they're not essential to the progress of the tension, we notice that one character is *always* leaning on things they shouldn't, another is *always* sorting through muddy gardening gloves for a matching pair, another *can't stop* dismantling and reassembling their fingernail clippers. It works its way into the dialog.

"Can I borrow your clippers?"

"Sure." Handed over in two pieces.

We finally get to the Climax, and we've planned it deliberately to be the one pickle these poor saps can't possibly get out of. We've backed them against a wall good this time—this is a bind for which none of the solutions they've used throughout the rest of the novel works. We've seduced the reader into our dreamland, and now we're walloping them with all we have like a two-by-four. *Whack.* And we throw ourselves into it, because this really is the very *worst* thing that could possibly happen.

Ezekiel and Ramona confess their love for each other the night before Ramona joins a convent.

Detective Spink has the suspect cornered after a long and nearly-impossible chase, when someone unexpectedly clobbers her from behind.

The dragons of Mallmart finally unite against the tyrant fairies, when an adolescent with uneven propane levels accidentally starts a forest fire that threatens the communal egg crèche.

"Why us?" our protagonists cry in anguish. "Why *now*?"

We put everything we've got into it—like a sea cucumber, we throw our guts in the reader's face. It's mesmerizing!

But then we read our entire novel through one last time before we let it go cold, with all its ups and downs, its drama and anguish, its shining characters, their humanity and pain, and their heart-stopping glory. . .and it turns out that, well, our Climax isn't quite as mesmerizing as we thought it was. In fact, it turns out that our final Conflict is still shaking the foundations of the story, while the rest of it just reads like—I don't know—*anticlimax*.

All that effort just to get here? But it's not worth it! Is our novel a *failure*?

Maybe.

Or maybe it simply isn't finished yet.

This is when we pull out our clipboards and fresh notebooks, find our favorite pens, take our manuscripts under our arms, and go sit under a tree. We bring hats. We're going to be there awhile.

We read through our novel page-by-page now—especially the beginning—jotting down our favorite telling details. What's the most gripping detail in the early scenes, the one we read and think, "Oh, how I love that detail"? Write it down and put a star next to it. Mark details that turn up repeatedly. Make notes on which characters they're associated with. Accumulate the data. Collate the findings. Categorize, prioritize, be hypnotized. This is research.

You know what's the most intensely flattering thing about being a writer? Not readers. No. Not even publishers. But spending all that energy researching *ourselves*. Narcissism can't even compare.

We must go through our entire manuscript this way, and we must find every single telling detail that might possibly be the key to the Climax. Because something in there is. Something is going to get the helpless victims of our authorial despotism into an impossible predicament.

Once we've got all our notes organized to our best abilities, we'll know which one or two or even three elements of our story it is. The more elements, the more exciting the Climax when they all come together.

> It's true that Ramona has a spiritual streak a mile wide and was raised among nuns. And it's true that Ezekiel is a poverty-stricken potter with nothing but his depthless blue glaze to his name. And it's true that Ramona associates the sight of blue water with the father she barely remembers, who committed her to the nuns' care when she was just a little girl right before he died. But who knew that when Ramona walks into the Mother Superior's office, she sees the Mother lifting dead flowers out of one of Ezekiel's precious blue bowls

on her desk and remembers in a flash that her father's last words to her were, "We're all human, sweetheart. . .we don't really walk on water"?

Honestly—who knew?
Our subconscious did, that's who.

Resolution: Succumbing to Dramatic Overwhelm

We come up with a great idea—"I'll have a brilliant but socially-malformed protagonist meet a creative savant, and they'll have to solve global warming before their romantic attraction wins out over their personality conflicts and the ex-President reveals himself as the incarnation of Sauron!" The more we think about it, the more we like it. "It'll be Phillip Marlowe meets *Rebecca* in Middle Earth!" It's keeping us awake nights.

We throw ourselves whole-heartedly into this story. We're taking notes in a whirlwind—everywhere we look, character traits both unexpected and riveting appear and adapt themselves almost effortlessly to our main characters, descriptive terms leap to mind, great plot elements are casting themselves at our feet, and our characters' dialog is sparkling, witty, disturbing, and profound.

Could life get any better? We always knew we were writers. And now we know why!

We've taken the time to learn to plot. We have Conflict Development to raise long hair on end, lightning flashes back and forth between the Conflicts, not just the inevitable final Climax, but inevitable cause-&-effect links from one Conflict to another, over and over again. We've got the reader in a barrel, and we're aiming them straight for Niagara Falls.

It's all so beautiful and meaningful and new! Nobody's *ever* written this novel before. Why hasn't anybody ever written this novel before? Years of our lives, and this story has become part of who we are. We will never want to let go of these characters. We will never stop loving just being with them.

But one day after years of faithful dedication, we reach that point. We've written every episode, polished every scene. There isn't a spare word anywhere. We are at the Climax. It's time to do what must finally be done. We've laid down cushions in all directions, enticing our reader to rest their weary head.

We've even finished researching the essential symbols that make up our theme. So now we write our Climax. And it's *perfect*.

All the strands come together exactly the way they should, and even we aren't quite sure where we got the words to create that image that knocks us backward out of our chairs every time we re-read it.

We have come to the point of Resolution. We write it. We are sated. We put our novel in a drawer. In six months, we will take it out and polish it once more, and then this phase of our lives through which we have lived so much will be over.

So in six months, we take it out, read from the beginning—it's so beautiful, so charming, so moving, so profound!—until we get to the end, past the Climax, and the Resolution is. . .what's that word? Oh, yes.

Hackneyed.

It's as though it were written by somebody else. All of that gorgeous tension and build-up and climbing the heights of Chimborazo to see the stars for what they really are, and here we are in some living room in the suburbs staring at glittery plaster on the ceiling.

What happened? Do we really, after all, have nothing to say?

This is called, in my own personal lexicon, *Dramatic Overwhelm*. And it is part of the writing process. It explains the conundrum in writing advice that we must both plan our novels and not plan them, both know where we're going and have not the foggiest clue, both plot a good, gripping, well-structured story and also let the characters take us where they will.

How do we make sure that our Resolution carries the greatest possible meaning of all potential themes in this novel, when we are simultaneously writing just to find out what we've written?

Dramatic overwhelm. It takes us down at the knees every single time.

The secret is that we *do* write every book to find out what we've written. But, even worse, we write every book to find out what we *know*. And this makes it difficult to write what we know, doesn't it? Because we don't actually *know* what we know.

This has been true for every single person on earth throughout the history of the human race. Nobody has ever known everything they really know.

And this is why fiction is not just a craft, it is art. Because art is about discovering the unknowable. It's about diving into that river of reality and fishing up what we find, turning it in the sun to make the light refract off it and show not just what it looks like, but what it resembles, what it's not, what it could be, what it might be, what, in fact—in the alternate universe in which we all simultaneously live without even knowing it—it really *is*.

We must dive deep for this. We must go over the falls. And once we've brought it up and explored what we found, we must dive once more, even deeper, because the truth does not come up in one piece. The truth always leaves its core behind.

So when we reach the point of *Dramatic Overwhelm*, we do not panic, do not despair. We're fine. We have simply reached the place in our novel at which we sit down with blank paper and begin to write—not the Resolution, no—but pages and pages and pages of dreaming about this situation and these characters and this Climax and that Hook and these plot elements and those twists and turns and impossibly inevitable Developments that have come to us by surprise, as well as about our lives and everyone else's lives and what matters most deeply and profoundly to us.

This is the moment when we have assembled all of the disparate elements that we want to illuminate, and it is time to link them all together in the essential.

You thought we were done after the Climax, didn't you?

But no.

We hunt with a magnifying glass for the invisible links between all things in the elements that we've incorporated into this novel. We look for what we've never realized is lurking behind those links. Most of all, we look for the ways in which this novel has taught us what matters to us.

Because what matters to us is why we're alive. And art is about learning why we're alive.

Two of my earliest clients were the authors of beautiful novels in which they dove deep, deep into the river and retrieved extraordinarily lovely and priceless things. And when we got to the Resolutions of both novels, we looked back through the stories at the characters and plot elements, the Hook, Development, and Climax, and all the beautiful, telling details to learn: what do these things show us about what matters to these authors? Why are these authors *alive*?

In both cases, we found that it was relationships. The characters' relationships had altered throughout the novels, they'd mutated from what the characters thought they were into something altogether different, they'd turned in the characters' very hands, almost letting the light reach their underbellies, there at the Climax. In each novel, there was a set of symbols that acted as catalyst. And we focused on this: how to fully and with perfect clarity show the light refracting off those beautiful underbellies.

No matter how wonderful and tense and profound our stories, it is at the Resolutions that we show the inevitable, impossible light refracting off the darkest parts. And we don't know what this looks like until we're done.

A story is research that allows us to learn the truth. And, like scientists, we plan our research.

However, learning this truth is why we write fiction in the first place.

Part 2

Line Issues

Chapter 12

Watching Your Language with P.G. Wodehouse

What is fiction? prose in scenes & exposition

I once stumbled across an article about a men's association in Hungary based entirely upon P.G. Wodehouse's imaginary Drones Club.

You remember the Drones. They play cricket with bread rolls in the Common Room, pop badminton birdies into the chandeliers, rustle up spontaneous conga lines to imitate mating newts, and ride around on each other's backs yelling and whacking indiscriminately in all directions with rolled-up newspapers. This is apparently what well-heeled gentlemen of London do with their spare time.

I find the Drones hilarious, in spite of their sad lack of female talent, and I love that Wodehouse named them after do-nothing male bees. My twelve-year-old thinks they're even more hilarious than I do. Adults acting like his dream twelve-year-olds are almost more than his budding imagination can handle.

But I will forever mourn that nobody has written a novel about those Hungarians *pretending* to be Drones.

P.G. Wodehouse liked to tell his friend Guy Bolton—with whom he collaborated on the Broadway musicals that made his fortune—that he only had one plot, but he used it over and over again.

And it's true. I can tell you exactly what that plot was: Bertie Wooster or one of his friends accidentally gets engaged against his will, requiring Bertie to steal something. Sometimes Wodehouse called him something other than Bertie, but the basic outline is always there.

Of course, this is a gross simplification. Not all of Wodehouse's wonderful little stories involve a failed theft. (Even the novels, for some reason, read like something you could tell over a glass of port after dinner to much companionable merriment.) Some of them involve a failed sale of a historic Georgian manor. Or a failed sale of a women's magazine. Or a failed sale of *soup*.

What makes each story charming isn't different plots. It isn't even different characters—Wodehouse is famous largely for using the same characters over and over again, especially the inimitable icon Jeeves, essential for bailing Bertie out of all those failures.

No, what makes Wodehouse's genius is the endless, sustained *consistency* of his language. There's hardly a loose word in all ninety-six publications.

Think about it: ninety-six books of fiction. Published. Widely-distributed over numerous decades. *Loved.* Even in Hungary!

How did he do it?

Well, the first thing he did was practice. He was already writing doggerel for London newspapers when he was a young man, supplementing his standard reporting duties with a wonderful series of poems called "The Parrot" based upon a contemporary import tax issue, in which a parrot flies into the windows of various characters croaking dolefully, poem after poem, "Your food will cost you more." This series even spawned a contest in which parrot owners brought their birds in to croak the necessary line, although it turned out that none of the birds would do it.

Wodehouse spent his apprentice years developing his ear for rhythm: an appreciation for the natural undercurrent of melody running through a well-told story, a willingness to let go the reins and allow words to stream out of him in the easiest, simplest manner possible. Line after line carries the rhythm through his stories. Word after word carries the beat.

Aside from becoming the literary style upon which Wodehouse built his name, this turned out to be a brilliant technique for popular lyrics. Bolton wrote the tunes, Wodehouse wrote the words, and between them they raked in money by the bale during the hey-day of Broadway musicals stretching all the way from the 1920s.

And the second thing Wodehouse did was learn to polish. Although he practiced his ear for language until he could pour it onto the page as though out of a bottle, he knew that there's no such thing as a writer with perfect pitch. So after he'd thought up a variation on his standard plot, run it through his lingual brain into words, and put the words down on paper, he went back through each manuscript conscientiously and meticulously, weeding out anomalies, antiphonies, and any and all tiny, jarring aural interruptions.

He taught himself to pace a paragraph by alternating simple declarative sentences with occasional long, complex ones. He ruthlessly cut every single word that didn't add significantly to the rhythm or sense. (If we're not part of the solution, we're part of the problem.) At the same time, he *kept* every single word he needed to make the translation from page to reader's mind transparent.

He trained his eyes firmly on the ideal of clarity.

Read a page of Wodehouse. Read another. And another. And another. Everywhere we look, there's that lissom flow of words hypnotizing the reader into submission.

Do we want to hypnotize our reader?

Yes, we certainly do.

Can you guess how? Same way we get to Carnegie Hall. Practice, practice, practice.

Prose

Chapter 13

Words

Use exactly the words you need, no more nor less

Braving the Dark & Stormy Night of Clichés

Clichés. Do all aspiring writers use them? Yes, pretty much. What a cliché.

Remember Snoopy's ambition to write a novel? Every now and then he'd appear up on his doghouse, typing away on his typewriter: "It was a dark and stormy night." He was great, up there randomly with no warning at all, typing the same old beginning over and over again.

Edward George Bulwer-Lytton, of course, wrote that greatest cliché of modern times and, with it, inspired the annual sport of cramming the highest number of intensely painful clichés into the smallest possible space, The Bulwer-Lytton Fiction Contest. Thank you, Professor Rice of San Jose State University. You have given the role of clichés in literature a whole other meaning.

The thing about clichés, though, is that they're not the simple, ordinary, dimwit stumbling blocks they appear to be. They are, in fact, one of the most complex, least easily-definable techniques in fiction.

Did I just call clichés *technique*?

Yes. Technique. And here's why: because they serve a purpose.

But what makes them complex? So hard to define? They seem agonizingly obvious. "She had a figure like an hourglass and an inviting twinkle in her eye. He had a powerful jaw and a steely gaze. She fluttered her eyelashes longingly, and he glowered threateningly. She pouted. He snarled. Her hips beckoned—"

Make it stop!

Clichés are fundamentally complex because they start life as colorful, brief alternatives to lengthier descriptive terms—the epitome of good description. Here's something you may not have realized: one of the things that makes international ("ethnic") literature so lovely in English is the unusual word choices, metaphors, and juxtapositions. Half of those are not interesting or unusual in the author's native language—they're simply translations of clichés.

You should hear how striking some of our English clichés sound in Spanish. "*Dentes como un caballo.*" Really? Teeth like a horse? So when she smiled she looked like a horse smiling? A smiling *horse*? Now there's an image to take home with you.

Clichés are also complex because they *work*. I'm sorry, but they do. When we say someone is "lovely as a rose," we use a simple, succinct image to communicate a great deal of information. And the whole point of good writing is to communicate a great deal of information as simply and succinctly as possible. A lot of what's now cliché came right out of great literature a long time ago. Look at Shakespeare.

So what's wrong with clichés? And how do we spot them in our own work?

This is why they are so difficult—there's no concrete definition.

We can't say, "Everything comparing one thing to another is a cliché." It's not—it's a metaphor or simile, which are extremely useful techniques in themselves.

We can't even say, "Everything comparing a young female to a flower is a cliché." It's not—a baby like a Venus flytrap would be an extremely interesting baby.

And besides, clichés cover a much wider spectrum than just young females and flowers. If we tried to pin the definition of clichés down example-by-example this way, we'd wind up writing lists straight out of Jean Kerr's *Please Don't Eat the Daisies.*

There is only one way to know what's a cliché and what's not, and that is to know as much as humanly possible about *what's already been written.* Identifying clichés takes the most exhaustive familiarity with our native literature that you can imagine.

Because this is the only definition: a cliché is something that has been done too many times before. It no longer conjures a specific, telling response in the reader, just the numbing effect of white noise. It has outlived its useful life.

How do we know whether or not it's been done too many times before?

Read. Read, read, read, *read.*

Read the great books to find out how they walked the tightrope between too simple and too bizarre. ("He had teeth like a large toothed mammal." "He had teeth like the Starship Enterprise.") Read crap to find out what's cliché. ("His teeth were pearly white.")

> *WARNING: This is the only time I will ever advise you to read crap. Do it only for a specific purpose, in controlled*

circumstances, under strict supervision, and while wearing a gas mask.

However, the *safest* way to guard against clichés is that standard of all great fiction—clean, simple, factual description.

Does she have a figure like an hourglass? Unless she's wearing a corset, probably not. (And if she is, it's not very attractive by modern standards.)

She might very well have large hips over which she wears tight clothes. Or she might move her body with a slow, deliberate motion. Or she might—more likely—have other features that communicate her allure in more telling detail, like a way of sliding her eyes toward the door when he comes in without actually catching his eye; or a short, sharp breath that she takes whenever he speaks even though her expression remains calm.

Facts. Stick to them.

We have a much better chance of avoiding the La Brea Cliché Tar Pits that way than if we load our work with whatever comes off the top of our heads, just hoping the plethora of those particular clichés in print hasn't yet reached critical mass.

Not Going Gently into that Adverbial Night

I blame Elmore Leonard.

Adverbs are out. So-called "-ly words" are out. Out of what? Out of the category of Things Writing Teachers Accept as Good Writing. Do we have an adverb or any word ending in -ly in a manuscript? For god's sake, get it out!

On the face of it, this makes sense. In Leonard's famous list of literary rules, he gives us #3, in which he sternly admonishes writers to use neither dialog tags other than 'said' nor adverbs with that dialog tag. In fact, he claims that using adverbs at all is almost a mortal sin.

Now, committing mortal sin by literary artifice is not something we want to get into. And it's definitely not something we want to get *caught* at.

Leonard had a good reason for these two rules. It runs along the lines of:

> "I think you want it another way," he insinuated sneakily and underhandedly.
>
> "Rip it up. See if I care," she taunted forcefully, dominatingly, and girlishly.
>
> "Don't kill me!" he warbled pathetically, sadly, hopelessly, paradoxically, and energetically.

We can try reading the number of manuscripts every week that agents wade through, chock full of such dialogic adverbial crimes, and see if we don't wind up throwing ourselves on Leonard's neck in abject gratitude.

However, Leonard's rule about adverbs in dialog tags does not translate into a wholesale ban on adverbs. Deleting all of the adverbs in a manuscript—even just the adverbs associated with dialog tags—is not the same thing as learning how to write good dialog, much less learning to write well.

This is just another of those of half-baked crutches offered to (or imposed upon) aspiring writers to save them the trouble of learning what good writing actually *is*.

So now more and more aspiring writers struggle to keep perfectly good adverbs and adverbial dialog tags out of their work without knowing exactly what they're doing or why. They wind up with monotone dialog that communicates nothing about the characters or their reactions to their situations.

On top of this, we start finding actual grammatical errors, in which adverbs are still used, only with their -ly endings lopped off:

> "I'd think you could guess," she said angry.
> "I don't want to," he said short.
> "Where did you leave it?" she said confused.

On the other hand, try this dialog tag:

> "I could have you tossed out," he said pleasantly.

Remove the adverb. Now what is he up to? Is he cagey? Is he businesslike? Is he mad? Is he kidding?

As it happens, "he" is a class-A freak in a highly-threatening environment arguing with the protagonist about the exact illegality of his behavior. If we remove the adverb, it's natural to assume that he's speaking threateningly. But that's not his style—it's not his *character*. A great deal of information about him is communicated through the adverb that tells us how he pronounces that sentence.

Or this adverb:

> He stared at me coolly. "Not the police."

Remove the adverb. How did he stare at me? Furiously? Sneakily? Suspiciously? Out of the corner of his eye? With amusement? With a wink? Is he about to attack me? Is he trying to get information out of me? Is he afraid of me? Does he think I'm funny? Is he trying to say something to me without saying it in front of someone else?

Or does he want me to know that he's not afraid of me, although in this context I'm telling him that I have something of his that the police would find very interesting, something secret, something dangerous, something illegal—in other words, he's staring coolly?

Or this one:

He looked vaguely at my hands.

Remove the adverb. How did he look at my hands? Hard? Intently? Leeringly? Rudely? Was there something on them he wanted to see? Was there something about them that mattered a lot to him? Did they turn him on? Was he showing me disrespect in a context in which I'd made it clear I didn't want anybody looking at my hands?

Or was he just looking at them to give him something to look at while he talked to me, maybe with a hint that, although he's focusing on something, it's not my hands—in other words, vaguely?

All of these examples are based upon lines out of Chapter Twenty-One of Raymond Chandler's *Farewell, My Lovely,* arguably one of the most vivid and intimidating chapters in the mystery canon. Chandler goes on to use the adverb "softly" three times in a row in the dialog tags on one page. He also uses "absently," "lightly," and the quintessential "bleakly."

Would this chapter be the work of art that it is without the adverbs?

Of course not.

Chandler was the master.

On the other hand, we can write for days such dialog as:

"Are you hungry?" he said.

"Not really," she said.

"I am," his brother said.

"What do you want to eat?" she said.

"I don't know," his brother said.

"Can you think of anything?" he said.

"Not really," his brother said.

"Good grief," she said.

If adverbs truly added nothing to language we wouldn't have them. There's nothing intrinsically wrong with adverbs, any more than there's anything intrinsically wrong with adjectives, prepositions, nouns, or verbs.

Not only that, but adverbs are not the only -ly words in the English language. We can't just tell writers to leave out all adverbs/-ly words, because we're telling them to leave out all apples/oranges. (And don't even get me started on the fad of leaving out the articles in poetry.)

The current fashion in crisp, clear writing uses far fewer dialog tags than writing of twenty or even ten years ago. Dialog tags (along with description) are being phased out, largely through the influence of advertising slogans and sound bites.

This isn't necessarily all bad. Good editing involves cutting out everything that doesn't add anything essential to the story.

Take the passage:

"Where did you get that?" she said, turning it over in her hand.

He shrugged. "I just found it lying around," he told her.

"Are there any marks on it?" she asked.

"Not that I noticed," he answered.

"What are you going to do with it?" she said before handing it back.

"Give it to you, I guess," he grinned.

Turn it into:

"Where did you get that?" She turned it over in her hand.

He shrugged. "I just found it lying around."

"Are there any marks on it?"

"Not that I noticed."

"What are you going to do with it?" She handed it back.

"Give it to you, I guess." He grinned.

(Please note: "He grinned" is a declarative statement, not a dialog tag, and must be punctuated as such. If you don't know what I mean, study it and you'll figure it out.)

Twenty years ago, we might have gotten away with a lot more dialog tags and still had fine writing. But extra dialog tags don't add anything, and they slow the reader down, even just fractionally.

It's a perfectly good exercise to go through a manuscript and remove every adverb we possibly can. What have we got to lose? Tighten up the language.

If an agent or editor really has bought into adverbophobia, that's okay.

When we find an adverb we sincerely need, we can always cheat:

"You're in my light," she said menacingly.

"You're in my light." Her voice was menacing.

It's an even better exercise to go through a manuscript and remove every dialog tag we possibly can. This forces us to make the dialog more specific to each character, and that in itself is worth a total revision.

And another really good exercise, just for fun—let's see if we can get a reference to mortal sin in there somewhere.

Then maybe we can work in the name Leonard.

Indulging in the Passive & the Active—Grammatical Voice

Now, adverbophobia is not the only modern literary phobia. There is also the dreaded passivevoiceophobia. . .oh, passivevoiceophobia. . .May our fingers curl backward and meet our knuckles if we indulge in this most heinous device.

But what exactly is passive voice? And what's wrong with it?

Active/passive grammatical voice is determined by the subject of the sentence:

Active voice: the subject of the sentence acts.
Passive voice: the subject of the sentence is acted upon.

And there are a few folks floating around out there who may or may not know what passive grammatical voice is but are *pretty darn certain* that we're not supposed to use it.

They occasionally turn this admonishment into: get rid of all "to be" conjugations. Of course, conjugations of "to be" don't always signal passive voice. I've actually got two separated by a single word in the previous paragraph, neither of which is passive. It's just that passive voice tends, in general, to use more "to be" conjugations than active voice does, which means active voice is, in general, shorter, clearer, and more succinct. And clarity, as we already know, is the goal of good writing.

Active voice:
I publish all the news that fits.

Passive voice:
All the news that fits is published by me.

Two extra words, one of them a "to be" conjugation and the other the mostly inevitable preposition "by."

But sometimes the admonishment against passive voice turns into: get rid of all auxiliary or 'helper' verbs. Auxiliary verbs include all those forms of "to be" (plus "may/might," "would/could/should," "must/ought," "shall/will," "can," "do," and, oddly, "have") that we use in English order to scoot other conjugated verbs around into exactly the correct positions. And these are also not necessarily passive voice.

Active voice without auxiliary verbs:
She gave it her all.

Active voice with auxiliary verbs:
She would have been giving it her all.

Passive voice:
Her all was given by her.

Like "to be" conjugations, auxiliary verbs are often quite helpful in managing passive voice. And, like "to be" conjugations, yes, they do sometimes make our sentences longer. Sometimes a little more complex, sometimes a little less succinct.

Sometimes. A little. That's all.

Yet these phobias—passivevoiceophobia, to-beophobia, and auxiliarophobia—continue to sweep the nation.

"No, no! Inflame us not with your nasty, two-timing little wases, shoulds, and hads!"

Doors are locked and barred. Red slashes are posted in windows. We cower in terror.

Has one gotten in under the door?

Well, *yes*.

If I had known you were coming, I would have baked a cake.

There are three main verbs in that sentence—known, coming, and baked—and a whole handful of little elves helping them out—had, were, would, and have.

You know what I love about the English language (and this sentence in particular)? Because we use contractions, we're perfectly capable of making certain auxiliary verbs, like "had," indistinguishable from others, like "would." And we do it *all the time*! Wacky us. It gives us great control over our rhythms. The real version of that classic sentence is, "If I'd known you were coming, I'd have baked a cake." And it's a heck of a lovely sentence.

We also use various forms of "to be" so often that we have a special grammatical rule in English, which states that subject and object take identical form when used with pure "to be" conjugations:

I am I. Not me.

Isn't that a nice little twist? These kinds of things add character to our language. And layered language is a wonderful tool for achieving layered stylistic voice.

The truth is that there's nothing wrong with passive grammatical voice, "to be" conjugations, or auxiliary verbs. Good writers use them all the time. They're unendingly useful in their own little ways.

Literary phobias are simply a symptom of our modern hunger for the quick fix. If we can identify which words not to use, we assume, we'll automatically be able to churn out salable writing, and it'll cut off years of having to mess around learning the actual craft. *Wot a savings.*

Shortcut Memo:
No adverbs or words ending in -ly.
No passive voice.
No "to be" conjugations.
No auxiliary verbs.

If we use these shortcuts, I guarantee that our writing will be. . .well, shorter. It just won't necessarily be any better.

Welcome to the twenty-first century.

Discovering Your Own Language—Stylistic Voice

Voice. Ah, voice. What is it? What do agents and publishers mean by it? Who even knows?

I do. They mean stylistic voice. And here's an exercise for identifying and beginning to understand stylistic voice:

First we pick three or more of our favorite authors. We come up with a scene or episode off the top of our head, the longer the better. Now we write that scene or episode over and over again, once in the voice of each author. We just try to put ourselves into the mindset of that author, try to use the words they would use, the imagery, the sentence structure, the details or lack of details, the tone (the feeling—dreary or passionate or pleased or arrogant). Whatever we do, we don't rush through it. This could take days, if not weeks. We're doing our level best to sound *exactly* like the author we're imitating.

Now we set them aside. They're cooking.

We work on other things for a couple of weeks or, better, months. I know it's hard, but being a writer is a lifelong career, not a hundred-yard-dash. We've got time. We must have projects in the works. So we go ahead and work on them.

When we've gone long enough that we've effectively forgotten the details of what we wrote, we get them back out and block off a couple of hours in which we will not be interrupted.

Now we read them through, lightly, casually, as though we were an objective reader. One at a time. Comparing them to writing by the original authors.

What underpins our imitative voices? What is common to all of the pieces, no matter how hard we tried to disguise it? (And no, I don't mean the errors. Those are common to us all.)

This is stylistic voice.

So mostly what we know now is that we have it. Which is good! A mute speaker has a hard time speaking. A writer without a voice has a hard time squeezing out words. We don't try to force it. We don't try to turn it into anything. Our stylistic voices are the ways in which we naturally express ourselves, even after plotting and revision and editing (yes, and grammar- and spell-checkers) have taken their toll.

Stylistic voice is not necessarily outrageous or attention-getting. It does not slap the reader upside the head with its self-importance.

It's just us. Saying what we have to say. When we say something interesting, and say it clearly, it really is identifiable.

What agents and publishers mean when they say they're always looking for a powerful voice is an author who's willing to dig deep into the world all around for the plot twists, characterizations, powerful cause-&-effect, telling details, gripping action, vivid dialog, and unusual insight that make a story fascinating to read. What they mean is that they've had enough of sloppy grammar and punctuation, lackluster dialog (And then I was like, "Whoa." And then she was like, "Whoa." And then he was like, "Whoa!"), trite description ("her hips beckoned"), unconvincing emotion ("He was as angry as a bull. She was as passionate as a kitten. Their lips burned with sexiness"), boring scenes ("I said whoa. She said whoa. He said whoa. Then we took a really long time to wash the dishes").

What they mean is self-assurance.

Stylistic voice is achieved by first learning how to write clean, clear, grammatically-correct and properly-punctuated sentences and then using them to show the unique, fascinating fictional world that is ours.

It's simply us.

Chapter 14

Techniques

Make your choices & stick to them

Tensing—
Past, Present, & Future Tense

Tense? Yes, I'm tense. What do you want to know about it?

Oh, you mean *tense*. As in: past, present, or future. How to use it, where to choreograph it, why not to mix it up.

We can use any tense we want in a narrative. I mean, there are only the three of them. We can have ourselves a field day! (Just as we can use our choice of first-, second-, or third-person narrative voice. This gives us a total of nine permutations. Boy, howdy!)

The issue is not how many tenses we use or which ones they are. The issue is: have we decided which tense to use and under what circumstances? And are we sticking consistently to that decision? Or are we just flying along on cruise-control bopping in and out of different tenses as the whim takes us, so that the final manuscript reads like time-traveling sci-fi. . .and not in a good way?

You see, I'm not going to revise this until tomorrow. It won't be early—I'm not an early riser—and I'll be a little fuzzy, a little slow, still a little blurry-eyed. I'll be thinking about whatever vivid dream I'm going to be in the middle of when I wake up. (*Why* will that happen?) I'll forget to bring a cup of tea upstairs from the kitchen and try to heat water for tea in the electric kettle in my office in the attic, which will be empty. So I'll have to come back down to the second floor and fill the kettle in the bathroom. My son will be sitting up in bed drawing track plans for his dream model train layout, and we'll wave to each other.

I'll say, "I'm still sleepy! How about you?" and he'll say, "I'm always a sleepy-head."

I know all this because it happens to me every day. I wake up in the middle of a vivid dream, lie there listening to my husband sleep undisturbed and trying to remember what it was in the dream that woke me, which I can never remember. After awhile I hear my son in his room singing to himself, and I realize it's morning. I get up and get dressed and start the whole eternal quest for a cup of hot water for my tea –

Except for this morning, when I remembered perfectly clearly what it was in the dream that woke me up. It took me ages to shake that dream. I had to dig my 1960s paperback mystery out from under my pillow and read about some skeleton being discovered in a supposedly unoccupied grave for almost an hour, and in the meantime the sun hit the tops of the redwoods across the meadow outside our bedroom window and gradually slid down the trees, until by the time I got out of bed and went to the window, my whole vegetable garden was in sun, and I could see the chipmunks making merry in my laughably inadequately-netted strawberry patch.

At least I knew what tense I was in!

Otherwise, if I don't make decisions on tense beforehand, I've often found I screwed up and will land my reader someplace I don't want them, like the past, when I really hoped to put them square in the present where they actually are right now and enjoying it and so, if I'm going to do it with passion, I'll suddenly be writing along, happy as a little clam, and find myself in the future. And I never knew what hit me!

That's what I'll tell you about tomorrow. In the future tense.

Because I do that. In the present and on-going tense.

As I have done in the past, in the past tense.

By which time this whole thing will be written in all three tenses, perfectly accurately—except for that one paragraph—each tense reflecting a different perspective on the narrative of my morning.

Here's an interesting point: when we talk or write about written work, we always describe its contents as existing in the present tense, under the assumption that the life on the page is eternal. Elizabeth Bennet is *forever and ever* telling Mr. Darcy that he could not have offered his hand in any way that would have induced her to accept him. I find this rule charming.

But not like this morning—this morning it was all in the past tense. The pre-hot-water-for-morning-tea tense. I *know*. I've simply got to relax.

Speaking— 1st-, 2nd-, & 3rd-Person Narrative Voice

"I" is first-person narrative voice.

"You" is second-person narrative voice.

"She/He/They/It" is third-person narrative voice.

And deciding in which voice to write trips us all up at one time or another.

First-person is most intimate. However, it requires a specially-developed stylistic voice for that one character, a level of consistency that can be painfully difficult to maintain all the way through 72,000 words.

Third-person is less intimate, but we get to write in our own stylistic voices.

And second-person is just funky.

So it is with a real sense of luxury that the reader sinks into Jessica Soffer's story "Beginning, End," which takes on all three dragons simultaneously, strings them out, complicates them, carries them beyond the limit, and finally delivers the reader upon a haunting shore, a shore that we all know is there but don't always know how to get to.

It starts out so easy, albeit unusually. Second-person. A paragraph of you.

The next paragraph switches. Now it's first-person. And it imposes even more distance between the reader and narrator than the second-person, through its ever-so-careful lack of interior perception.

Then a brief paragraph, just four sentences: first-person, second-person, first-person, second-person.

And the rich, inevitable next paragraph: first-person plural.

So the story begins in earnest, long, full paragraphs of first-person plural split into first- and second-person singular whenever there's a squaring-off between the characters, a divergence in their lives, arguments and fights and separation, the anguish of trying to live life with another and never knowing quite how to do it the way it's meant to be done—only to come back over and over again to the first-person plural, first-person plural, the enmeshing of lives that is partnership, until the two are thinking as one.

And just when we imagine Soffer's taken this wonderful exercise in voices as far as it can go, she goes one step further. The person is suddenly both first- and second-person singular, speaking dialog. And it's *important*. The separation is no longer in the hands of the characters.

So when first-person singular returns, it's from a completely different perspective, the voice of a character—an I—who has begun as one person, gone through a metamorphosis, and come out another person, all the while retaining the I of I.

When the story ends on an asymmetrical series of first- and second-person singular sentences, the reader knows how that's come about, not because it's been explained (but isn't exposition explanation? no, it is not) but because the reader's been through the transformation, too.

The reader is the I who has changed.

Seeing—
Limited, Unlimited, Omniscient Point-of-View

So let's talk about the different aspects of point-of-view (POV). Because this one, too, is quite a sticky wicket.

'Limited aspect' means limited to the POV of one character.

'Unlimited aspect' means that we can use the POVs of more than one character.

'Omniscient aspect' means that we can screw around with POV as much as we want so long as we stick to one narrative voice (first-, second-, or third-person).

Beyond this, we're off into the realm of experimental fiction.

The simplest, commonest, most straight-forward POV is third-person narrative voice, limited aspect: the whole story told from the POV of just one protagonist—but not the narrator, who is the author. And there's a really good reason for this.

Because it *works.*

Once upon a time it was *first*-person limited. *Great Expectations, Moll Flanders, Moby Dick,* all riveting, all first-person limited: protagonist as narrator.

However, first-person got kind of beaten to death over the millennia, so these days we use third-person for everything but the most specific situations.

It's true that third-person is not as immediate and intimate as first-person. But it does have the benefit of allowing the reader to feel they're in the room with the protagonist, going through the protagonist's experiences alongside them like another character, rather than having to do it all from inside the protagonist's own head. 'Alongside' is absolutely the most vivid way for a reader to experience a story, and authors who are really good at first-person have to cheat to keep the story largely outside the protagonist's head as though it were third-person. (Except for James Joyce. He didn't try very hard.)

Fortunately, keeping the aspect limited—rather than unlimited or omniscient—*also* optimizes for immediacy and intimacy. The better the reader knows a particular protagonist (and it's hard to know them better than exclusively or 'limited'), the more deeply they become invested in that character's welfare, their fate, their decisions and actions and accidents, the urgency of meeting their *needs.* So—to the extent that it's possible to keep the immediacy and intimacy after all these years without getting bored with the technique—we've retained the limited aspect with the move from first-person to third-person.

Third-person limited.

We like to call this in professional circles The Best of Both Worlds.

But what if we have more than one character we're crazy about? What if we want the reader to be able to bond with more than one protagonist? I mean, here we are, locked in our little windowless rooms for ninety-nine years, walking with these characters, talking with these characters, learning their needs, their desires, their hopes, their fears. Learning to *care* about them.

They must meet their needs! They must! *All of them!*

So we weigh the alternatives. On the one hand, the greatest possible immediacy and intimacy by sticking to third-person limited (without getting into the specialized realms of first- or second-person). On the other hand, diffusing the reader's experience with third-person unlimited or omniscient for the sake of. . .what?

Not our personal feelings. Never for the sake of the writer. *Always* for the sake of the reader.

But say we've weighed the alternatives, and it turns out that our story really does need to be told from the POV of more than one protagonist. There's no way around it. It's simply what the story is.

In this case, we wind up using something called 'unlimited aspect,' which is really sequential limited. ('Unlimited' implies that we can see into everyone's perspective simultaneously. But that would be 'omniscient.' Which implies that we can see into anyone's perspective from any POV. But that would be *anarchy*.)

So instead, like Carson McCullers in *The Heart is a Lonely Hunter*, we put one protagonist after another under the spotlight and set the reader dreaming alongside first one character, then the next, then the first, then the second, et cetera, et cetera. Sequentially. Not simultaneously. Unlimited characters, but still limited to one character *at a time*.

This technique requires incredibly careful design. We need a pattern that highlights the main protagonist, as well as illuminating that character's relationships to the other protagonists. Who's closest, who's most detached, who's most distinct, who's got a conflicting agenda? We must be freakishly sensitive to the ways in which these characters interact. We must treat their very relationships as characters.

When designing such a pattern, we must remember that:

1) The reader imprints on the first character they meet. Unless either this character is given barely a passing mention or, as in *The Heart is a Lonely Hunter*, the structure of our story is absolutely solid and thoroughly integrated with the story itself, *this had better be the main protagonist.*

2) The reader feels intuitively the links and contrasts between the personality of one protagonist and another. This is *enormously* helpful. That's the juxtaposition that gives our story layers.

3) Every single technique we use must have its purpose. *Why* do we absolutely need the reader to experience this particular character's POV? Because *we* enjoy imagining it? Not good enough. Miss Havisham must have been great, rollicking fun to be during the writing of *Great Expectations*, but it would have diluted the immediacy and intimacy of the story to include her POV, and since he had no other purpose for it, Dickens was ruthless. Miss Havisham is a kick in the seat not because the reader gets to pretend to *be* her, but because the reader gets to actually *meet* her.

The best way—hands down—to show our characters is from the outside, not the inside. Show them as if they were real people the reader were meeting in the real world.

We only use a character's POV if we absolutely cannot tell our story any other way.

But what about other POV techniques? First-person, unlimited and omniscient aspect? Second-person, limited, unlimited, and omniscient aspect? Third-person omniscient?

Let's assume for the sake of argument that second-person is such a wildly specialized technique that we're not using it at all, in any aspect. If you are, drop me a line. Otherwise, we'll let this one slide.

Let's also assume for the sake of argument that first-person unlimited is unusual enough (although not unheard-of—John Gardner used it beautifully in *The Wreckage of Agathon*) that we're not using this, either. If you are, see above.

And first-person omniscient is complex to the point of complete insanity. "I was myself, but I was also everybody else"? We could *sprain* something.

This leaves us with third-person omniscient narrator.

Talk about a bugaboo!

You know how one dimension is a dot—limited aspect—and two dimensions are a line—unlimited aspect? Omniscient aspect is three-dimensional. That's (x,y,z) graphing, for all you computer graphics engineers.

Here's how we do third-person omniscient:

Massive research. Relentless practice.

Seriously. We must devote ourselves to a minimum of one year of conscientiously researching (finding, reading, and analyzing) only the most accomplished novels written in third-person omniscient, dissecting them POV switch by POV switch, looking for patterns, looking for relationship illuminations, looking for the ways in which the authors have used the transition from one POV to another as a technique in-&-of itself to show the reader something they couldn't possibly have shown any other way.

Try Elizabeth Bowen's short stories or James Clavell. Do not try F. Scott Fitzgerald.

And for every pattern, illumination, and transition technique we learn, we must practice. Practice, practice, practice. We write the same chapter multiple different ways. Write the same characters into different scenes with different patterns. Set up different characters with different relationships and use the techniques of the greats to illuminate those relationships with the switches. By the sweat of our brow.

Sound like a lot of work? It is. But omniscient narrator is so much more specialized than even the other specialized techniques, and yet so commonly misunderstood and misused and (dare I be so dark?) *abused,* that there's no point in attempting it if we're not going to do it right.

Or just stick with the obvious: third-person limited. The Best of Both Worlds.

Scenes are *Showing*

Chapter 15

Description

Give your characters a world

Moving from Proust to Haiku

There was a time when a brilliant writer could sit in bed day and night between cork-lined walls, years on end, writing seven volumes of fictional memoir containing two thousand characters, steeped to the eyeballs in meticulous description of things as ephemeral as the instant just before falling asleep.

But we don't live in Proust's *Remembrance of Things Past* anymore.

These days it's more like haiku: say it simple, say it on the wing, and leave what the reader can infer unsaid.

Why?

It's the times. Flash fiction, one of the staples of contemporary literary work, didn't even exist as a genre at the turn of the century. When Virginia Woolf wrote her fragment-like short-short stories, she was working a vein that wouldn't be seriously revisited for almost a hundred years.

And what's fascinating are the mechanics behind that.

Woolf began experimenting with fictional forms in the wake of the first World War, when Europeans found themselves waking from what appeared at the time to be an endless dream of Victorian realism into the horror of their world gone totally surreal. Cubism wasn't only an artistic school. It was a very real illustration of how Europeans felt about life in an era in which they woke every day without brothers, fathers, and sons they'd never expected to lose, to bomb craters and collapsed homes and ruined cities, with the inescapable knowledge of modern Europeans methodically slaughtering other modern Europeans decades after they all believed the German-English-French extended family of aristocracy had finally learned how to sit down to Christmas dinner without automatically going after each other with the steak knives.

It couldn't happen here, they thought. *It couldn't happen now.*

But it did.

And hand-in-hand with that historical earthquake came post-Industrial Revolution technology, when not only domestic servants but also multiple-daily mail, visiting cards, weekly At Home days, *salons,* and nearly-endless stays in each others' country homes all became obsolete practically overnight in the wake of such stunning inventions as telegrams, telephones, cars, central heating, and vacuum cleaners. It wasn't just about factories and Luddites anymore.

Do you hear the tiny bells ringing?

We're living right now in the wake of 9/11, the first wake-up call to the US since Pearl Harbor.

It couldn't happen here. We all knew. *It couldn't happen now.*

Coincidentally, the Information Age has already, within our adult lifetimes, given way to the Digital Age, in which it's not information that owns the airwaves, but technology that owns our actual time.

Flash! flash! flash!

Joseph Esposito has theorized on the O'Reilly Publishing Tools Of Change website that we need an even newer genre, what he calls 'interstitial,' a fictional form designed specifically to be read on personal devices during fragmentary moments of waiting throughout the average industrialized day, in which private life and business are becoming increasingly indistinguishable. (After all, nobody wants to get *too* far from their lifeline to social media, even on vacation.)

And meanwhile we writers are off in the corner plugging away at those heart-wrenching novels.

Even as late as Raymond Chandler's era, the 1930s and '40s, he could still burn up the whole first chapter of a book describing a house. He could describe the color, the roof, the chimney, the trim. He could describe the front walk, the flowers, the trees, the lawn, the statuary. He could throw in any old thing he felt like, whether it moved the story forward or not. Dashiell Hammett could describe every character in detail as they appear, even their clothes. *Especially* their clothes. Chandler did it, too. You'd think these two tough guys were a pair of *fashionistas*.

However, we writers can't do that anymore. Readers have no time for stasis, no patience for a pause in the storytelling. Readers want action. They want things to happen. They want them to happen here. They want them to happen *now*. Just give them the most telling and significant details, and let them extrapolate the rest.

There's simply too much going on constantly all around them in their real lives. They desperately need to be shown the unintelligible historical moment they're living through in this instant, as it flashes before their very eyes.

Creating Layers of Meaning

In John Gardner's *The Wreckage of Agathon*, Agathon yells to his hanger-on Peeker to break the jug. So Peeker *breaks* the jug, much to Agathon's dismay. It's the wine jug, and Agathon is speaking figuratively.

A good metaphor is a wonderful thing—flexible, subtle, transparent, fraught with intent. I admit to a cringe when Juliet insists on cutting Romeo up into bits and pieces, but her point, his beauty, does carry over. Some of the most wonderful titles ever are metaphors, comparisons of an object to a story in order to illuminate the common essence of both: *The Fountain Overflows* and *This Real Night* from Rebecca West, "Pale Horse, Pale Rider" from Katherine Anne Porter, *The Sheltering Sky*, *The Spider's House*, and *Let It Come Down* from Paul Bowles, *The Big Sleep* from Raymond Chandler, and of course Flannery O'Connor's magnificent use of aphorism in her titles, "The Life You Save May Be Your Own," "A Good Man Is Hard to Find," and, "You Can't Be Any Poorer Than Dead."

Isak Dinesen embedded in her story "The Roads Round Pisa" the complex metaphor of a play, *The Revenge of Truth*. In exactly the same way, Shakespeare embedded in *Hamlet* the slapstick mummers' play of the poisoning of the king. Using the metaphor of a work of fiction within another work of fiction in this way is an old and time-tested technique that creates depth and illumination with great style. Dinesen, in fact, was a master of this technique, so that her stories are packed to the gills with storytellers.

With a metaphor, we rely upon our reader's ability to differentiate between what we say and what we mean. *The Spider's House* isn't actually about a spider.

With simile, though, the writer is slightly more helpful. A simile is "like" or "as" something. We give the reader that little lift under the elbow they might need.

For this reason, simile is often considered a bit of a coarser tool. Thomas Hardy could say that a character courted in a voice like milk and mean it, but this particular simile works as well as it does because it's both so different from the expected amorous comparison and so particularly apt to the milkmaid character, Tess.

Clichés, the ultimate in coarse technique, are usually similes.

Graham Greene conscientiously weeded almost all metaphors out of his work. Raymond Chandler, on the other hand, wrote some of the best similes ever. His subject matter (the LA underworld of his era) was specific, and what he was attempting (creating pulp fiction of literary quality) was highly unusual for his time. Also, he had a heck of a sense of humor. If you can write similes like Chandler, I say have at it.

Symbolism, on the other hand, is metaphor taken to extremes.

When Flannery O'Connor explicated her story, "Good Country People," to show the use of symbolism, she explained her symbol, saying that she intended the reader to understand the protagonist's lack of religious feeling as akin to the wooden leg that she so highly values.

Now, I love O'Connor and get enormous pleasure from reading her work, but frankly I find it more entertaining without understanding the religious implications she intended. Her books are chock full of references to God's grace and the Devil's temptations, and without the logical explanations they're simply chock full of wholly inexplicable and hilarious metaphors for real life. As her neighbor chided her, her stories just showed what some people *would* do.

The minute we decide to write fiction rather than nonfiction, we step into the world of layers of meaning. How far we proceed—how carefully we choose our materials, how many layers we attempt, and how delicately or solidly we arrange them—is entirely up to the writer. The best fiction functions on both the shallowest and deepest levels simultaneously.

The shallowest level lies within the concreteness of our details, the appropriateness of them, their significance, their uniqueness, the way they carry the story *forward*:

Telling details.

The deepest level lies within the juxtaposition of our details, the meanings that juxtaposition reveals, the hidden agendas, the layers, the movement *forward*:

Juxtaposition.

Layering with description is really quite simple—if we just keep those two levels in mind.

Chapter 16

Action

Give your characters life

Transcending Language

How do we write an action scene? How do we get a character from the beginning of it—a sudden acceleration of activity—to the end—wherever we need to get them through that particular action?

Short sentences? Long sentences? Incomplete sentences? Onomatopoeia?

Honestly, how many of us even know what onomatopoeia *is*? I had to look it up. My writing friend who helps me with such things thought the term was "wizbang."

Zip! Back to the subject at hand.

> She threw a right hook at my chin and connected with it. My head snapped back against the wall. It hit and made me see stars. I staggered toward the couch, holding my head in my hands. Wow, it hurt! I leaned over the back of the couch and fell into the cushions. I started thrashing around. The cushions entangled me so much that my feet flew up and hit the chandelier hanging low over the back. It shattered it into a million pieces. She was running after me to hit me again. I think

she wanted to kill me. Obviously, stealing that money out of her bank account was a bad idea. Her foot landed on a large piece of broken glass from the chandelier. She slipped and fell into the radiator, which was standing in her way. Her head hit it with a loud noise. Her eyes rolled back in her head. Her tongue lolled out. She collapsed in a pile on the floor. I staggered back to my feet again. I looked around for a weapon to defend myself with. I finally noticed that she was knocked out cold on the floor against the radiator.

Or:

She threw a right hook. My head snapped against the wall. I staggered, stars whirling, to the couch and fell over the back. My feet flew up into the low-hanging chandelier in a shower of glass. She slipped on a large piece as she ran at me, there was a loud noise, and by the time I got up she was out cold against the radiator.

Paragraph #1? Or paragraph #2?

June sat down on the couch and read her magazine, turning the pages slowly. After a long time the door opened, and Reginald wandered into the room. He sauntered around for awhile with his hands in his pockets. He went to a table by the window and picked up a book that was lying there with some others. June watched him finger the gold lettering on the spine, although she knew he didn't know she was there. She stopped turning the pages of her magazine so that he wouldn't look up. He lifted the book to his lips, curling and uncurling his fist, let a tear run down his cheek in the afternoon sunlight, and kissed it with his eyes closed.

Or:

The door opened. Reginald didn't see June when he came in, but moved forward, paused, and moved forward again through the afternoon sunlight. He picked up a book from a table by the window, fingered the gold lettering on the spine, closed his eyes, and raised the book to his lips.

Paragraph #1? Or paragraph #2?

Which paragraph gets the characters from the initial adrenaline rush to the end, where the point is, with the greatest tension?

The point of the first scene is that this character gets decked by someone who, in the act of decking them, accidentally clocks herself unconscious. We want that protagonist where they are at the end: on their feet, swaying dizzily over their incapacitated attacker. This sets them up for the next step. What are they going to do about what's just happened?

The point of the second scene is that June sees Reginald kiss the book without him knowing. We want them where they are at the end: June watching, Reginald unconsciously kissing. This sets them up for *their* next step. How are they going to react?

The action scene is just a means of getting them to that set-up.

Think about the purpose of the scene. What do we hope to accomplish? Some character needs action—for whatever reason, whether it's pacing between chunks of dialog, a wake-up after exposition, an increase in tension—and we *also* have a plot to follow. What next step are we aiming for? What do the characters have to know when they get there? What does their relationship need to be?

At the end of the first scene, the protagonist has learned how the other character feels about them and what she intends to do about it. Their relationship has gone from not-dangerous to very dangerous indeed. The next step is how the protagonist deals with the *consequences* (bing!) of their *actions* (bing! bing!).

Plot is cause-&-effect: actions and their consequences.

At the end of the second scene, June has learned how Reginald feels about that book. Reginald, however, has not learned about June. Their relationship has developed an enormous imbalance. Now June has a power over Reginald that she didn't have before. The next step—we can see this coming—is how June and Reginald deal with the *consequences* (this new imbalance) of their *actions* (June's silence, Reginald's kissing proclivities).

Action scenes change things between characters. Our characters move around each other, they influence each other, they alter their shared chemistry. Readers want to read about people whose relationships keep changing. This is fascinating stuff to the human animal.

Remember about keeping things in context. The action of this scene might very well be for the sake of the characters, but the overall forward motion of the plot is *always* for the sake of the reader. We never inadvertently interfere with the forward motion of the plot. When we do it in a first draft, we don't worry about it, but we always line edit afterward with an eye for *forward motion.*

Be aware of repetition. Repeating the same words happens a lot in first drafts. It's because we're thinking. Which is fine—

we all think sometimes while we're writing, although a lot of the best stuff gets written when the writer's keyboard is on fire and their fingers have to keep moving to keep from being burned. But don't fall into the trap of assuming that just because repetition is used in hypnosis this means littering a manuscript with it makes the work hypnotic. You know what happens to people inexpertly hypnotized? They fall asleep.

Also keep in mind the rhythm of the sentences. The rhythm in action scenes is an essential part of managing the tension. And tension is what action scenes are all about. Long, drawn-out sentences can slow things down, but so can too many short, choppy sentences in a row. What we want is rhythm, always rhythm, carrying the reader relentlessly forward into the set-up for the next step.

When in doubt, go ahead and use a simple meter: two shorts and a long, or two longs and a short. By the time the reader gets to the end of the last sentence, they're not sure how they got there. All they know is that they're with these characters where we intended them to be, their head whirling, their heart unexpectedly pounding, ready to be flung again.

We did it! We transcended language.

Entangling Your Characters

The first thing we decide for an action scene with more than one character is: whose scene is this?

> As I came down the hall with Detective Pincher, the sound of running feet approached up the stairs. Benny Jackrich appeared, her hair wild, her hands out, tears running down her contorted face. She nearly blundered right by without seeing us.

"Benny, what is it?" I grasped her arm.

"Don't touch me, damn you!" She shook my hand off and ran on, sobbing.

"Go see who's downstairs," I instructed Pedro, at my elbow.

Mr. Anderson came up the stairs behind Benny Jackrich. "I need to talk to you," he said to me.

Whose scene is this? The first-person protagonist? The investigating detective, Pincher? The master of the house, Mr. Anderson? The convenient Pedro? Someone unseen?

No. This scene belongs to Benny Jackrich.

On her way through the house, the protagonist witnesses a startling event: Benny Jackrich comes running full-tilt up the stairs on her way to her room looking as though her heart were broken. Even when grabbed, she doesn't stop, just jerks free and runs on. Benny's got something going on!

What do the characters need to know by the end of the scene? The protagonist (and, by extension, Detective Pincher) needs to know that something devastating but not violent has just happened to Benny. Not only that, but she also needs to know that Mr. Anderson *knows something about it.*

Benny—Mr. Anderson. Mr. Anderson—Benny. What's up? That's the set-up for the next step.

The next step is that, as Mr. Anderson is about to tell the protagonist, Benny has almost confided the solution to the mystery to him. Holy cow! Benny knows!

We need this scene in order to introduce Mr. Anderson telling the protagonist about this. Would Mr. Anderson's news have worked as well without the action scene? Not at all. Why not?

Because the reader wants to be *involved.*

Through the protagonist, the reader not only hears from Mr. Anderson that Benny knows something, but gets to be a part of Benny's anguished refusal to cough it up. In this way, the action scene serves to drag the reader into the room with the characters. The reader is caught up, themself, in the action, so that when Mr. Anderson delivers his news to the correct listeners, the reader is right there listening as well, and the curiosity of the moment isn't just the character's, it's the reader's.

What the heck? the protagonist thinks. *What could mousey little Benny Jackrich know that I, the housekeeper in charge of running this house, do not know?*

What the heck? the reader thinks. *Why is Benny tearing around with her hands out, yanking herself away from the housekeeper, swearing in her panic to get where she's going?*

Let's try it without Benny:

> As I came down the hall with Detective Pincher, Mr. Anderson came up the stairs.
>
> "I need to talk to you," Mr. Anderson said.

Are you working up a sweat? I'm not. What do we care what Mr. Anderson has to say?

There's another important point about allowing the reader to witness Benny's anguish first-hand, and that's the standard issue of all storytelling that *people lie*. We don't know whether or not Mr. Anderson is going to lie about what just happened between him and Benny to cause such a reaction. But we know for a fact that the reaction exists. We were there.

We were there.

This is absolutely crucial. If we weren't there, then we're not invested in whether or not someone's upset over something that Mr. Anderson said. Could happen every day, for all we know.

By the end of Benny's scene, not only are the characters set up for the next step, the reader is as well. Our curiosity and empathy have been aroused, so what comes next will matter to us in a personal, emotional way.

Now, even though the protagonist is obviously the main character of this story, notice how little the focus is on her in that particular scene. It's not her scene. It's boring if every single scene belongs to the protagonist.

It's Benny Jackrich's scene, and the protagonist only gets enough action to entangle her in Benny's problems. The protagonist stops Benny. She asks her a question. She relays instructions to another. But Benny gets to do all the running, shaking, and sobbing, not to mention thundering up the stairs in the first place. She also gets to have a wild hair, outstretched hands, facial contortion. And she gets to swear at her boss.

Good for Benny! She's having quite a day.

Choose a main character for each action scene. In dialog we can get away with shifting the focus back and forth between characters—she said, then he said, then she said—and each piece is hard-hitting, fascinating stuff. But in an action scene the reader needs a physical response, which means a personal connection, and jumping around between characters confuses and diffuses that connection. Let the reader's heart leap into their throat with one character's heart. Let them blurt out that character's impolitic exclamation. Let them feel the strain in their own body, just like that one character.

Action scenes are about getting the reader's blood pumping. To do that, we've got to suck them right into the core of the scene. This is no time for pussyfooting around.

Make the reader *be* that character, and then feed the both of them the juice.

Chapter 17

Dialog

Give your characters their voices

Structuring & Punctuating Dialog Correctly

My favorite antique dialog tag is "interpolated." Isn't that a terrific word? Ellery Queen was a great one for interpolating conversation.

The thing is that we can use any verb as a dialog tag that is, in fact, a vocal act involving words. This means "moaned," "babbled," "sang" (but only with lyrics), and—yes—"ejaculated." They all, technically, qualify.

The real question is: *should* we?

I have a very limited list of verbs that I use for dialog tags. Granted, it's not as limited as Elmore Leonard's, but whose is? And I limit them for a different reason than he does—not because I'm a minimalist, but because dialog tags are largely unnecessary. I highly recommend that you do the same:

said
cried
yelled
shouted
shrieked
whispered

That's pretty much it.

If the occasion really calls for it, I sometimes use others:

muttered

murmured

hissed

snapped

I only rarely use variations on "said" that indicate the speaker's relationship to their respondent because, again, it's simply unnecessary:

asked

replied

answered

The reader's already supposed to know about that relationship.

I do not—unless I am writing humor—use "screamed." This is because in my experience when someone is screaming that's all they're doing. Words do not come into it. If I'm in enough control of myself to enunciate dialog, however profane, I consider that shrieking.

When we get into the area of limiting dialog tags, we immediately also get into the area of adverbs. If we aren't going to use a variety of verbs for dialog tags, we often need adverbs to qualify the verbs that we do use. On the other hand, if we aren't going to use adverbs with dialog tags, we often need a wider variety of verbs.

This is a messy area. Given the choice between "she said quietly" and "she whispered," we must choose based upon exactly what we mean.

I would strongly advise against, however, "she insinuated," "she trumpeted," or "she lilted in the voice of a wilting flower."

The ideal is for the speaker's voice to ring in the reader's head without reference to it being dialog at all. Our goal is for the reader to feel as though they're in the room with the characters, determining for themself how to feel about what's being said.

Like verbs, adverbs used with dialog tags should not draw attention to themselves.

As far as punctuation, we're past the era of gratuitous experimentation, and this I consider a good thing. Dylan Thomas could, as an experimentalist in the 1950s, dispense with quotation marks and use dashes instead, but it makes his work confusing to read until you get used to it. (Yes, Charles Frazier does it too, trying to place his novel in history, but I think it's a mistake. It's not a true historical issue.) Earlier than Dylan's era, single and double quotation marks were reversed, but there's standard punctuation now, and we need a pretty compelling reason to deviate from it:

> Double quotation mark.
> Dialog.
> Ending punctuation mark.
> Double quotation mark.

This is all we need.

> "Will you stop?"
> "Make me."

Sometimes the British still use the old-fashioned style of single quotation marks instead of double. So if you're in Britain, enjoy yourself!

And, like attention-getting verbs and adverbs, I rarely use exclamation marks. It happens—particularly in first drafts—but I find upon editing that I can almost always do without them. They go with "shouted," "yelled," and "shrieked," although we can get interesting effects with those dialog tags without exclamation.

However, there is one other punctuation mark with which we normally end a piece of dialog, and that is the comma.

We always use a comma instead of a period when ending a piece of dialog before a dialog tag:

> "Will you stop?" she said.
> "Make me," he whispered.

That's all. A comma instead of a period and *only* before a dialog tag. That means a verb that describes a vocal act involving words. Never before anything else. This is an iron-clad rule. Ellery Queen notwithstanding, nobody interpolates words anymore. Ever. For any reason.

Some of the other things we don't do with words are laugh, grin, giggle, smile, frown, or throw them. We don't rebuke them, either, although I've seen people try.

> "I'll make you, all right." She laughed diabolically.

So here's the other thing about the structure of dialog: most editors these days don't like to see the dialog tag first. It used to not be an issue. Even as late as the 1960s, we could find a plethora of dialog beginning with its tags in, say, John Updike's *Couples*. Those days are past. It is now considered incorrect to begin a piece of dialog with anything but dialog. Today we would alter the perfectly-correct '60s dialog:

> He looked at her and said rudely, "If that's the only reason."

to the correct twenty-first-century dialog:

> He looked at her. "If that's the only reason," he said rudely.

Now, I know Elmore Leonard litters his manuscripts with dialog tags before dialog, but he's breaking the rule for a reason, and I consider it a sloppy reason—to make his stylistic voice sound more *cazh*. However, if we can't make our voices sound casual without drawing attention to ourselves as writers, then we should probably work harder on our voices. Especially if we're known for making up even more restrictive writing rules.

Dialog tags before dialog are old-fashioned. So it goes.

Something else that we used to be able to do, which we don't anymore, is put two characters' dialog in the same paragraph:

> "It was last summer," he said, and she answered, "Is that supposed to make it all right?"

Nowadays, each character gets their own paragraph. When characters interrupt each other, we have to be creative. I tend to use dashes:

> "It was last summer—" he said.
>
> "It that supposed to make it all right?"

Interestingly enough, up until about the turn of the century dialog tags were frequently used to break up dialog and create pauses that mimicked actual speech:

> "We used to have time for each other," she said, "before I took this stupid job."

In fact, it was common to the point of being standard to break off the first phrase of dialog in order to lead into the dialog tag:

> "If it were me," he said, "I'd have given up on that garden a long time ago and laid down Astroturf. Ask Harriet."

We can still do this, although I once heard of a self-titled "editor" so allergic to breaking up dialog that he actually altered such constructs even when there was a necessary action involved in mid-dialog. (This is not editing. This is tampering.)

But the more invisible dialog tags become and the further we move from using a variety of verbs and adverbs for them, the further we move into the real forefront of the dialog world, and this is the elimination of dialog tags altogether.

"What? How can you tell who's speaking?"

"With action."

One of the most interesting things about dialog is that people almost never sit around talking solely with words. Even on the telephone, we tend to pause, sniff, clear their throats, scratch, cough, and perform other noise-worthy functions in the course of speaking our minds.

In person, the spectrum of activities is awe-inspiring. Glasses, ears, hair, noses, lips, teeth, fingers, hands, elbows, even eyelashes provide plenty of opportunity for the speaker to indicate an attitude or reaction. I was talking to my elderly uncle one evening when he simply stood up and walked away.

There's a reason written conversation over email, IM, and texting so quickly acquired emoticons. Speakers don't like to do without visual cues.

Given this—that speakers feel distinctly hampered without action during dialog—and given that dialog tags in fiction draw attention, however passingly, to themselves and therefore interfere with the dialog, it's a simple and straightforward step to substitute actions for dialog tags.

Not:

> "I have to go home," he said. "Right now, before it's too late."

But:

> "I have to go home." He jumped to his feet. "Right now, before it's too late."

We bring our characters more vividly to life while retreating, as writers, further out of the reader's line of vision.

This leads to one other punctuation issue, unusual in the realm of dialog tags and therefore commonly misunderstood. That is inserting an action into the middle of a dialog sentence. If a character's going to jump up between sentences, well and good. We have no problem. However, if they leap up in mid-sentence, we're stuck with a situation in which one full sentence is embedded in another full sentence.

The following are incorrect:

> "The water," she climbed on her chair, "is rising too fast."
>
> "The water." She climbed on her chair. "Is rising too fast."

Use dashes to indicate one complete sentence embedded into another complete sentence.

The following is correct:

"The water—" She climbed on her chair. "—is rising too fast."

This is one downside to substituting action for dialog tags. And it must be taken into consideration.

The other, of course, is the over-use of actions so that they, even more than dialog tags, interfere with the characters' dialog. For this reason, many writers do their utmost to limit the number of characters in any given conversation to two. With only two characters, we can give quite limited speaker indications every few lines and leave the rest of it up to the dialog. When we do this, we indicate who's speaking by giving each character their own paragraph, whether they speak or just act:

He sighed and leaned on the table. "They might."

"I hope not." She picked at the splintered Formica.

"It's a possibility."

"I don't think so."

"You have to be open to it."

She looked at him.

"I'm just saying."

She glanced at the piece of Formica she'd broken off. "I know."

It's tempting, once we begin using actions to identify our speakers, to go whole-hog. Speakers are capable of packing several actions into each pause in speech, and if we visualize our characters carefully enough we'll see them performing them all.

The next thing we know, our readers are so busy scrutinizing gestures and mannerisms that—once again—the thread of the dialog gets lost:

> He put his head in his hands and sniffed, and a tear fell on the carpet between his feet. He rubbed his chin with the back of his wrist. "It was a matter of minutes."
>
> "We saw it coming." She stood in front of him, her hands helplessly by her sides, and touched his shoe with her toe.
>
> "It doesn't help!" He looked up, stretching his neck.
>
> She sat on the couch next to him and sighed. "I'm not saying it does. I'm just saying—"
>
> He dropped his hands between his knees and stared into her eyes, his face twisted. "You should have been there." He took her wrist in both hands and sniffed again. His tears ran along the line of his jaw and down his neck into his collar. "It was—it was—"
>
> "I understand." She reached out with her other hand but didn't touch him.
>
> He dropped her wrist and turned away, the arm of the couch solid under him and his arms wrapped around his head. "You don't. You couldn't. He wasn't your father."

As much as each of these actions might contribute to the scene, there are just too many of them. Some of them have to go.

The goal, of course, is to write dialog so unique to each character that the speaker can be identified by their words alone. In real life, this doesn't work. People who belong to the same social groups tend to talk about the same things in the same way, using the same slang and the same rhythms.

However, in fiction our characters' ways of expressing themselves must sound as least reasonably distinct, enough so that dialog between two characters can go on for several lines without total confusion.

This is the subtle art of writing dialog. This is where proper structure meets the internal ear, word choice, character focus, intentional design and inference, and the joy of talking at cross-purposes.

Hearing What Your Reader Reads

What's the first thing you say when you wake up in the morning?

"Where am I?"

Yeah, me too. But, unfortunately, when the same line of dialog happens every day, it stops being newsworthy.

Even a classic line such as the one that Joseph Conrad put into Kurtz's raving, delirious, yet shockingly honest mouth at the end of *Heart of Darkness*, if repeated constantly over and over again, becomes worse than banal. It becomes trimmable.

Forget everything about creating the looks of characters for a minute. Forget about reality. Forget about taking meticulous notes. Do you know what most people say all day long every day? Not, as Edna St. Vincent Millay quipped about life, one damn thing after another.

The same damn thing over and over again.

Try it. Sit down at the kitchen table and note every word that comes out of the mouths of your family and friends for, oh, half an hour. Maybe an hour if they're not very talkative. (In my extended family, your hand would lose all mobility after five minutes.) Fascinating stuff, no?

> "Hey, uh, is there any more coffee?"
> "Yeah. Um. I don't know."
> "Well, but did we drink the last of it yesterday?"
> "I don't know. Huh. Maybe. I can't remember."
> "So—did you move the filters, do you know?"
> "Um. No."
> "Well, I'm looking, but they're not here."
> "Yeah, I think they are."
> "No, uh, they're not."
> "Um, they're probably there."
> "I'm telling you, huh, I'm sorry, I don't see them."
> "Hey, guys, who's the president of Tasmania?"

I won't torment you any longer.

Something that's happened in fiction over the last few decades is the emergence of excruciatingly lifelike dialog. I think it's supposed to show that the author knows how real people talk. What it actually shows is that the author knows how to put real people to sleep. We didn't get this in the 1700s. When Moll Flanders quoted herself, it was because she'd said something worth quoting. Everything else that came out of her mouth during the course of her long and extraordinarily conversation-worthy life she wisely kept to herself.

On the other hand, there's that great Uluru of literature, which was generally unknown in the early life of the novel and without which no modern writer can survive: readers like dialog.

Readers like dialog enough to skip everything in between if it's not absolutely riveting, including action. Readers like dialog enough to read enormous amounts of that excruciatingly lifelike drone, even while it's putting them to sleep.

I'm hanging in there, the reader's thinking as they nod off. *Any second now, someone's going to say something amazing that I've waded through all this to hear.*

There are two reasons for this.

The first and foremost is that most dialog is short. You can test this. Write a whole story in dialog. Just put quotation marks at the beginnings of your paragraphs. Then see if readers are more likely to read it in that form.

Not really. In fact, readers skip long paragraphs of dialog as reliably as they do non-dialog. They're looking for a quote, not a lecture.

The other reason is that dialog is people. People interacting. We're social creatures, and we *like* it when people interact. It makes us feel safe. The shunned, isolated, and ostracized do not hear a lot of dialog in their home lives. Who wants to be them?

Because of this, aspiring writers are often advised to work exposition into their characters' dialog.

"Don't tell us. Have them tell each other."

And, in this way, we wind up with the wonderful world of dialog that reads like billboards, only not as concise:

> "Hey, Ken! Put on your grey tweed jacket with the leather elbows, grab your Meerschaum pipe and those spiffy J. Crew Wellingtons that make you look like a guy who's comfortable both in the board room and shoveling shit, and join us over here by the body that's leaking blood all over this deep-pile faux Art Deco wall-to-wall carpet, made to order by a fabulous retro factory in Fruitvale, only minutes from trendy downtown Oakland."

We got the news. Now all we need's the weather report:

> "Watch out for the mud Gloria tracked in from that terrific thunderstorm going on outside, worst one we've had since 1984 when the church tower was struck by lightning while pastor Frank was tolling the bell and he disappeared in a puff of smoke, a mystery that's never been solved even to this day."

Fortunately. From this quite compelling human preference for dialog in storytelling, plus the sensible ban on extraneous exposition, we can extrapolate one essential piece of information: excellent dialog is both tight *and* crucial. Ignore realism, ignore working in exposition, ignore anything we can leave out that the reader will infer from the context.

Say only what the character has to say to make the story move forward, say it like a person, and say it quick.

> "Sorry." Her tone wasn't particularly convincing. "The alliteration was on purpose. I just wondered if you were still paying attention."

Getting a Grip on Dialect

Years ago, when I was young and foolish, I spent a winter in Australia. It's my understanding that the further south you go in Australia and the closer to Melbourne, the milder and more generic the accent becomes. However, I lived in Brisbane, up on the northeast coast within a long day's drive of Townsville and the Great Barrier Reef, in the heart of Queensland.

And let me tell you, *those* people speak serious Aus.

Even worse, by comparison, I speak serious American. I'm third-generation Californian, meaning that I speak with the TV accent people around the world know as American. So I came in for some taunting.

I had two men friends who'd learned what they considered American from watching reruns of *Roseanne*.

"Gimme a beer, Coot-er," they'd say, sending each other into fits.

"Gyit it yersef, Buuuh-buh."

Then they'd look at me hopefully.

I'd shake my head. "You're doing it wrong."

So they'd beg me to say it, and since my native part of California is Bakersfield I can do Roseanne as well as she can.

They'd listen intently. "That's what we said!"

"No. You said, 'Gimme a beer, Coot-er.' It's, 'Gimme a beer, *Coot-ur*.'"

Actually, I was just messing with them. Their accent was perfect. But they didn't need to know that.

By the time I left, I was told that I'd finally begun to lose my accent. This was because I'd learned to talk in the highest part of the back of my mouth, in a voice that curled and looped up at the end of every word as if all the world were just a friendly question. I wasn't doing it on purpose. I was simply tired of being mocked.

"G'dai, awl! Whait's ap?"

But apparently I didn't know when I'd had enough. I went on to New Zealand. Just when I'd gotten used to all vowels being variations on a sharp i, suddenly I found myself in the land of the long e. I had a conversation about deeth for five minutes before I realized we were talking about dying.

I came home. All the vowels were short u's, the words run together.

"Whut'suhp? C'mon."

I had lunch with a cousin from the South. All vowels were short a's. Loooong short a's.

"Whah dahn't y'ahl jahn us fah a beer latah?"

And I realized, in a flash, how truly impossible dialect is.

Because, really, who defines it? Does anybody pronounce the words that we spell so confidently, in all their Latinate, old Germanic, holdover French, the way that we write them? Can you imagine?

"Whee air yoe-uh guh-ees in theh gar aje? Whoh'ss buh-reeah-uh? Cahn I tuhrn ohn ah lig't?"

It's not even readable.

So who gets to say, "The way *I* pronounce it is the way it's spelled—the way *you* pronounce it is dialect"?

We have to wonder what the native speakers of what's commonly considered 'dialect' think of the way their spoken language is represented in literature, particularly when it's written by writers for whom that dialect is not native. Does it feel a bit like having people throw peanuts at you in the zoo?

Mark Twain researched the dialects of his native region meticulously before trying to put the language into words.

Margaret Mitchell was horribly insulted when the dialect in *Gone With the Wind* was questioned, saying that she'd studied it with care.

Emily Brontë gave her freakish character Joseph, an elderly Yorkshire servant around the turn of the nineteenth century, entire speeches in the dialect of her town's local people. It's thick wading.

And there's a wonderful scene in a Canadian movie from about 1987 in which a teenager's grandmother says severely to her, "What is this wah-ter? It's *woe*-tuh. Speak the Queen's English!"

My own German grandparents spoke with heavy Okie accents, but I never noticed until I was in my thirties. It turns out that an Okie accent—for probably good reason—bears a striking resemblance to a German accent when in the mouth of a first-generation German.

My Canadian grandmother liked to tell the story of how she asked my American grandfather where he was from, and when he said, "The Stayte o' Tex-as," she said briskly, "Well, la-di-da."

Flannery O'Connor quoted Eudora Welty, a fellow Southerner and a native Mississippian, on the wonderfully idiosyncratic details of local imagery. But O'Connor didn't say, "We write the way we hear people pronounce their words." (Certainly not, "We write the way we *think* we hear people pronounce them.") She said, "We use our local idiom." What is cliché to one region is distinctive and surprising to another.

Dialect is rarely a simple matter of pronunciation. The important stuff—the telling details that indicate origin, the meat of the language—is in the words, the catch-phrases, the terminology. And those speak most powerfully to readers when spelled in a way they can understand.

So we don't waste time trying to figure out how to make inner-city/rural poor/faux British/redneck hick/old moneyed New England characters pronounce their words the way we imagine. We don't struggle to portray accents that are not native to us and never will be.

And when we write our native dialect, we make our spelling match, as closely as possible, the spelling our readers themselves would assign to the words. If we must indicate actual differences in letters, we're sparing:

"I gi'ya a gud heent abowt that. Ponees're ya beyst bet."

"I give ya a good hint about that. Ponies are ya best bet."

"I t'ot yew wointed ta warsh yer hyands."

"I thought you wanted to warsh your hands."

Even better, we try to work in a long word that can be spelled conventionally, to off-set the labor of reading a phrase that really needs to be spelled unconventionally:

"Y'make it like ya momma, Betty Crocker?"

The contrast makes the sentence.

And, beyond all that, we focus on collecting and using the metaphors and verbal shorthand that are the true indicators of regional speech.

We stop listening to the letters in the words. We listen to the sentences.

Focusing Characters with Their Words

I cannot tell you how I *love* Heathcliff's fight with Catherine on her deathbed. Talk about a match made in hell!

Who tears into their beloved as she croaks out her last breath? And who wastes their last breath ripping their true love to shreds?

Emily Brontë wrote some of the most powerful, emotional, *painful* dialog in the English language. Her characters are bigger than life and tortured to the core. And anybody who's tried it knows that brutally honest, distraught dialog is the hardest thing in the world to write without sinking into melodrama.

How did she do it?

With laser-like focus. Forcing her characters to talk at cross-purposes, with intent, inference, tension, and immediacy, and ending each piece of dialog on a little kick off the rainbow of the scene.

There is a reason we're including this dialog exchange. What is it? We identify that, begin the exchange in a way that makes the reader curious, engage them both intellectually and emotionally throughout, and leave them with an ending that they didn't expect. It doesn't have to be a big surprise. But it has to make the effort of reading this piece of dialog worthwhile.

Intent:

First Brontë made sure she *intended to accomplish* something with every single piece of dialog. Here, she needed a scene in which the reader experiences exactly what things are like privately between Catherine and Heathcliff. In spite of hundreds of pages on either side all about the two of them performing in front of witnesses, *this* is that scene. This is the core of her entire novel.

Cross-purposes:

Brontë also made her characters *talk at cross-purposes*. Notice what Heathcliff does in this scene? He *contradicts* Catherine. Here the woman he loves is dying, seven months pregnant with someone else's child, raving like a madwoman—and he, by god, is going to win this argument!

"*I* didn't do it, *you* did it. *I'm* not going to feel sorry for you, *you* have to feel sorry for *me*!" He is perfectly willing to use spaghetti-logic to accomplish this goal. ("Poor old me for having to live!")

Inference:

Now guess what Brontë left out of that scene. *Backstory. Explanations.* Who really did what? Who cares? Catherine's dying—so let's get those cards on the table! *It's all her fault!*

Guess what else Brontë left out. *Transitions. Rationale.* (Who need rationale? We don't need no stinkin' rationale.) So much as a pause for Catherine to answer Heathcliff's question. (He couldn't care less what she thinks.)

Brontë lets the reader *infer the facts from the context.*

This is possibly the single most important aspect of writing dialog. Our reader doesn't want us hanging over their shoulder explaining the scene to them. They want to live this experience for themself. And exercising the capacity to pick up clues, to follow hints, to understand body language and verbal hints, is what feels good about the act of reading. That's the part that's just like hanging out with friends.

So we give the reader as much of this as we possibly can. They're smart. They like that about themself.

Tension & immediacy:

Also, Brontë used *em-dashes,* not *ellipses,* to break up the dialog and keep Heathcliff from using complete sentences. He's choking these words out, trying to cram everything he has to say to Catherine into these last few moments while she's still alive to hear him. He doesn't have time for sentences. He barely has time for words.

Intensity is always better than diffusion.

Kicker:

And when Heathcliff comes to the emotional core of their situation—Catherine's imminent death—he breaks off, unable to say it. He skips right over factual information straight to the point, for him, which is quite profound and unnerving and an excellent place to drop-kick the reader off the little rainbow –

He expects to lose his soul when she dies.

It's not a pretty picture, considering that we've already seen that he does, indeed, appear twenty years after her death to live without either conscience or humanity. The reader is completely ready to believe he's lost his soul.

And now we know why!

Brontë drags us by the hair through this excruciating fight and then dumps the clue to the entire conflict of the novel (Heathcliff's inhumanity) right in our laps.

Now *that's* dialog.

But what if our characters don't live their lives at full-tilt on the brink of madness? Well, *some* people don't.

Ivy Compton-Burnett is the undisputed queen of English-language dialog. Her books (twenty of them, all of which I own and cherish) are almost entirely dialog. Her characters are dry, witty, deadpan, dealing incessantly with life in enormous Victorian families that revolve around lies, deception, forgery, theft, tormented marriages, secret parentage, and untimely death. And yet there's not a spare word (or an ellipsis) in the lot of it. Every *single* sentence counts.

I picked a scene randomly from one of her books picked randomly off the shelf, in which Compton-Burnett used just three lines of dialog between a mother and her son as a hook-development-climax to first give us something to wonder ("Where are the others?") and tell us a brief, tragic story ("Things will never be so bad for them [after this death] again"), even including the pivotal character at the source of the mother's internal conflict ("In with the governess"). Then Compton-Burnett unexpectedly bounces the mother off our foreheads with insincere praise of her son illuminated by the immediate retraction of that praise. ("You're such a priceless boy. Get your hands out of your pockets.")

What is the mother doing as she praises her son in this troubled time? Looking him in the eye? Touching him? Making sure that he hears her? No.

Walking away.

Intent:

Did Compton-Burnett have a particular *intent* in mind for this piece of dialog? She certainly did. It shows exactly how the mother responds to her children's problems. This relationship is pivotal to the novel.

Cross-purposes:

Did Compton-Burnett stick to *talking at cross-purposes*? Yes, she did. The mother's first line is two questions in a row. She doesn't give her son time to answer, and in this way she shows us how interested she is in what he has to say. (Remember Heathcliff.) The boy answers his mother when he's given a chance, but he doesn't just tell her what she wants to know, he tells her what she hasn't asked and what (we know from the context) she's not going to enjoy hearing. The family has gone to their governess rather than their mother for help with their grief. Then the mother responds not with sympathy or comfort, but with rather oddly overstated praise (why is he such a priceless boy just because he knows where his siblings are?) illustrated by *leaving* and the parting shot that, actually, he's not doing so great in her opinion, after all.

Inference:

Guess what all Compton-Burnett left out. *Backstory, explanations, transitions, rationale.* Just like Brontë.

Let the reader *infer*.

Tension & immediacy:

Guess what else Compton-Burnett left out. *Ellipses*. The boy is rather subdued, not in the biggest hurry to have this conversation with his mother. Many aspiring writers would want to use ellipses to communicate his hesitance. However, Compton-Burnett uses a very simple action—the boy lifts his eyes to the ceiling. Subtle, significant action communicates hesitation with far great tension than any words or punctuation.

What else did she leave out? (Compton-Burnett managed to write twenty full-length novels of mostly dialog as a minimalist.) *Extraneous words*. Does the boy say, "They're in with their governess"? No, he does not. He says, "In with the governess." That's on purpose. The elimination of that one word matters.

She also left out either character's *internal dialog*. (Brontë didn't include a word of Catherine or Heathcliff's internal dialog in her novel, either.) What do the characters think of each other? We have to figure this out from how they speak and behave. Compton-Burnett also left out almost every physical clue—we don't even know that the boy's got his hands in his pockets until his mother mentions it.

Surprise!

That's tension.

Kicker:

Like Brontë, Compton-Burnett's characters drop-kick us off the end of this dialog exchange with that double-take on the boy's hands not belonging in his pockets. His mother walked away from his grief saying what?

But what if our characters aren't grappling with such monumental issues? What if they're not tormenting each other over death? What if, well, nobody in our story *dies*?

Try Jane Austen. Wit—one of the most wonderful uses for dialog ever.

In a classic exchange, Mr. and Mrs. Bennet of *Pride and Prejudice* argue about whether or not Mr. Bennet is going to call upon their new neighbor, and Austen captures, in a nutshell, the entire relationship between these old married people. We could waste pages and pages, entire chapters, explaining at length what Austen managed to squeeze into a few dozen words.

Intent:

Did Austen have a particular *intent* in mind for this dialog? Absolutely. The tension between the elder Bennets fuels a major thread of conflict throughout the novel, driving the essential wedge between their contrasting influences on their daughter Lydia and resulting in the complete disaster that triggers the Climax. This is our introduction to that tension.

Cross-purposes:

Do the characters *talk at cross-purposes*? Beautifully. Even while he's pretending to agree with his wife, Mr. Bennet is arguing with her. ("You don't!" "Yes, I do.") We know from the context that she's arguing with something he's said previously, but we could almost guess this because she's so far gone on the attack. So he argues back. And he does it not by holding to his previous line of argument ("Stop whining about your nerves and address the issue, for heaven's sake"), but by adroitly turning the tables on her so that she's suddenly losing this new argument without having won the last one, either.

Inference:

What did Austen leave out? You guessed it: *ellipses, explanation, transitions, rationale*.

Mr. Bennet does take the opportunity to fill in a bit of *backstory* (his wife has been complaining of her nerves for a very long time indeed), which is fine. Sometimes dialog is used to add backstory, and these characters don't happen to be at the height of passion here, so they have time to mention things like this. And, importantly, he uses it as an opportunity for wit.

But does he try to *explain* his position? ("We were talking about our daughters, not you, and besides that I was reading.") *Transition*? ("Why would you say such a thing?") *Rationalize*? ("I have nerves, too, you know, and, no—I already said it, but I'm saying it again—I will not go visit that guy.") Not a bit.

We can *infer* all that from *the context*.

Tension & immediacy:

Austen, also, left out her characters' *thoughts*. We won't find a single piece of internal dialog in all her work (some internal monologue, but not much in *Pride and Prejudice*, a particularly dialog-heavy novel). Search for it. We know her characters almost entirely through their narrators' eyes, and yet they are icons of our culture, figures so vivid and lifelike that they're still being stolen by modern writers.

Kicker:

Austen did use dialog as an opportunity to develop character, illuminate the relationship between the Bennets, and—yes—drop-kick us off the end of the exchange with an unexpected laugh over Mr. Bennet's crack about his old friends, Mrs. Bennet's nerves.

Note on ellipses:

Now, as far as *ellipses*, it's true writers like Colette and Jean Rhys used a lot in their dialog. It's a specialized tool for a specialized style. Unfortunately, it doesn't happen to be a style much in vogue these days and was never, even in their time, terribly useful, just a mostly French mannerism. They wrote a lot about timid and inexperienced young women coping with the world of overbearing men with the passivity expected of women then.

There's simply not much call for this type of fiction anymore.

Designing Dialog with Intent

All dialog must be designed with a specific intent in mind, not just used to fill up pages while we wonder what to do to our characters next.

One of the best purposes for dialog is to uncork the djinni's bottle in a moment of conflict. We can use description to set a mood, action to engage the reader physically, and exposition to catapult the reader into an epiphany. But dialog is terrific dynamite for blowing a plot to pieces.

Brontë saved up Heathcliff's and Catherine's declarations of undying love for Catherine's deathbed. Then she let the fur fly.

Compton-Burnett passed on to the reader the information about the children's loyalty to their governess over their loyalty to their mother, along with the mother's attitude toward her children, through dialog. She could have simply told us, but she wanted to break the story wide open at this particular point.

Austen yanked her characters first one direction—the Bennet girls will not be introduced to the rich young dandy who just moved in next door—and then the opposite direction—

psyche! yes, they will! – through dialog. This is how their parents always affect them.

Dialog can also be used to develop and deepen character, to show contrast between characters and how they grapple with it. It can reveal hidden agendas and characters' blind spots. It can show characters circling around each other, feeling for each others' weaknesses.

But whatever we use dialog for, it's powerful precisely *because* it needs more than one layer. No matter what purpose we have in mind for any particular piece of dialog, it must *always* move the plot forward.

Catherine is dying, and Heathcliff is losing his soul. Guess what happens next.

The children are hiding from their mother, and their mother isn't pleased. Guess what she's going to do.

The Bennets are locking horns over the new tenant of Netherfield Park. Guess where this is headed.

Remember that good dialog is always, always crafted so that every single word absolutely needs to be there. We don't have our characters say anything that the reader can *infer* from the context, and certainly we don't have them repeat themselves unless we're using repetition to make a point. And, with repetition, we keep in mind that a little bit of any technique goes a very long way.

We cut out every word of dialog that we can, let it go cold, and then cut again. Sometimes when we re-read weeks later, we've lost a word that we need for rhythm, and if this is the case, it's fine. We just put it back in. But not unless we simply *cannot* live without it.

This isn't the way we talk, but life doesn't have to make sense, and fiction does. Life is a whole lot longer than 72,000 words.

Fiction is experience condensed.

Talking at Cross-Purposes

The best way to create tension is to create suspense, make the reader lean forward turning those pages, wondering—worrying!—how this is all going to turn out.

And the best way to create suspense in dialog is to make our characters talk at cross-purposes.

But what does that mean?

> "Will you hand me that wrench over there?"
> "Sure! Which one?"
> "The one with the black handle."
> "Here you go."
> "Thanks!"
> "Do you want me to help?"
> "Okay. Can you hold this just like that?"
> "You bet. I see you're pretty used to doing this."
> "Yes, I am."

The reader doesn't know who these people are, only that they're pals. Good for them. Very helpful to each other. But how does this benefit *us*?

Well, aren't we interested in character development?

Sure. But this isn't it. These two characters are pretty much interchangeable. There's no development of their differences.

Doesn't this show a detail about their relationship—that they work with tools together?

One of them works with *one* tool. How many people in the world could identify a tool by a black handle? That doesn't narrow the field much.

Doesn't it establish camaraderie?

No. It establishes good manners. Rather dance-lesson good manners, at that. I'll be honest, the last time *I* had a wrench in my hand, the words that came out were not ones I learned from Emily Post.

So let's try that scene again:

"Hand me that wrench. No—that—with the black handle."

"Can I help?"

"Learn this at Frankie's?"

"I just washed rags. You know. But I've got a good wrist."

"Hold that."

"Hey, you're good!"

"I better be."

Characters? Details? Atmosphere? Let's take it apart:

"Hand me that wrench. No—that—with the black handle."

"Learn this at Frankie's?"

"Hold that."

"I better be."

"Can I help?"

"I just washed rags. You know. But I've got a good wrist."

"Hey, you're good!"

Does this develop the characters?

The Mechanic has an agenda: authoritarian, gruff, minimally-communicative, focused on the job, confident enough that they're not interested in compliments.

The Helper has their own, separate agenda: eager, questioning, reluctantly honest about their lack of experience, self-promoting, complimentary.

Character development shows how characters are distinct and separate people, with their own needs and interests and priorities. When they speak only in harmony ("I'm fine! How are you?" "I'm fine, too!") there is no distinction drawn. Why show a piece of dialog that indicates no distinction?

Everything our characters say that does not delineate them blurs them. Bad idea.

Does this piece show details about this relationship?

More than just details, it creates an image: a black-handled wrench, an absent character named Frankie, rags to be washed, a (supposedly) good wrist. All without explicit description. These details bring the scene to life in the reader's mind and allow them to visualize the characters in action.

Does it establish an atmosphere of camaraderie?

More than camaraderie, it shows the power balance between the characters ("Hand me that," "Hold that"), as well as differences in skill and experience, in self-esteem, even in the relationship each has with the elusive Frankie. By the end, we know which of these characters we identify with and how we feel about the other. We have *emotional reactions* to the differences.

We are there.

Can we create this reader investment in a cozy scene at home between loving family members?

> "Hi, Mom! I'm home. Where are you?"

> "I'm in the kitchen, honey! Would you like some fresh coffee cake?"
>
> "You bet. I love your coffee cake, Mom!"
>
> "Thank you! I made it just for you. How's school?"
>
> "Just great!"

It's nice that family members love each other. And it's true that we might very well have had this exact conversation just yesterday. But what purpose does it serve in our fiction?

Doesn't it develop these characters?

No. Again, these two characters are indistinguishable. That's not development.

Doesn't it show a detail about their relationship through the coffee cake?

Maybe. In a rambling and unspecific way. But if we want to show that Mom makes coffee cake for Junior and Junior likes it, we can do that in one line: "Coffee cake—humdinger!"

In fact, we can do that in one action. It should be a noteworthy action, like Junior plunging a hand into the coffee cake or crashing into the door in an all-fired hurry or dropping to the floor and throwing both arms around Mom's knees. We read to learn something we don't already know, and we all know how to say, "Thanks for the coffee cake."

Doesn't it establish a warm family atmosphere?

A warm cliché atmosphere, maybe. But again—we all know this stuff. If it's not like this at our houses, it's certainly like this on TV commercials. Is this an authentic atmosphere? Does it give us details and complexity true to life? Not a bit. This is white-washed dialog.

> "I'm home! Mom, I'm home—wow, this whole place smells like coffee cake—"

"That's hot, sweetheart."

"Never stopped me before. Holy cow!"

"How was school?"

"Scraped my knee—"

"Not on the table, honey. Can you wash your hands before you touch that?"

"I'm just going to stick my face in it—"

Do you see the difference?

Let's take it apart:

"I'm home! Mom, I'm home—wow, this whole place smells like coffee cake—"

"Never stopped me before. Holy cow!"

"Scraped my knee—"

"I'm just going to stick my face in it—"

"That's hot, sweetheart."

"How was school?"

"Not on the table, honey. Can you wash your hands before you touch that?"

Does this develop the characters?

Junior has an agenda: active, good-humored, smart-aleck, focused on themself, *needing Mom*.

This is a teen.

Mom also has an agenda: cautionary, authoritative, questioning, affectionate, focused on Junior (and keeping the eating area at least slightly clean). She even refrains from saying, "I told you so."

This is a parent.

Does this show the details of their relationship through the coffee cake?

Sure. But it shows more than that. We've got the details of the scraped knee, the dirty hands, the kitchen table. Again—a whole scene to visualize, without explicit description.

Does it establish a warm family atmosphere?

It establishes not only the affection between the characters, but, again, their power relationship ("Not on the table"), their ease with light-hearted sparring ("Never stopped me before," to which Mom doesn't even respond), and which of them carries the responsibility to protect and care for the other. By the end, we can predict that Mom is not going to be flustered by Junior's plan to "stick my face in it."

We know them now.

And that's the key: *we know them now*. Not because they're generic ha-ha good-time stock characters, but because we've had a chance to see them deal with cross-purposes.

What do *you* do when you ask a question and don't get an answer?

> "Who was it at the door?"
> "Why can't that kid put her shoes away?"

Do you let it go? Answer the second question? Get mad? Get sulky? Laugh? Get up and go answer your question for yourself? Your reaction tells us about your character.

Could we learn this about you if nobody ever crossed you? Of course not. (Dream on.)

People are interesting when they're in trouble. Readers read to find out how to cope with problems.

We put our characters at cross-purposes in dialog to see what they'll do when their nicey-nice official personas are *off*.

Because what they do then tells us who they really are. And who they really are tells us what's likely to happen to them (their worst nightmare). And what's likely to happen to them is. . .our story.

The events in a story tell us what our characters will do when they honestly don't know what else to do, revealing the real people inside, in all their complexity and stupidity and grace and, ultimately, overwhelming humanity.

Which—as we already know—is the whole point of fiction.

Exposition is *Telling*

Chapter 18

Sketching in Story

Use telling details

"Show, don't tell." If the world of fiction has a motto, that's it.

This is because the reader is interested in the story, not the storyteller, in following the flow of the plotline forward, always forward, and *inferring* the deeper meaning rather than pausing to have it pushed under their eyeballs by an ingratiating narrator. Yes, it's easy enough to read stuff *telling* it rather than *showing* it (so long as it isn't boring to the point of pain). But it's corny. It makes the brain feel flabby. It's like eating Pabulum, and by the time a person can read, you know, they're a little too old for that.

It doesn't feel like a real *experience* unless the reader is using their own senses and intelligence to pick up sights and sounds and smells and interpret them the way that they do in real life, without authorial voice-over.

And fiction is all about creating an experience for the reader. There truly is no other agenda.

"Show, don't tell."

But, at the same time, you know, we don't always want to show *everything*.

Remember *Ramona the Pest,* Beverly Cleary's masterpiece? We used to know a couple of kids just like Ramona and Beezus, right down to the blunt-cut hair on the Ramona girl's little brow. Every time that child came over to play, I thought of the day Ramona's teacher read *Mike Mulligan and His Steam Shovel* to her class, and Ramona was the only one who asked the obvious question about Mike settling down in the basement at the end: "How did he go to the bathroom?"

Lots of our characters' daily lives we're going to skip right over without mentioning. Even Mike Mulligan's.

So what if something simply has to happen—it's essential to the plot (remember that time we put a couple of bumblers in a car from New Jersey to New York City to pull a heist?), it can't be implied—but it *detracts from the forward motion* to take a detour and show it in full?

We must never, *ever* lose control of the flow of the plotline.

So sometimes we use exposition.

Say we've got a story about a couple in dire financial straits, and the guy's got a rich brother, and the issue is the couple fighting over their money problems. At one point, the guy agrees to try to borrow from his brother, but his brother refuses, and this touches off the Climax, which is the woman throwing a cheap old ugly vase the man inherited from his great-aunt and breaking it and the great-aunt's diamond jewelry falling out.

Would we use exposition in that story?

Well, first we have to decide whether this is a short story or a novel. Because, although short stories need to be vivid and gripping and pretty much everything up to a stick of dynamite in the reader's face, they have this one overriding limitation, and that's that they're. . .short. Whereas, a novel has lots of room. It's like the old woman who lived in a shoe. We can cram an almost endless number of scenes into a novel so long as we keep the reader intrigued with *every single one* of them.

Which means that short stories, for all their punch, sometimes wind up with a lot more exposition in them than novels. We just don't have room to show it all.

I read "Brokeback Mountain" recently. (I know—I'm right on the cutting edge of new fiction.) It's a perfectly competent story told by a professional who obviously knows her way around a reader's expectations. But I was disappointed to find that it's largely exposition.

I think this is why Proulx has run into so much trouble with real Montana shepherds who take quite serious umbrage with the idea that she knows anything at all (*at all*, they're saying) about how they pass the time out there on those lonely, isolated mountainsides. Because, even though she tells us that Jack and Ennis have a profound emotional bond, even though Jack and Ennis tell each other more than once, "I ain't a queer," even though Ennis' wife finally leaves him because, she tells him, she knows what he and Jack are up to on their habitual fishing trips, we see almost nothing of the actual development of Ennis and Jack's relationship.

"Fishing trips?" the reader is left saying to themself. "What fishing trips?"

Yes, short stories can depend more heavily on exposition than novels. But still, Proulx could have done herself a big favor if she'd focused more on scenes developing Jack and Ennis as unique individuals, showing us their unique times together rather than relying so much on exposition, which lends itself to interpretation, and leaving it open for the reader to assume she thinks Montana shepherds in general go in for the ole homosexual slap-&-tickle.

Anyway, let's make our story about the financial *brouhaha* a short story, to give us an excuse for exposition. We need to keep the focus *sharp*, we need to keep it *tense*, we need to keep it *moving forward*. We'll structure the story in a series of scenes containing both the wife and husband, always aimed at the wife throwing the vase. We'll even go so far as to make them all scenes of the wife and husband fighting. Fighting over money.

But we won't give them a phone, much less email. We'll make the guy get up and go over to his brother's house on that ill-fated bid for sympathy—just to be pissants. We'll force a situation involving a scene for which we don't have room.

> Mickey went to Bernard's to get it over with as soon as he woke up the next morning, and the minute he walked back in the front door Eunice knew he might as well not have gone at all.

> Mickey went to Bernard's and came back. "It's all your fault," he said to Eunice.

> If Mickey hadn't hated Bernard before, he certainly hated him by the time he got back from visiting him the next day.

That's all. We just let the reader know he made the effort and get on with what's happening between Mickey and Eunice that's going to end up with her giving the heave-ho to the right piece of bric-a-brac.

However, you'll notice that each of these examples of simple exposition contains more than information—it contains significant, telling details: morning, minute, walked, front door, "your fault," even hate.

That's essential: **layering**. More than one purpose to that snippet of prose. Exposition can't stand up without layering.

But how about in a novel? What if the bashing of the vase is only the beginning of Mickey and Eunice's problems? Maybe this is a story about how the family found out that Mickey and Eunice have Great-aunt Zelda's diamonds and the ensuing the tussle over rightful ownership, which winds up revealing the blood kinship between Great-aunt Zelda and the girlfriend for whom Bernard's been thinking about leaving his wife. The girlfriend who's convinced Bernard she's carrying his child, even though it's actually someone else's. And it turns out she's an escaped convict. . .

Well, these people might have enough problems already, without involving the long arm of the law. But anyway.

Newspapers have this wonderful convention called the Editorial Section. It's generally section B, after the hard-hitting news (which is of course section A). On dinky little newspapers like the kind I used to run, it's page two. And, although it's not actually facts—readers really like facts—it's everything that the editor thinks the reader ought to know in order to properly understand and interpret the facts in the correct light and with the correct emphasis.

"The President is resigning office under threat of impeachment. And, yes, we can quote him saying, 'I'm not a crook!' But face it, people, even though we don't have those 18 1/2 minutes of tape right now, we all know the reason they were erased is—Nixon's a crook!" (And it did turn out that Nixon was, indeed, both a liar *and* a crook.)

In fictional terms, section B is Chapter Two or Three, a quick detour after Chapter One.

We give the reader the news in section A:

> Mickey and his brother Bernard are going at it hammer-&-tongs over a pile of loot Mickey may or may not have legitimately inherited from their Great-aunt Zelda. Mickey hates Bernard. Bernard hates Mickey. In fact, as Mickey mentions, Bernard actually refused to lend Mickey a helping hand to avoid bankruptcy, even though Mickey *came* to him, dammit, with his hat in his hands, apologized for their estrangement, admitted he does love Bernard, and *humbly and politely asked*. But Bernard scoffs at Mickey when he mentions this. He doesn't argue. He knows it happened. But he scoffs! Bernard is kind of a turd.

That's Chapter One, your Hook. Whoa! Conflict!

And we want to keep going with this trajectory, because we've got a whole novel plotted out based upon this fraternal stonewall between what Bernard has that Mickey wants (brotherly love) and what Mickey has that Bernard wants (the shiny pile). But we do have to explain how Mickey wound up with the diamonds, which would be a fabulous explanation if it could also prove Mickey's claim about having been stone-cold broke and having gone to Bernard to mend the rift before the diamonds ever came to light. So while we're giving their backstory in flashback scenes in Chapter Two or Three, we sketch in briefly Mickey and Eunice's fight and how Bernard reacted.

There's that key to exposition again: layering. Multiple purposes.

And the keys to layering are *telling details* in *juxtaposition.*

Exposition must always do more than explain—it must illuminate. Like dialog, it must accomplish more than one goal at once. And if we're going to take longer than a very few words, it must do it very specifically:

> It was a long walk across Bernard's acre of spiky manicured lawn, avoiding the lawn sprinklers with his bare feet, and an even longer drive to the end of the paving and onto the gravel road that ran across the railroad tracks, back to where Eunice waited with her chin to her knees on the second step of their weather-beaten porch. Mickey was older and greyer when he got home, the shadows under his eyes bleaker.

1) Does our exposition illuminate *character*? (While we're sketching in backstory, can we simultaneously establish that Mickey's a basically truthful, decent guy?)

2) Does it illuminate *conflict*? (While we're mentioning Mickey and Bernard's past, can we show how Great-aunt Zelda taught them to fight over her?)

3) Does it illuminate *a secret*? (While we're explaining how the ex-con went to prison, can we drop a hint about who knew where she was hiding out when she was arrested?)

4) Does it illuminate *more than one* thing?

Exposition is about exposure, anything the reader needs that they can't get from the scene, illumination from within.

Use it with tact and just a *soupçon* of grace.

Part 3

Copy Issues

Chapter 19

Learning Simplicity with Hemingway

What is correct usage? grammar & punctuation

One day years ago, my husband walked through a room where I was reading *The Complete Short Stories of Ernest Hemingway,* and in a flash he'd unrolled his sleeves and was dangling them, empty.

"Get me," he said. "A Farewell to Hands."

That joke is one of my favorite things about Hemingway, because, honestly, he has a lot to answer for:

1) Teaching aspiring writers to write repetitious, deadpan dialog that goes nowhere in particular.

2) Teaching the same poor innocents to write as though words come out of the mouths of invisible characters and hang in the air in—yes—nowhere in particular.

3) Teaching that if the hero drinks enough whiskey and says the same banal thing often enough the story will take on resonance.

4) Using the fictional short-story form as a thin disguise for a *laboooooorious* technical manual on fly-fishing.

It's true that Hemingway taught us to apply the rules of journalism—keep it clear, sharp, active, and to-the-point—to mainstream fiction, thereby helping to usher in the age of postmodernism. He learned this partly from his newspaper writing, partly from Ezra Pound's imagist work, and partly from the minimalist theories of his friend Gertrude Stein. He often took the edict of brevity to the extreme, resulting in sentences that can hammer in your head until you have to stop reading and go lie down, but at least he showed us that there are a whole lot of words in first drafts that can safely be edited out.

Hemingway also wrote about something he knew quite well, European battlefronts during the Spanish Civil War and both World Wars, thereby giving his war novels both authenticity and complexity, two of the hallmarks of great literature.

Hemingway wrote some lovely exposition, and he put it in exactly the right places—only where he needed emphasis.

And Hemingway helped bring the flawed anti-hero to the forefront of popular fiction, to the extent, anyway, that he was able to admit that his heroes were both anti-heroes and flawed.

What Hemingway really did right, though, was work at fiction as a craft to be learned thoroughly and painstakingly throughout his life. He focused not just on his plots (full of action and hair-raising danger), his themes (the isolation of the human soul, notably that of a pre-suicide, and the inherent instability of the human condition), and his descriptive passages (okay, he didn't focus on them so well), but also his paragraphs, his sentences, even his words.

He thought and spoke and wrote about the work obsessively, pushing deeper and deeper all the time into what makes craft into art, what makes fiction into literature.

When Annie Dillard advises us to become writers only if we like sentences, she is talking about Hemingwayesque dedication. When Gary Lutz builds prose sentences with a poetic sensitivity to word choice and order, he is working with Hemingwayesque compulsion. When Flannery O'Connor says that, because you use ten fingers instead of two, she considers the typewriter to be the more personal instrument and also because you can read what comes off of it, she is speaking with Hemingwayesque practicality.

However, Hemingway was not by any means the only, or even the pivotal, American writer of the early twentieth century practicing these literary virtues. And his literary crimes sometimes met and exceeded his shining qualities.

What makes him important is that, a generation after Jack London, Hemingway was the mainstream literary writer who spoke in simple, straight-forward, correct language to the taciturn, non-literary-type American male. In doing so, Hemingway encouraged the interest of one of the most hard-to-reach sectors of the literate public, helping to spawn a tradition of reading among generations of men who otherwise might never have known that art has anything to offer or that sensitivity to the human condition makes any difference to the über-manly. Many of the men who were first introduced to literature through Hemingway went on to make irreplaceable contributions to the canon of American fiction. And many continue to do so today.

If Hemingway had not spoken so powerfully of a man's internal experiences to their fathers, would the men of the 1960s have been able to join the feminist movement in as great of numbers as they did? In minutely observing his world, did Hemingway bring observation to generations of men un-used to receptivity? In using craft to communicate with his fringe audience, did Hemingway actually alter modern culture?

Because that's *literature.*

Hemingway also gave us books and books and books full of simple fiction sentences, modeling the basic rules of grammar and punctuation to an audience that might never have made it through the lesson alive if we had to rely solely on such writers as the eminently correct—but cruelly verbose—Henry James.

Chapter 20

Grammar

Say what you mean to say

Parsing 101: Making Sense with Sentences

The only way to know whether or not we're writing clearly is to understand sentence structure. So writers learn to parse, or at the very least learn what parsing is. You don't have to study or even read everything in this chapter, but you should know that it exists.

That that was was not what that was but that that was not was what that was.

Read this and identify where the one piece of punctuation goes.

That that was.

There's a noun. It's something that was. We're calling it 'that' and giving it the further definition that it's the thing that used to be or, in short-hand, 'that that was.'

And since it's acting as the thing that does something in this sentence, that makes it the subject.

That that was.

It did something.

What did it do?

It *wasn't* something.

That that was *was not.*

Subject, verb. A thing and what it does: that's a full sentence. We can put the period there. We can be done now – what a *relief.* We have learned the basics of all good grammar.

Or. . .(and this is your choice) we can dig a little deeper. What wasn't it? Give that basic subject-verb sentence an object.

What.

That's right. **That that was was not** *what.*

But what?

Well, it wasn't what it was. Or, with a slight redirection of emphasis, it wasn't what *that* was.

That that was was not what *that was.*

Again – we can put a period there. Termino. Finito.

Or. . .(again, entirely your choice) we can ask ourselves for a more concrete answer. I mean, all we've got right now is a negative statement. We know what it wasn't. But what if we want to know what it *was*?

But.

So here it is, the little golden prince lost in the Impenetrable Forest of Words, the one necessary piece of punctuation.

We always put a comma before 'but' when it connects two contrasting clauses. That's all. (There's one exception to the comma-before-but rule, and that's when 'but' is used as another word for 'except.' We use a comma everywhere but there.)

So now we know where our one piece of punctuation goes: between the two complete sentences that have been joined by 'but' to make one compound sentence. Just a little indication, a flag, to let the reader know they've actually read a whole sentence and can stop here if they've got better things to do.

That that was was not what that was, *but—*

And here we are, in the second clause, which can be treated as an entirely new sentence:

That that was not was what that was.

That that was not. Again, we've got something we're calling 'that,' but in this case we're defining it as the thing that *never was* so, in short-hand, we call it 'that that was not.' It's the noun this second clause of the compound sentence is about. The subject.

Hear the echo? "That that was." "That that was not." There it is: the contrast. The reason for that 'but.'

That that was. . . but *that that was not. . .*

What about *that that was not*? What did it do?

It *was* something.

That that was not *was.*

There's the verb for that subject! Want to put the period there? Let it be over? Call it a day? Have you had enough? We can.

Or. . .(choices, choices) we can keep going. Give this sentence an object, too. Into the jungle, the mighty jungle.

What was that that was not?

What.

That's right. **That that was not was** *what.*

But what?

It was what *that was.*

That that was not was what *that was.*

So simple for something that looks so complex.

That that was was not what that was, but that that was not was what that was.

And for my next trick, I'll admit there is one type of full sentence that, while sticking to the strict grammatical law of subject-verb, doesn't actually include the subject.

That's the imperative form: commands. When we command someone to do something, the subject is *always* assumed to be 'you' and therefore left off.

Remember that!

Parsing 102: Writing With Clarity & Manners

On June 25, 2009, Farrah Fawcett, who made history in The Burning Bed *and earned her first Emmy nomination for it 25 years earlier, died of cancer in Santa Monica at the age of 62.*

Is this news lede incorrect? Grammatically flawed? Factually impossible? *Wrong*? Would we be willing to get involved in a hot-headed wrangle with strangers over it?

Hey, that sounds like there might be something controversial about this!

So let's parse it and find out.

Subject-verb:

Farrah Fawcett died.

Good enough. What's the subject?

Farrah Fawcett

What did the subject do?

Farrah Fawcett **died**

Let's parse the verb and its modifiers. When did she die?

On June 25, 2009

where?

in Santa Monica

why?

of cancer

how?

at the age of 62

So that's pretty clear. What, when, where, why, and how. All present and accounted-for in perfectly clear English, all the information the reader needs, in modifying phrases either set off by commas, in the common (American) journalistic practice of putting the date before the subject, or without commas, in the common journalistic practice of eliminating every comma humanly possible. (Be thrifty with your quads.)

Now let's parse the subject and *its* modifier:

Who did something?

Farrah Fawcett

How about that long clause modifying the subject?

who made history in *The Burning Bed* and earned her first Emmy nomination for it 25 years earlier

Let's parse the clause.

subject-verb:

who made and **earned**

Any modifiers for those verbs? Yes. A prepositional phrase for the verb **made.**

made **in *The Burning Bed***

Both verbs take objects, so let's give them those.

who made **history** and earned **nomination**

So far so good. Any modifiers for the objects? Yep. Some adjectives for the object **nomination.**

her first Emmy nomination

Any problem with those modifiers? No. It's clear that history was made in *The Burning Bed*. It's also clear that the nomination was her first Emmy.

What could anybody find to complain about in this sentence? How could anyone think it was incorrect, grammatically flawed, factually impossible, *wrong*?

It's that last adverbial phrase in the modifying clause:

25 years earlier

Earlier than what?

Enquiring minds want to know.

The way the sentence stands, that adverbial phrase **25 years earlier** could apply to either:

1) both verbs of the modifying clause, **made** and **earned**, or

2) only the second, **earned**.

It *could*.

1) If **earlier** applies to both verbs, that makes its antecedent (the word it refers back to) the main verb, **died**, whose point in time is stipulated in a modifying phrase at the very beginning of the sentence, **June 25, 2009**:

Fawcett both **made** history and **earned** the nomination **earlier** than **June 25, 2009**, the date on which she **died**.

Given the commas that set those two verbs in their own little modifying clause, this would be the obvious interpretation.

2) However, if **earlier** applies *only* to the second verb of the modifying clause, **earned**, that makes its antecedent either the main verb, **died**, *or* the first verb of the modifying clause, **made**. Both of these verbs either appear or have their relevant data stipulated earlier in the sentence.

2a) In the first case, again, **earlier** refers to **June 25, 2009**, the date on which she **died**. You see, again:

Fawcett **earned** the nomination before she **died**.

2b) In the second case, though, **earlier** refers to **made**:

Fawcett **earned** the nomination before she **made** history with the role.

Interestingly enough, a handful of amateur critiquers in a large online critique group some years ago took the stand that in such a sentence that adverbial phrase, **25 years earlier**, could *only* apply to the second verb, **earned**. Not only that, they claimed that the adverb **earlier** could *only* refer to the antecedent of the first verb, **made**. They were completely, absolutely, beyond a doubt positive, and let me tell you, they didn't mind saying so.

Why?

Because, on a purely surface reading, that's how it might easily appear, based on the proximity of that adverbial phrase, **25 years earlier**, to the second verb, **earned**, and the appearance of the first verb, **made**, in the sentence shortly before the second.

What this would mean is that the sentence states Fawcett won her first Emmy nomination for *The Burning Bed* 25 years before she appeared in it. Strange timing indeed.

However, as we've just seen, the sentence also states Fawcett won her first of Emmy nomination for *The Burning Bed* 25 years before she died.

But hang on! It also states Fawcett both made history in *The Burning Bed* and won her first Emmy nomination for it 25 years before she died.

This is, of course, the interpretation meant by the writer.

Granted, the best sentence is the perfectly-clear sentence, the sentence for which there are not multiple possible interpretations but only one. The right one. And we do expect journalists to hew to the perfectly clear, no matter what deadlines they're trying to keep.

But does lack of clarity make a sentence *wrong*? Is any refutation of that verdict *nonsense*? Are we obliged, as writers, to either produce sentences of one and only one interpretation or accept that the worst of all interpretations is the only interpretation possible?

The sentence above was not published by an international news outlet, but another of identical structure was, and, wow, did some folks make hay of it.

Why?

Well, geez. Some people just like to make hay.

The truth is that there will always be amateur critiquers looking for ways to prove professionals wrong. It's a hobby. And it's conveniently easy to get bogged down in wrangling over little-understood technicalities in order to keep from having to focus on laying our *own* guts out on the table in simple and straight-forward language.

But when we're looking for grammatical *faux pas* that lead to factual dark matter, before we pitch in our sterling opinions it's a good idea to set our surface reading gently aside and go straight for the grammar.

Parse it. Is there anything in there we're missing? Probably.

Can we find it if it is? Sure we can.

Parsing 103: Unwinding Henry James

Feeling brave? Ready to jump into the deep end of the pool? Swim with the sharks? Grammatically, this means the inimitable

Henry James. Let's paraphrase a sentence out of "The Aspern Papers" and parse it.

> *He himself had been living in Venice for two weeks and had bought a large number of shoes there; but the scope of his mission did not involve the three small, dark, and, as it could sometimes appear, rarely frequented shops (the owners were thought to have misplaced on their last journey all shop keys, besides having had, as their business showed, some odd lapses in their memories), that sold no socks and displayed no merchandise.*

All righty, then.

The thing about James is that, convoluted as his sentences became toward the end of his career (and this is by no means the most convoluted), I have yet to find a single instance of grammatical or punctuation error—not a single mangled verb or misused semicolon, not even a misplaced comma. The man was a grammatical *machine*. I think he avoided simplicity just for the exercise.

First off, this is a compound sentence, joined by the coordinating conjunction, **but**. So we'll be parsing the two combined sentences one-by-one.

First sentence:

> *He himself had been living in Venice for two weeks and had bought a large number of shoes there;*

Subject-verb:

He had been living and **had bought**

Any modifiers for that subject, **He**? Yes. A reflexive pronoun acting as an adjective:

He himself

We have a few auxiliary verbs there, putting the main verbs **living** and **bought** into the pluperfect (my favorite grammatical term—it sounds like it was made up by a three-year-old). James used auxiliary verbs with aplomb.

Note the coordinating conjunction:

and

Any modifiers for those verbs? Yes. Two adverbial prepositional phrases for the first verb, **had been living,** and an adverb for the second verb, **had bought**:

had been living **in Venice. . .for weeks**

had bought **there**

Any modifiers for those? Yes. An adjective for the second prepositional phrase, **for weeks**:

for **two** weeks

Any objects for the verbs? One object for the second verb, **had bought**:

had bought **number**

Any modifiers for that object? An article, an adjective, and an adjective prepositional phrase:

a great number **of shoes**

That's nice! He sounds a real treat.

But! On to the second sentence:

> *but the scope of his mission did not involve the three small, dark, and, as it could sometimes appear, rarely frequented shops (the owners were thought to have misplaced on their last journey all shop keys, besides having had, as their business showed, some odd lapses in their memories), that sold no socks and displayed no merchandise.*

Now that's a beaut.

Subject-verb:

scope did involve

Any modifiers for the subject, **scope**? Yes. An article and an adjective prepositional phrase:

the scope **of mission**

Any modifiers for the object of that prepositional phrase? A possessive pronoun:

of **his** mission

That's the subject, then.

The auxiliary verb, **did**, is necessary in order to include the negative adverb, **not**. That's how English negative adverbs work:

did **not** involve

Any objects for that verb? Yes.

did not involve **shops**

Any modifiers for this object? Holy cow, are there! Now we're right in the thick of things. Let's start with the simple adjectives—an article, a quantity, two regular adjectives, and a participle, which is a verb acting as an adjective:

the three small, dark, and **frequented** shops

Again, note their coordinating conjunction:

and

Any modifiers for these adjectives? Yes. An adverb for the participle **frequented**:

rarely frequented

(Weirdly, anything modifying either an adverb *or* an adjective is an adverb. Don't ask me why—but it's in the OED.)

Any modifiers for this adverb? A lovely adverbial clause for the adjective's adverb, **rarely** (triple-layer adjective!), long enough to need its own commas:

as it could sometimes appear

Subject-verb:

it could appear

Adverb for the verb:

could **sometimes** appear

Note the subordinating conjunction:

as

And now we get to an even more fun part. A parenthetical adjective clause for the object, **shops**!

(the owners were thought to have misplaced on their last journey all shop keys, besides having had, as their business showed, rather odd lapses in their memories)

Subject-verb:

owners were

That's all for the subject verb? Yes. That's all.

Any modifiers for the subject, **owners**? An article and two participles:

the owners were **thought** besides **having had**

What's that word in between? That's called an adverbial conjunction:

besides

James loved unusual conjunctions. (This one allows him to transpose the participles—otherwise the second one would have to appear right next to the noun they both modify.) Now, can a participle take an object like a regular verb? Yes, it can. The first one has an infinitive verbal direct object, another participle:

thought **to have misplaced**

How about modifiers for these participles, **to have misplaced** and **having had**? (You see how he's got participles working on two layers here, a complex, rather risky design, like grammatical cousins once-removed.)

Yes. Two prepositional phrases:

to have misplaced **on journey**

having had **in memories**

Any modifiers for the objects of these prepositional phrases? Two possessive pronouns and a regular adjective:

on **their last** journey

in **their** memories

Very tidy.

Any objects for those participles, **to have misplaced** and **having had**? Yes, indeed. One for each:

were thought to have misplaced **keys** besides having had **lapses**

Any modifiers for these objects? Two adjectives:

shop keys

odd lapses

Any modifiers for these adjectives? Two more adverbs:

all shop

rather odd

Any *more* modifiers for these participles, **to have misplaced** and **having had**? Yes. Another lovely adverbial clause for the second participle, **having had**:

as their business showed

Subject-verb:

business showed

Adjective, a possessive pronoun:

their business

Subordinating conjunction:

as

Whew! Any more?

Yes—two verbs for the object, **shops**:

that sold no socks and displayed no merchandise.

sold and **displayed**

These are introduced by a demonstrative pronoun:

that

Any modifiers for those verbs? Mercifully, no.

But note their coordinating conjunction:

and

Any objects for the verbs? Yes.

sold **socks** and displayed **merchandise**

Any modifiers for those objects? Two negatives:

sold **no** socks and displayed **no** merchandise

Are we done?

Yes. And lived to parse another day!

You see why James has a reputation as the King of Spaghetti Prose, a man who could knot a sentence just by folding his arms, picking up the ends, and unfolding his arms again?

But listen to the rhythm he achieved! Like the rolling sound of thunder.

Chapter 21

Punctuation

They're just dots & squiggles

Using Punctuation Marks Correctly

Punctuation is often seen by aspiring writers as a sort of Chinese finger trap—don't stick your fingers in, or you'll never get them back out again.

There's nothing like a good stack of punctuation to sink our teeth into first thing in the morning. So let's get this out of the way once and for all:

comma ,

A comma indicates a break between phrases. The most common misuse of the comma is placing one in the middle of a clause—a phrase with both a subject and verb—either between the subject and its verb or between the verb and its object.

Don't do this, no matter how long and convoluted one of those elements might be. Just because "Uncle Frank's pointed and unusually yellow teeth that stick out nearly at right angles" is a long subject, it is not correct to work a comma in there before the verb, even if that verb turns out to be as long and unusual as the teeth. We use commas to set off part of this subject as a phrase if we must, but we use one comma for the beginning of the phrase and another for the end.

The following is incorrect:

> Uncle Frank's pointed and unusually yellow teeth that stick out at nearly right angles, first bit and then wrangled for fully twenty minutes the sinewy pulp of the aging mango.

The following are correct:

> Uncle Frank's pointed and unusually yellow teeth that stick out at nearly right angles first bit and then wrangled for fully twenty minutes the sinewy pulp of the aging mango.

> Uncle Frank's pointed and unusually yellow teeth, which stick out at nearly right angles, first bit and then wrangled for fully twenty minutes the sinewy pulp of the aging mango.

The second-most-common misuse of the comma is in lists.

This misuse can be traced directly to journalists, who have their own brand of correct punctuation related to the historic need to cram as many letters into as small a space as humanly possible. For this reason, journalists have developed a code whereby they eliminate certain commas and instances of 'that' normally included in correct writing.

We let them have their day—they've earned it. But we don't write in journalese unless we're writing nonfiction.

In fiction, put a comma after every single element in a list (except, of course, the last one), unless that list contains only two elements, in which case don't bother with any commas at all.

The following is incorrect:

> Julia took out her false eyeball, wrapped it up in her handkerchief and lobbed it to Harriet. Harriet caught it, and polished it well.

The following is correct:

> Julia took out her false eyeball, wrapped it up in her handkerchief, and lobbed it to Harriet. Harriet caught it and polished it well.

In nonfiction, eliminate the last comma in the list. It's called the Oxford comma, and it is one of the few concrete elements of writing that distinguish fiction from nonfiction.

semicolon ;

A semicolon is a weak period (or full stop). It indicates that, although these two clauses *could* be independent sentences, we prefer them to be linked in order to emphasize some commonality between them.

In Emily Brontë's day, we could use semicolons with impunity. We could throw them like rice at a wedding. They served an elegant purpose, fully as common as either the comma or the period, and served it enthusiastically.

Of course, in her day the comma was also misused to the point of inanity, so we can't really base our standards of punctuation on those guys.

Besides which, Brontë herself was terrible at punctuation.

The most common misuse of the semicolon is to link sentences without enough in common to earn the link. It's often misused with a vengeance in gimmicky works that are supposed to be constructed entirely out of a single sentence.

The following is incorrect:

> Uncle Frank ate his mango; belched; turned to Julia in confusion; a bluebird landed on the windowsill and sang Handel's *Largo*.

The following is correct if either the mango or the belch is what confuses him:

> Uncle Frank ate his mango and belched; he turned to Julia in confusion. A bluebird landed on the windowsill and sang Handel's *Largo*.

The following is correct if the bluebird is what confuses him:

> Uncle Frank ate his mango and belched. A bluebird landed on the windowsill and sang Handel's *Largo*; Uncle Frank turned to Julia in confusion.

Please note the cause-&-effect that necessitates the correct order of events.

Semicolons, I'm afraid, are not currently much in fashion. I blame Hemingway. He was so obsessed with short sentences that he really ruined it for the rest of us, and now whenever confronted with a choice between a series of short sentences and a single long sentence using semicolons, the modern editor will almost always throw their hat in the ring for the short sentences. Yeah, me, too.

The following is not only correct, but most likely:

> Uncle Frank ate his mango and belched. He turned to Julia in confusion. A bluebird landed on the windowsill and sang Handel's *Largo*.

colon :

A colon, unlike any other punctuation, indicates the meaning of the term previous to the punctuation. There is a direct association between the before and after, so that the defined term *always* comes before the colon and the definition after it.

You'd think nobody but the author of a dictionary would have much use for it, but it does turn up in fiction more often than seems probable.

The following (and any similar permutation) is incorrect:

> Julia would have winked at Uncle Frank: but her false eye was missing.

The following is correct:

> Julia would have winked at Uncle Frank, but for one problem: her false eye was missing.

Note the defined term "one problem" and the definition of that term "her false eye was missing." Colons are interesting and useful little things, but remember that too much of any technique is too much of a good thing and use them sparingly.

en-dash -

An en-dash is used to create hyphenated words.

The en-dash and em-dash date back to the era of typesetting. They actually date back to the era of setting type *by hand*. Quads are the spaces occupied by letters, and certain letters such as 'm' and 'w' simply take up more space than the rest of the alphabet. Therefore the different sizes of dash became associated with the sizes of the quads they used, either an 'm' quad or a regular-sized quad such as m's counterpart 'n.' (They could just as easily have become known as 'w' and 'u' quads.)

There is also the little-known 'i' quad for i's and lowercase l's and t's, but since nobody's ever wanted an i-sized dash nobody talks about it. (This is actually a joke—there is an industry distinction between an en-dash and an i-dash. However, Word ignores it, so it's relatively useless to those of us writing in the modern world. Typesetters know what I mean.)

The following is incorrect:

> I love a good literary—marsupial conundrum. It's too bad Wordpress has the propensity to turn em-dashes-probably trying to account for i-dashes-into en-dashes.

The following is correct:

> I love a really good literary-marsupial conundrum. It's too bad Wordpress has the propensity to turn em-dashes—probably trying to account for i-dashes—into en-dashes.

em-dash —

The correct modern structure of an em-dash is to begin immediately after the previous word (no space) and end immediately before the next word (again no space). In normal typing, this is accomplished with two hyphens in a row. In Wordpress, though, it takes three. And in early versions of Word it's done wrong. I'm sorry about that—Word was created by computer engineers, not writers.

An em-dash, as you might have gathered, is a strong comma. It's used to set aside a phrase within a sentence with greater emphasis than a simple comma can offer. I'm quite fond of em-dashes and use them with a liberal hand. They give sentences a graceful bendability that no other punctuation mark really accomplishes.

The following (and any similar permutation) is incorrect:

Julia would have mentioned this to Uncle Frank—although he hadn't asked, but she was too busy with her shoelaces.

The following is correct:

Julia would have mentioned this to Uncle Frank—although he hadn't asked—but she was too busy with her shoelaces.

An em-dash can also be used to replace the poor benighted modern semicolon. It's not the most elegant use of it, but I do it all the time. It can even be used to replace a colon, if we're desperate.

The following is incorrect:

The bluebird—had untied them.

The following are correct:

The bluebird—blast its feathery little head—had untied them.

The bluebird had untied them—blast its feathery little head.

The bluebird—it had untied them.

ellipses. . .

The correct structure of ellipses is to begin immediately after the previous word (with no space), insert a space between each dot, and end immediately before the next word (again with no space). Again, early versions of Word do it wrong. Those darn computer engineers.

Use three dots, no more, no less. Anything more than three is wasteful. Two looks silly. And anything less than two, of course, is a period.

Ellipses are used to indicate a pause, normally to reflect or make a decision. That pause is called an ellipsis.

Ellipses are relatively common in many writers' dialog (not mine). They are far less common in narrative. This is because the reader generally expects the writer to have already done all their reflecting and made all their decisions before they come to the table. (We don't have those kinds of scruples about characters.)

Personally, the minute I discovered that Emily Brontë accomplished so much power in her dialog by using em-dashes instead of ellipses, I made the unilateral switch.

The following (and any similar permutation) is incorrect:

> If Harriet hadn't for whatever reason. . .thought to tell Uncle Frank, he might still be there to this day. . .worse luck.

The following is correct:

> If Harriet hadn't, for whatever reason, thought to tell Uncle Frank, he might still be there to this day. . .worse luck.

The following is also correct, but comes across as indecisive:

> If Harriet hadn't. . .for whatever reason. . .thought to tell Uncle Frank, he might still be there to this day. . .worse luck.

(parentheses)

Parentheses are used to set aside a phrase so inconsequential (however fascinating) to the meaning of the entire sentence that the sentence could safely do without it altogether. For this reason, we cannot refer back to the contents of a parenthetical phrase.

The following is incorrect:

Uncle Frank (who could smell something was up) turned on Julia and Harriet, because his nose never lied.

The following is correct:

Uncle Frank, who could smell something was up, turned on Julia and Harriet. (His nose never lied.)

An interesting and rather playful little thing about parentheses is that we must decide whether to include the parenthetical phrase within the punctuation of the sentence or give it a sentence of its own.

We decide this based upon whether or not the parenthetical phrase is, in fact, a sentence in its own right, as Uncle Frank's nose is above. It can get tricky when we want to put a complete sentence into parenthesis inside another sentence. There's no real standard for this that I know of, as there is for dialog. I try to avoid it.

The following is incorrect:

Uncle Frank wagged his nose at Julia (he wasn't interested in Harriet).

The following are correct:

Uncle Frank wagged his nose at Julia (uninterested in Harriet).

Uncle Frank wagged his nose at Julia. (He wasn't interested in Harriet.)

"quotation marks"

Quotation marks are for dialog and short quotes, as well as stories, poems, and other citations of short works. They are not quotes themselves. Quotes are what we put into quotation marks. When we must nest one set of quotation marks within another, we alternate between double and single quotation marks.

The following is incorrect:

> Julia sighed. "Uncle Frank," she said, "Harriet has been telling me for years, "You've got to keep that thing cleaned." So I let her clean it."

The following is correct:

> Julia sighed. "Uncle Frank," she said, "Harriet has been telling me for years, 'You've got to keep that thing cleaned.' So I let her clean it."

There's a complication with quotation marks around short quotes at the ends of phrases and sentences—complicated because the rule is different in the United States and Britain.

In the United States, an ending comma or period is included inside the quotation marks, even if only *part* of the sentence is quoted.

In Britain, that ending comma or period goes outside the quotation marks unless the *entire* sentence is quoted.

In both parts of the world, ending colons, semicolons, question marks, and exclamation points go outside the quotation marks.

The following are incorrect:

Uncle Frank was beside himself with excitement over what Julia meant with that bored comment, "nothing important!"

Was Julia wondering what Uncle Frank meant by, "I'll be the judge of that?"

The following are correct on both sides of the ocean:

Uncle Frank was beside himself with excitement over what Julia meant with that bored comment, "nothing important"!

Was Julia wondering what Uncle Frank meant by, "I'll be the judge of that"?

The following are correct in the United States:

Harriet agreed with Julia that it was truly "nothing important."

Uncle Frank snorted, making Julia think it was "nothing important," indeed.

However, the following are correct in Britain:

Harriet agreed with Julia that it was truly "nothing important".

Uncle Frank snorted, making Julia think it was "nothing important", indeed.

italics

Italics are used for emphasis, as well as book titles, plays, epic poems, and other citations of long works. Italics take the place of ALL CAPS in *all* works of fiction, except maybe certain situations in children's literature. They are also useful for avoiding the proliferation of exclamation points, which should be used sparingly (and never, dear god, multiply at one time!!!).

Interestingly enough, acquisitions editors sometimes prefer italics to be indicated in manuscripts with underlining rather than actual italics. Again, this dates back journalism and the era of typesetting, in which newswriters and editors needed to communicate with typesetters through the means available. Typewriters don't have italics. You've probably noticed. But typesetting machines *did*. So we all took a vow to recognize underlining in typewriting as equal to italics in typesetting and let it go at that.

The following is incorrect (outside children's literature):

> Harriet let out a scream you could hear in Peoria. "JULIA! The BLUEBIRD!"

The following is correct:

> Harriet let out a scream you could hear in Peoria. "*Julia!* The *bluebird*!"

Note that the italics apply to the words and the words alone. The punctuation (in this case the exclamation point) remains stolidly unmoved. *The Chicago Manual of Style* reversed itself on this point between the Fourteenth and Fifteenth Editions, and, because they've prevaricated, I do usually put the punctuation in italics if it applies to a full sentence. However, quotation marks always remain unitalicized.

And for our finale, we'll clarify 'vs.' This is the abbreviation for *versus*, which means 'as opposed to.' It's Latin, from the past participle of the verb *vertere*, 'to turn,' meaning to turn toward or away from something. So let us turn away.

Living & Dying by the Period

And here we are, innocent writers coming down the pike with heads full of ideas and itchy pen fingers. The words are just rolling off our tongues. Ideas come tumbling down the chute in perfect order: Hook, Development, Climax, scene after scene, and each episode, each chapter, each scene, has own its hook, development, and climax. In our minds' eyes, our novel follows a gorgeous arc of inescapable cause-&-effect. And it works! Tears of joy come to our eyes. *It works!*

Unfortunately, we're feeling at this point as though the Spaghetti Prose Posse lurks eternally behind the rocks on the steep bank up ahead, and any minute now we'll be flat on our backs, perfect stories in shards around us, while the wicked Imps of Punctuation tear the shards viciously into smaller and smaller bits, words and logic and meaning and resonance streaming everywhere. *The gore, the gore!*

There's a way to avoid this.

The period.

Like a clove of garlic, the period can be worn around the neck of the writer. All we need to know are those two magical words of the incantation: subject, verb; subject, verb; subject, verb.

We hold the period out in front of us as we pass under the shadow of the Valley of Punctuation Despair.

Subject. Verb. Period.

This is especially important when we're struck by a fit of loquacity and find ourselves rambling on, line after line, clause after clause, phrase after phrase, adding and embellishing and detouring and meandering in and out of side comments and secondary references, which—while they may add everything in the way of color and texture and robust illustration—

immediately subtract it again in complete impregnability, particularly when we start needing really unusual words (or unusual forms of normal words) in order to communicate our meaning within the context of such baroquisations.

What are we trying to say?

It's okay!

Just *spit it out.*

Part 4

Revision

Chapter 22

Gaining Distance with Time with Truman Capote

Let your manuscript go cold

Truman Capote supposedly said that he liked to let a manuscript go cold for a year before revising it. I have done this. It's enormously—even shockingly—helpful. But it makes writing a novel take a really, really, *really* long time.

Books do take a long time to write. They take years and years and years to learn how to do properly. The greats dedicated their entire lives to this craft.

The only way to minimize those years is to hire a skilled independent editor, relying upon the many years that the editor has already spent accumulating specialized writing education and experience and understanding of the craft. It took me *decades* to figure out through trial-&-error just how much to cut out of dialog in order for it to sound both authentic and essential. It took even longer to figure out how to apply that to narrative. This kind of experience makes a huge difference.

Also—those wonderful canonical books we grew up on, the ones that taught us to write, the ones that made us want to *become* writers?

All edited.

However, before we break open the piggy-bank, let's learn to self-edit: let the manuscript go cold.

We finish our novel to the best of our abilities and put it in a drawer. Then we stay away from it for as long as humanly possible. Start other projects. Pull out other manuscripts that have been going cold in their own drawers. Play sudoku.

When we're ready to go back to the cold manuscript, we make sure that we have a large block of uninterrupted time, at least several hours. We sit down and read it straight through without stopping.

We mark it up as we go with a pen in a distinctive color—like red: 'cut,' 'add more,' 'move X over there.' We don't try to write additional scenes or even snippets, unless it's a word or two that are obviously necessary. Just mark it: 'more.' If we know what that 'more' should be, we scribble ourselves notes, but we keep moving. We let our guts talk to us.

This is our chance to get a feel for the overall flow of the plot. If we used a plot outline (yes, we did), does our manuscript actually follow it? Does the story fit into classical three-act structure from Hook through Development to Climax? Is the Hook surprising and intriguing? Does the plot Development hold the reader's interest all the way through? Does the story have boring spots? Can they be fixed? Is there a solid, moving design of Conflicts and Mini-Resolutions and even greater Conflicts throughout? Does the tension increase from start to finish? Have we taken into account the Faux Resolution? Where does the story punch the reader hard? Are those punches where we want them? Is there a really good reason to turn every single page? Is the Climax worth turning all those pages for?

Does it work?

This is a good situation in which to know standard typesetting shorthand. If we don't, we make something up and create a legend for it.

We keep a notebook nearby and jot notes to ourselves as they come to us. We brainstorm about the characters, their motivation and where it succeeds or fails, the cause-&-effect of the plot design and how it's played out in the episodes, chapters, and scenes. We comment on where the grey areas are and our ideas for how to explore them.

Do we have trouble seeing just why one character would do what they do? Why they couldn't possibly do anything else? Or what they would do at all? Do we have an intuitive sense that it might have something to do with a particular aspect or event or symbol?

We jot this down. Jumping to conclusions is very helpful at this stage. The deeper meanings come out of these intuitive leaps.

Does the plot lose cohesion after awhile? Do we become confused about where exactly we were going with all this? Do we look up and think about other things? Are we asking ourselves after awhile why we should even care?

We scribble a sentence for the Hook at the top of a piece of paper and the Climax at the bottom. We sum up the Faux Resolution right before the Climax. Then we re-cap the three Conflicts, one sentence apiece. If the problem's not obvious, we break each one of those down into their own little hook-development-climax. We probably won't have to go far to find the disconnect.

We brainstorm ideas about how to fix it.

A cold manuscript is a rare gift, to be cherished and handled wisely. If we use this technique too often, our perspective will never be crisp enough, plus that novel will never get done. If we don't use it often enough, though, we'll find ourselves bogged down indefinitely in the details of dialog tags and adverbs and punctuation and how much description is too much description, and we won't ever be able to see the big picture.

Once we're done marking up and making notes on our cold manuscript, we'll have a mountain of material to work with, and we can spend the coming weeks or months (or years) going through it all and crafting the pieces we've decided we need to add, and smoothing gaps around parts we've decided to delete. And the next time we let the manuscript go cold we'll see a *huge* difference.

Then we can send it to Truman Capote and ask him what he thinks.

Chapter 23

Cutting & Trimming

Don't fear the Grim Reaper

Killing Your Darlings

Graham Greene called them leopards in the grass and said that he and his wife went through his manuscripts eradicating them. Metaphors.

Personally, I like metaphors.

Personally, I know he's right.

Many years ago I wrote a scathing essay for myself on learning to write that involved writing my heart out, then reading really bad fiction, and then going through my manuscript eliminating anything that smacked even faintly of that bad fiction. I congratulated myself on the one word I'd wind up with: "This is the first word of the rest of my writing life."

When I was young, I used to write all day long, churning out stories in an irrepressible gush, saying absolutely anything that came into my head, all in the blissful knowledge that I could always go back later and scratch it out. I was a paragon of the written word. I was invincible!

Then I grew up and spent the next twenty-five years feeling each word I put down with all my soul, polishing it, petting it, loving it because it was mine. The one thing I didn't do was cut it.

You know what they say about a second childhood? Get yours now.

We launch into writing as though throwing ourselves out of a plane. Go ahead. Write like a fiend. We have tons to get down, more material than we can possibly record: backstory, agendas, mannerisms, gestures, personal twitches, blow-by-blow action, panoramic descriptions, dialog that goes nowhere (because the characters just woke up or they just met each other or they have a lot on their minds or, hey, they just like to talk). We have vistas to imagine and rooms to detail and walks to follow our characters on.

They're not going to wait around for us. We'd better get going.

The thing that amazes me most about aspiring writers is the way some react when I tell them to write.

"I want to write a book," they say. "I don't want to write *everything*."

But that's the way it works: writers write *everything*. Unless we want to wind up with just that one word.

Wuthering Heights is approximately 120,000 words long, every single one of them essential. *Jane Eyre*—hold your breath—is closer to a whopping 190,000. (And that's just one novel, not a series.) Can you even imagine how many words must have wound up on the floor of the Brontë parlor? They must have been wading in it.

The average professional fiction writer cuts 25-100% of the words that they put into their first drafts. This is how Mark Vonnegut can say he knows from growing up with his father that two paragraphs are a good day's work.

I couldn't do the trimming day-by-day like that. I'd hang myself with my poor little disintegrating typewriter ribbon.

We must write as though our lives depend upon it. We must try not to listen to ourselves. Just let it go, let it flow, let it run through the goose. Then when it comes time to cut and trim, we'll have so much material that we'll gladly go after it with a machete, chopping and hacking every single thing out of our way that's not a stepping stone or an essential swinging vine or someone behind a tree with a really wonderful haircut. We won't be circling things to take out—we'll be circling things to leave *in*. Clear-cut the jungle! Slash and burn! Have a blast! (Save the originals on backup.)

My husband and I bought a house once that needed a room demolished before we could live in it, and my father happened to be with us when we made the decision.

"Maybe I should help," he said wistfully, his fingers twitching. "This looks like fun."

We could see *the joy of the sledgehammer* reflected in his eyes.

Fearing the Reaper

Sometimes we writers worry that we're cutting too much. I mean, where do we stop? We want to cut as much as possible. But we can't cut it *all*.

So I am not going to expect you to rush out today and try to reduce a 72,000-word manuscript to something that could fit on a recipe card.

Learn from my experience.

Here is the big secret that someone should have put on a neon billboard hundreds of years ago—we can always write more words.

Not only that.

But the new words we write have a very good chance of being better than the old ones.

This is the exercise that I devised so long ago as a guideline for cutting and trimming:

1) Write something. It doesn't matter what. Just huck it out there on the page, the more the better.

2) Go away.

3) Read something really, really terrible by one of the canonical writers. F. Scott Fitzgerald's *This Side of Paradise* and *The Beautiful and Damned* spring to mind. (Never, *ever* include your own juvenile attempts at poetry in a novel.)

The truth is that an awful lot of the greats rushed into publication before they had—how to say this politely?—earned their chops. And a certain number of them lay back on their laurels and did their dribbling after they'd gotten everyone's attention. Elizabeth Bowen was a genius with the short story and wrote some beautiful things into *The Last September*, but *The Little Girls* could have been written by anyone. *Interview with the Vampire* was groundbreaking both in plot and style, but Anne Rice's work can take a serious downhill turn whenever it isn't edited. Radclyffe Hall's *The Well of Loneliness*, which made such a huge splash—excuse me—when it came out in the 1920s because it deals with lesbianism, is a dreadful, maudlin book.

4) Now *dash back to that manuscript* and, with pen in hand, take out every single thing even a tiny bit similar to the tripe we just read. *Everything.*

5) Ta-da! We are the proud authors of one, two, maybe even three little words.

Yes, it depressed me, too: the Grim Reaper in the doorway, sickle in hand, saying, "I'm here to pick up a manuscript?"

But it works.

People, fear of cutting has no place in a writer's life.

Why? Because we can always save, that's why. I have a whole folder for each of my novels in which I collect what I call out-takes—bits and pieces and scenes and whole chapters that, for one reason or another, just didn't work. And you should see the clippings from my typewriter days.

Not only, that but I've used this material, too. Sometimes I cut out a scene, not because it doesn't work, but because it interferes with the flow of the story. I've taken out lovely scenes, stashed them, and, after a manuscript's gone cold and I'm in revision, reached a point somewhere else where I thought, *It could use a little breather here, something with character development. Wasn't there a scene once about how they went to that thing that time?* I went into my out-takes files, and, lo and behold, there it was, waiting for me.

One time I cut out a seventy-page chapter because it was set on the other side of the planet from the rest of the story. I thought I'd lost my mind when I'd written it. Later I saw why it was essential and an interesting plot twist and put it back, and now it's one of the major cornerstones of that novel.

Don't fear the Reaper, folks. It is our friend. When we re-read a cold manuscript, we do so with the intention of removing every single thing that rings the slightest false note, makes us blink, wakes us up from the suspension of disbelief for *even an instant.*

We take out extraneous words and extra phrases. ("I stood in the doorway with my hand on the door knob standing and watching him walk away from the door.")

We take out whole paragraphs if they interfere with the flow of the plotline. (We've got a good head of steam up, the action's moving along at a terrific clip, we're on the edge of our seat, and suddenly we're wading through a paragraph of internal dialog explaining how the protagonist feels about all this—*cut cut cut*).

We take out great scenes if they don't add to the forward momentum. (Scene: She meets Him. Scene: She has a fight with Ex-Him. Scene: She accidentally emails a letter to Him meant for Ex-Him. Scene: She pays her bills.)

Cutting and trimming is not tearing down the house. It's mowing something that's going to grow right back.

I want to make a special note here about internal dialog and exposition. I highly, highly, highly-infinity recommend doing a pass on the manuscript before letting it go cold specifically in order to remove *all of it*. You heard me. Pull it all out. Put it in its own little "Internal Dialog Out-takes" and "Exposition Out-takes" folders. Make a note of where it came. But cut that manuscript down to the bones. We just lost thirty percent, didn't we?

So we let the manuscript go cold, work on something else, take up a hobby, get a real job. (Radical words to say to a writer, I know.) We come back months later and re-read. The spots where we need either a breather for pacing, backstory, or a little illumination — just a little! — will stand up and tap us on the nose.

And remember: we don't limit ourselves to our out-takes when filling those spots. First we write new scenes.

This is our chance to luxuriate in our fictional universe.

Chapter 24

Editing & Critiquing

Get professional help

Maybe this would be a good time to talk about the differences between editing and critiquing.

Critique groups and workshops help toughen writers up to the reality that we have no control over how readers take fictional works. A lot of our readers' untrained reactions are going to be ignorant at best and destructive at worst. For those of us who publish, this is the reality.

But critiquing—simply trading impressions of each other's drafts—is not the same thing as professional mentoring. Flannery O'Connor called critique workshops *the blind leading the blind.*

When I first read this, I was in Hawaii whiling away my carefree single childless years with a manuscript, a manual typewriter, and almost infinite avocado face-plasters. I'd just had dinner with Richard Brautigan's ex-wife Ginny, who happened to be friends with my landlady, and she'd instructed me to send a copy of my manuscript home for safe-keeping while I traveled, fixing me with stern eye when I was flip about it: "You did say you were a *writer,* didn't you?"

I found O'Connor's canonical work, *Mystery and Manners,* in the Kona library while looking for an obscure novel by someone

one of my friends had known back in San Luis Obispo, California. She'd told me that he spent a lot of time at the coffee kiosk where she worked flirting with her and asking people what they thought it would take to sell a book to the movies for a million bucks, and then he sold a book to Disney for a million bucks. And I was curious to see what a book worth that much money looked like.

I needed reading material for the plane to Australia, but after the first page I knew it would not be *Demonkeeping,* so instead I read O'Connor's firm, considered collection of essays, in which she discusses critiquing.

At that time I was fresh out of a protracted college education and the veteran of not a few writing workshops. In fact, I'd made rather a notorious name for myself in the poetry workshops at Cal Poly San Luis Obispo and been an original member of a fiction-writing group that wound up on the wrong side of the university authorities, for which I'd embroidered the words 'Renegade Fiction' in black Courier on the back of my denim jacket.

I'd just left a warm and supportive poetry group in San Jose who'd been meeting every week for a year. (Only a few years later, fellow poet Greg Keith would die of cancer at the age of fifty, leaving behind his collection *Life Near 310 Kelvin* and a devoted Santa Cruz following, while Kristy Nielsen would go on to well-deserved cult status for her extraordinarily lush experimental prose poetry novels, *A Girl Needs Something of Her Own* and *We All Fall Down*.)

I also didn't know it at the time, but within a couple of years I'd be attending the Community of Writers at Squaw Valley, receiving a personal critique from Anne Lamott during her meteoric rise to household name after the publication of *Operating Instructions* and while she was promoting her new book, *Bird by Bird*. I would become friends with then-unpublished Sasha Troyan and then-unpublished Lucia Orth in Squaw Valley workshops.

I considered myself *definitely* a fan of the critique group.

So you can imagine I raised an eyebrow at O'Connor's assertion that the aspiring writer is better off taking nobody's advice over just anybody's.

I have never believed the old saw about writing being a talent that we must simply be born with. I certainly wasn't. I've always considered this the literary equivalent of a "bad magic number."

When I studied computer science at Cal Poly, one of the most common errors we got back on programs that crashed was "bad magic number."

"Don't you ever wonder what that means?" a professor finally asked us.

We nodded.

"Job security."

If nobody knows what a bad magic number is (and none of us aspiring computer engineers did), the one chowderhead who invented it gets to keep their job.

This is similar to my mother's advice about being an office manager. "The minute you get hired," she told me, "rearrange their filing system. They'll never find anything without you again."

So I shook my head over O'Connor. "I love you, Flannery," I said, "but you're a dog in the manger." Then I landed in Australia and mailed her book back to the Kona library (yes, well before its due date).

However, when I returned to critique workshops fifteen years later, after a lucrative career as a salaried writer and editor, I was taken aback—is that a strong enough term? knocked on my hoopie-doop – to discover what passes for advice in critique groups these days. Maybe I hadn't noticed before. Or maybe the plethora of terrible advice went viral with the explosion of the blogosphere and took over the aspiring writing community while I was out of the loop.

No matter how you look at it, things got B.A.D.

Now, it's true things that have never been the same for the small, in-grown, mentally-deranged quasi-club of the aspiring literati since a certain 1930s writer-who-shall-remain-nameless told her readers, "You're already a writer because you have feelings."

Feelings? Really? Just throw them on a page and demand money for them? Well, I guess there are the Romantics.

The logic is the same for critiquing. Got an opinion? Well, who *doesn't*?

People, people, people. Dear innocent, dedicated, aspiring people. The ability to write well is not a god-given talent that we are issued, like our feelings, along with our navels and fingerprints. And the ability to offer useful constructive editorial criticism is not something that we inherit along with literacy like a side of fries at the Gutenberg A&W.

These are professional skills. They can be learned – pretty much *anything* can be learned, even poodle-grooming – but we have to actually devote our apprenticeships to it, just as for any career.

Editorial apprenticeship involves years of research into proper structure and the documented rules of written English (including the differences between American and British standards), extensive study of great authors and their distinctive styles and techniques, careful line-by-line deconstruction and analyses of scores of novels and stories from canonical to experimental, as well as trained professional editing experience under professional supervision.

In order to edit other writers' fiction, I must be able to talk about all aspects of the craft and its genres with intelligence and insight, understanding such fine distinctions within my chosen genres as reverse mysteries, forensic mysteries, cozy mysteries, classic mysteries, and psychological horror mysteries.

I must be able to identify and diagnose practically *all* fiction issues reasonably quickly and accurately and express this diagnosis in simple, clear language.

Since I am a developmental editor, I must understand what makes a story gripping to a reader, what keeps the reader intrigued, what establishes characters as icons of the reader's imagination, what makes the reader intensely grateful— when they reach the end of a novel or story—that they've discovered this particular writer. I must have a sterling grip upon the intricate complexities of plotting, primary, secondary, tertiary, even quaternary subplots, plot layering, and techniques like resonance and lit fuses. I must know how to take a wonderful idea with exciting events and a cast of unique characters and turn it into a fully-developed fictional journey.

And since I am also a line editor, I must also have a sort of freaky developed ear for the rhythms of language and a ruthless eye for only those words absolutely necessary to polished literature. I must be able to rearrange scenes for optimum arc, sentences within scenes, words within sentences. I must be able to pick from a variety of choices only the most vivid and telling details, and when there are none vivid and telling enough I must be able to elicit more powerful details from the writer. I must also know exactly how to identify a writer's unique voice and bring out the full beauty of its greatest strengths, while pruning with all tender delicacy its weaknesses.

In addition, I must have a certain amount of background in basic psychology and the human response to support and criticism as it applies to the artistic impulse, including separation of self and creation, transference, self-esteem issues, and vulnerability.

I must have a sense of confidence, not in my desire to become a wannabe 'guru,' but in my professional skills—as well as security, not in my ability to fool others into thinking that I'm skilled at something I haven't properly learned yet, but in my ability to be good at what I do without fooling *anybody*.

Donald Maass has made the excellent point that the rise of independent editors in this era brings a level of professional help to aspiring writers that's never been available before. It's there now.

People: get help.

Chapter 25

Despair

Survive it

You're floating face-down over a river of nightmare, and in the bottom of the river lies your beautiful Frankenstein. You stick your arm into the nauseating goo and reach for it. You reach for it and reach for it, and it's receding. It's fading away—that shining, burning spark of life—and you can't get your arm in deep enough. There it goes. . .your story, escaping you. All of this work for nothing. Your dream, the passion you've built your life upon, your very identity, and it all turns out to have been a mistake, after all.

The despair is crippling.

And it's so bright and brilliant and poignant, far away down there. It was all going to have been so much more than worth it.

Revising Unto Death

Animal House. The first time I saw that it was 1979, and I went outside afterward and watched someone drive over the concrete base of the theater sign in the parking lot. In a Chevy van.

Those were the days.

I've never forgotten the Donald Sutherland character's apt summary of his life's work in one brief, succinct term: "a piece of shit." Maybe because he lisped. More likely, though, because it was uttered with such glib bitterness. This was a novelist who'd just done that one last revision before he went behind the barn and shot himself.

I spent a lot of time on this issue back in my twenties, when I had a lot of excess energy and fuel and *time* to expend on wrestling the craft, like wrestling an angel, into submission.

Revision is a mercurial tool.

The first few times through revision is pleasant, a sort of aromatherapy on the exhausted psyche of the deservedly-proud parent of a tiny baby book. Sure, we can let that multiple adverb go. Yes, let's take out most of the "oh's" and "well's" in the dialog (except where they're really necessary for character development, of course). And we understand that we didn't need quite so many lines to get the main characters out of the room in that pivotal plot point scene.

It's a diamond in the rough—a little elbow grease honing every single gorgeous facet never hurt anyone.

Hey, we're *Writers.*

After awhile it starts being less like aromatherapy and more like sit-ups. *One* more time through. How'd we miss that typo? Woops, her name used to be Janet. And, hang on—wasn't the symbolic color lavender? When did it become puce?

But we're still feeling pretty good because, after all, we're still improving it. Granted, it needs more improvement than we were expecting. We all but called Molly Friedrich the day we typed *The End* to see if she wanted to get a spot before our future filled up, and now we're glad we didn't. That would have been one expensive trip to NYC to tell her that we're still in the middle of "giving it a last once-over." We're such perfectionists.

We've stopped laughing out loud at the humor. We don't need to pause anymore and let the glory sink in when we come to really incredible turns-of-phrase ("lava leaked slowly out of his heart"—how come nobody ever thought of that image before?). We're taking it in stride. Only now and then do we allow ourselves a soft, clear murmur—leaning across the desk to change the writing music—"We're really good."

We write because we love to write. Isn't that the way it works? So we keep revising as long as we love to revise. And we do enjoy this! It's a heck of a book! We'd buy it in a *hot second.* Molly Friedrich is going to be so pleased.

And then there comes the night when we find ourselves reading over words that have acquired such resonance in our mind that they're no longer in English. We wake from the daydream of fame with a start ("Sorry, Oprah—that's my phone"). We have apparently written a heck of a book. In Martian.

We blink and re-read that line. Words in English. Meaning by telepathy. Syntax in. . .well, it looks a lot like a dead language. Are we channeling someone?

We try whispering it out loud to break the spell. "He had a brain flamed with meaning. His eyes reflected fire. Hot lava poured from his sternum. His heart followed it, wincing."

It's fly-fishing for romantic volcanologists.

In a flash, it sinks in. This is not a heck of a book. This is a heck of a piece of shit.

We're not going to be able to revise this. Flaubert's friends made him burn *his.*

Uncontrollable weeping is not humiliating when it's accompanied by sincere, bittersweet regret and an unshakable commitment to never repeat such a humbling mistake again. We will go on with life, we vow. We will stick to our last. I mean, how many people saw this coming? How many well-meaning advisers said, "It's nice for a *hobby,* honey—"? How many of them did we dismiss as callow unbelievers?

A part of us has died.

So we weep our heart out. Us and Ophelia both. You think she threw herself in the river over that nickel-plated nutcase, Hamlet? She was too good for him.

No. She'd just finished her one last revision.

Returning from the Dead

But what if we survive the Self-Loathing Phase of Revision? Do we come back as Writing Zombies?

Actually, I'm tired of zombies. I wasn't really into them in the first place, and for some reason they've just exploded into a kind of unbelievable dawning—of the. . .uh, dead. . .

So let's call ourselves Writing Mummies instead, shall we? Staggering hither and thither in our unwinding windings, exhaling a little cloud of dust like Pigpen with each attempted breath, grasping blindly at everything we run into (because of course we can't see through our bandages), leaving a trail of bits of tooth and bone in our wake.

That's pretty much how it feels the day after we give up on a novel, isn't it?

We stumble into the kitchen, where some compassionate loved one has left the tea pot simmering, pour a cup of yerba mate (I know you probably drink coffee, but the day after we die everything really is different), and dump it down our mouth opening into our stomach cavity, where it siphons onto the floor between our skeletal feet.

We turn and drag ourselves up the stairs to our office. Our manuscript is waiting. We collapse into our chair, several limbs let go their grip on their neighboring bones, and they fall off. It's morning, and we are now legless, one-armed, and drenched in libation. Not so different from a regular workday, after all.

That's right. It's still a workday.

I'm now going to give some strict instructions, and woe unto you if you ignore them: *do not* touch your manuscript. As my son used to say in his piping, dictatorish, Mary Poppins voice when he was about two years old, "*No*, no!"

Leave that poor thing be.

I know everyone tells us to keep at it: "Write every day! Successes are people who never accept failure! Have faith in yourself!"

Hogwash. Forget the faith. Don't be a raving idiot. We've found errors too big to be fixed, plot devices like snapped masts, lack of motivation to make Beckett weep. What do we want? A frontal lobotomy? (Yes.) Use a little common sense. That manuscript sucks.

Put it in the bottom of a drawer and close it. Stop the torment.

Instead, let's spend some real quality time using both hands to lift first one shin bone and then the other—even if we have to lean over and fish them out from under our chair—up to rest our poor bulbous heel bones on a nice comfy stool. We prop the ends of the broken shin bones on the corresponding knee caps. It won't hurt them. We adjust our pelvis carefully so that we can lean back without dropping all our vertebrae in a shower of hollow clatter to the floor. That's right. We prop our broken armbone up on our shoulder socket, and we rest the elbow of the whole arm on the arm of our chair. We lay our finger bones out across our keyboard. See what a nice pattern they make? Like the spokes of pretty little bats' wings.

We let our jawbone hang down on our chest if it wants to. It's not bothering anybody.

Now we just sit. We are a skeleton. We feel our eye sockets. Big, aren't they? We feel the roots of our teeth in our jaw. We've got a lot of them, don't we? We breathe through our nose holes. Two's a pretty good number, isn't it?

Our sternum rises and falls with each breath. Our collarbone tips gently forward and backward. Every now and then a vertebra settles.

We keep thinking that our whole spine's going to come tumbling down all over our lap, spilling ribs we'll never get back, but it doesn't. Our broken bones stay balanced on the joints they're propped upon. Our feet might fall over, but they don't fall off. Even our skull manages to stay upright on our scrawny excuse of a neck.

We keep thinking that the white electricity of shame is going to finish us off, but it doesn't.

Another breath, another rise of the sternum, another tip of the long axoidal collarbone. And back down again. Over and over. We can forget the novel we've been so immersed in for so long, the characters we've come to love, the amazing plot points, the rich tone, the vast, complex, shifting, colorful world that those characters inhabit.

We can forget about wanting to throttle every single person who ever raised an eyebrow and said, "A nice *hobby*—"

We can forget about waking in the middle of the night last night to weep helplessly over the agent queries we've spent so many heady hours crafting and polishing and sticking—all ready to go the instant our novel was ready—into their sweet, pristine little envelopes. We don't have to look at them there in their place of honor on our desk. We don't have eyeballs anymore.

We left our inner organs in jars somewhere in another room. We're not going to need them.

Letting our sternum rise. Letting our collarbone tip. Letting our sternum fall back again. Letting the collarbone settle. We can spend the day this way. The light through our windows appears on the wall, moves slowly and with complete indifference across it, meets the floor, crosses that, slides up the other wall and eventually disappears, all without caring whether it makes it or not.

Our eye sockets get bigger, get smaller, become rounder and less round. It doesn't make the slightest bit of difference. We still have all those teeth. We still have two nose holes.

Our wrappings might get a little looser, and some of them might unwind a little. That's all.

At the end of the day, when the light is gone and twilight is making it hard to see the pretty little bats' wings on our keyboard (we didn't need to move them—lifeless fingers have no need to move), we finally do something. We sigh.

Then we grip the arms of our chair and heave ourselves, clanking, to our feet. We don't need to hold onto the desk to get across the room, like we did this morning. We can make it to the hall with just a hand out to steady ourselves in the doorway. We go on downstairs, and taking the steps is a lot easier when gravity helps. We hear the voices of our loved ones in the kitchen. The light's on over the kitchen table. Someone's at the stove, and it's starting to smell good. We come around the corner, and they look up.

They smile. They've missed us.

"Long day, honey?" Someone is handing us a glass of wine. I guess they don't know mummies can't drink.

"*Long*." We put a hand on our child's head, and the hair is soft and familiar. We sit down and cross our knees and take a sip. You know, it tastes nice, considering that we don't have any tongue.

"I understand," our child says kindly. "I had a long day, too."

And we take our child onto our lap and hold them close, smelling their hair, feeling our heart beat against their lovable little back. The lamplight shines down on the beautiful face under our chin, and the high voice goes on with whatever endless, convoluted story they were telling when we came into the room. Our loved one goes on cooking. The cats come in and sniff our feet.

None of them seems to notice our loose windings, at all.

Running with the Chipmunks

Yesterday we were five-thousand-year-old skeletons losing our wrappings. We had a manuscript in the bottom of a drawer—the vivid, lush, poignant, *devastating* story of wonderful, struggling people doing impossibly brave things with beauty, anguish, and humor. All that time and energy and insight and humanity.

All done wrong.

We spent a day being dead over it. So what do we do now?

Well, the first thing *I* do is go off and have some completely unrelated, unexpected, hair-raising adventure that has nothing whatsoever to do with writing. That puts a few things into perspective.

The other thing I do is lie on my face in the garden thinking about how short life is, how many things I meant to do that I'll never have time for, how long the humiliation of being a terrible writer is going to last in my memory after I'm gone.

And the *other* other thing I do is read some advice on writing until something happens in my head, some little spark ignites, and I think, ". . .that kind of makes me want to put some words in a row and see what happens—"

Scientists have been able to determine so much about the origins of life. We know now how old the earth is, what the first life form was (and it's still here, taking over my pond), when that happened, and a whole lot about what's been going on since. But what we can't do is pinpoint the exact mechanics of what started it. Why? What made certain chemicals, when bumped into each other, suddenly *automate*?

They woke the chipmunks.

That's what happens in my brain when I've read enough interesting books on the craft of writing to clean out all the old ego and anxiety and hope and nerves and sheer fatigue from the piece I've had to put away.

The chipmunks wake up.

Now, I don't know about you, but my chipmunks are not necessarily all sweet and soft and cuddly. My chipmunks are really quite bony little guys under that ephemeral fluff, with claws and teeth and tiny poky elbows. And they're busy. They don't sit around waiting to be petted, like my cats. They're on the *move*.

They have enormously high metabolisms, which means that they have to be constantly eating. They dash around like their tails are on fire, yanking down grass stems, looking under loose brush, *pillaging my strawberries*! (Yes, these are real chipmunks.) They sit up on their hind legs in full sight of the windows, hold their booty in their miniscule fingers, and chew it up as fast as they can.

Have you ever watched a chipmunk chew? They're *fast*!

Then they're off and running again, and the cats are dashing hysterically through the house, from window to window, after them.

And here's me, sitting at my desk surrounded by books I'm half-through reading or re-reading (I've just re-awakened my long-standing passion for Jane Bowles), listening to John Gardner's classic words ring in my head, listing off the *self-destructive qualities* necessary to the truly dedicated serious writer, all so awful and familiar.

I look out the window. Chipmunks. Destroying my life.

I look back at the book, where he's talking about *shame* and *humiliation.*

I've got those. I've got them in spades! My dead manuscript is right there on the desk in front of me.

He goes on in excruciating detail about *the anguish of failure.*

Even the chipmunks look annoyed about those weedy little strawberries. We were both hoping for so much more.

He quotes F. Scott Fitzgerald on *the sheer drudgery of the life of fiction.*

And suddenly the chipmunks and I are one.

See how this works? I have lots of files of ideas and partial starts and old pieces gone cold waiting for a rewrite, but I don't care about them. There's something going on in my head, the chipmunks have found a wheel, and words are coming out of it. What I really want to do is pull out a fresh pad of yellow legal paper and start writing:

"Phoebe leaned over and took Leo's hand. 'I'm so sorry,' Marcus said gently from across the desk."

Who are these people? I have no idea. Where are they that they need a desk? Beats me. What is Marcus sorry about? Your guess is as good as mine. But you know what would be really fun? Writing a novel about three people based on the personalities of my *cats*.

That was, in reality, some years ago, and I had to write on a yellow legal pad because I had a little boy and his life-sized toy skeleton in my lap discussing with great interest the illustrations in *Winnie-the-Pooh*. I know all about Phoebe and Leo and why they needed a desk now, and I know exactly what Marcus was sorry about, although he wound up a lot sorrier about other things later.

What a great novel that's been to write! And how *long* it's taken—it's certainly spent plenty of good, nutritious time composting in the dark of that drawer while I was busy reading Pooh to the little boy and the skeleton. Plus writing a new children's book to read them every year. And then working for a living. And then working on another novel. And then building a house. And then learning to write mysteries. Getting older. Switching careers—

But it was Exciting. And Educational. And Alarming!

Although there were times I didn't want to be writing it, there was never a time I didn't want it written. I take Toni Morrison to heart every day and write the book that I most want to read.

Yes, the craft of fiction is a wonderful, bizarre, exotic, and yet intensely intimate angel. Yes, it is heck of strong. And, yes, it's going to slam us on our backs and knock the wind right out of us.

Sudden inhalation!

That's inspiration.

Book II

BEING A WRITER

Chapter 26

Facing The Bad News with Flannery O'Connor

Should you become a writer?

I'm going to tell you the bad news now and get it out of the way. If you don't want to hear it, I don't blame you—go ahead and skip this chapter.

When Flannery O'Connor was asked whether or not she thought universities stifled writers, she famously answered that she didn't think they stifled enough of them. She thought there were quite a lot of best sellers that could have been headed off by a half-way decent writing teacher.

It was the late 1950s, and O'Connor was seriously worried about the state of American fiction. She should know—one of the most intelligent of the fiction writers of twentieth-century America, she was also one of the most talented, creative, and hilarious. She was a devout Catholic, with an immovable belief in the grotesque as the path to enlightenment and a sense of black humor as big as a barn door. What we cannot learn about great literature and human nature from following Enoch Emery on his quest to shake the hand of the man in the gorilla suit perhaps cannot be learned.

O'Connor also held the immovable belief that there is no such thing as The Writer. However, she was, at the same time, a pragmatist, and she understood that the world was—and is—absolutely chock full of people desperately eager to *become* The Writer. She blamed the growing influx of writing classes and MFA programs for turning out legions of mediocre writers capable of being published without being particularly good.

She also knew that it's sometimes the ability to write *badly* in just the right way that actually gets aspiring writers published. Fiction as an art mattered too much to her to look kindly on this situation. She strongly suggested stifling such people the minute you lay hands on them.

I've been reading up on the writing advice available on the Internet. I've found some smart, funny, excellent advice by people with sense and experience. I have also found some people who give the worst advice possible. On two of the more visible sites, writers are told to replace normal, useful, active verbs with clichés like "snatched," blurry actions like "retreated," and the horrifying "hips" that "beckoned." (Please. Swear that you will never, ever have a character in any book whatsoever *whose hips beckon*.)

Naturally, everywhere I look I also see aspiring writers crying: "We get conflicting advice! How do we know whom to listen to?"

I know from my own personal experience that it's agonizing, when suffering from an image of myself as The Writer (or even A Writer), to understand that writing fiction is rarely—if ever—a career. However, it's also nearly impossible to shake the conviction that Writing is the Greatest of All Arts and that I, personally, am destined for my place in the canon.

After all, it's so easy to find proof that such ambition works.

We are raised to list the arts alongside other professions when we're asked as children, "What do you want to be when you grow up?"

Few if any little children answer, "A stamp-collector!" "A spelunker!" "An amateur ham radio operator!" Nobody points out to children that answering, "A writer!" is akin to saying, "I hope to become a professional hobbyist!"

This is because it would lead to the next inevitable question, "And am I the one who's going to be supporting you?" (Granted, my own twelve-year-old yells, "A model train enthusiast!" but that's because he knows his father and I will let him live in our attic.)

Oh, I know—not *every* fiction writer must treat their calling as a hobby. Look at O'Connor. Wasn't she a writer? Didn't she achieve fame and fortune? Isn't she remembered decades years after her death as one of the great Southern writers of all time?

Yes, she was a fiction writer. Yes, she was paid for her stories and invited to give talks on fiction to classes and Catholic groups. And yes, a thousand times yes, she is remembered as one of the greats.

But fiction writing was not her career. O'Connor lived at home with her mother, raising peacocks with possibly as much energy as—certainly more angst than—she put into her writing. She had lupus, a hereditary disease that killed her father when she was a teenager and would kill her at thirty-nine. Her place in history did not find her while she was still alive to enjoy it.

She wrote fiction because, as she said, she was good at it. And for no other reason.

Virginia Woolf ran a publishing house with her husband Leonard, conveniently situated to publish her work without vetting by either agent or editor. Jean Rhys was a helpless drunk who lived as a kept woman for part of her life. Raymond

Chandler was an executive in the oil industry. Edith Wharton came from a family of money and also sold her services in landscape architecture and interior design. Faulkner, Fitzgerald, and Chandler all worked as scriptwriters in Hollywood when they got tired of living hand-to-mouth, even when they hated themselves for doing so. Graham Greene, it turns out, was a spook. (Hemingway was a *failed* spook.)

Decade after decade, the authors of the canonical books on writing advice—Flannery O'Connor, John Gardner, Syd Field—remind us to write fiction either because we're good at it or just because we love to.

We cannot expect the masses to make it worth our while. We can ask them, and they'll tell us honestly: they don't want to.

But what about Stephen King? What about Anne Rice? What about that darling of the desperately-aspiring writerly masses, J.K. Rowling?

Yes, those people write fiction. Yes, they are hugely read. Yes, they make a lot of money at it. But mostly what they'd be doing if they were starting out today—like us—is marketing.

It is a different world now. The combination of the Internet and the economy has changed everything. The innocent new fiction writer these days winds up spending an *unbelievable* amount of time promoting themself. They write endless blog posts, newsletters, and emails, they talk about their writing incessantly, they get sucked into Twitter and Facebook and LinkedIn. They hire independent editors to help them get a foot in the door and, sometimes, publicists after they've done it. If they're lucky, they eventually get invited to business meetings, where they drink bad coffee and eat stale pastries. If they're really lucky, they deal with professional marketers, who may be the nicest people in the world and best at their jobs, but still—

they're marketers. They're not interested in great literature, they're just interested in marketing, and when writers meet with them and they tussle over what they're going to talk about. . .guess what? The marketers win.

The innocent new fiction writer can then, if they're still lucky, face what seems like an eternity on tour, a literary vaudevillian, traveling until they're exhausted, staying in cheap hotels or sleeping on couches without family or favorite armchairs, dragging themselves to conferences and book readings and signings with the stoicism of stage actors and not even the adrenaline rush of footlights and a theater of echoing applause.

I have traveled for work as a writer. I have stayed extensively in hotels paid for by writing. I have even brought my husband and son along.

Take a good hard gander at the countenance of the next big-name writer you meet at a book signing and see just how brave and desperately cheery it is. When I met Ray Bradbury at the bookstore where I worked in 1991 and told him he knew my aunt, he looked at me with the eyes of a bull at the end of a bull fight. The man was bled dry.

Truthfully, that life is not very different from working a job in corporate America, traveling for work and writing on the side. We get a few more hours for writing during the day. Not all of it. Sometimes not even half. Just some. When I worked in an office, I could usually pick up that much time by avoiding co-workers on coffee breaks and cutting down on my night-life on the weekends.

And the pay in corporate America is *much* better.

But convincing those of us longing to be The Writer of any of this is like discussing the odds with aspiring gamblers—"I could win big!" we cry, "I could score thousands!"

"Yes," comes back answer, "but if we factor in time, expenses, and the possibility of repeat performance, we still don't get enough to live on."

We have to look at the highest success possible in our line of endeavor. Eating stale pastries with marketers and calling our children at bedtime to hear them ask when we're coming home, just so we can pay our mortgage? I have worked at IBM, and I have been published, and believe me, when it came to making a living I went with IBM.

Writing fiction is not a lucrative profession. Truly. We don't get into it for the fame and fortune.

It is an obsessive compulsion that would reign unchecked in our hearts our whole lives long. . .whether anyone ever found out about it or not.

Chapter 27

The Good News

How to become a writer

So now I'll tell you the good news.

There has never been a better time in history to become a fiction writer—literacy rates around the world are spectacular, traditional cultural limitations are dropping away as technology becomes global and daily communication between countries commonplace, and the ebook and Print On Demand (POD) revolutions have brought publication back to the people who make it all worthwhile: readers and their writers.

Fiction writers just need to accept the same facts that publishers always have—a good book needs a writer, editor, book designer, promoter, and financial backing—and once they do, they'll tip the scales and we'll see a jaw-dropping amount of incredible literature hit the airwaves. I see it in my clients' work right now.

It's going to alter our perceptions of literature itself.

Truly—an amazing time to be alive.

Aspiring

It is my experience that talented teenage writers, by the very nature of their lack of experience, are generally better writers than aspiring adult writers. This is because they haven't muddled their heads with a lot of useless and destructive advice and models of terrible writing. Talented teenagers may be confused about life in general, but they are often far less confused about putting the right words in the right order than people who have figured out how to live. Most writing teenagers don't have that distraction.

So, no matter how old you are, when you begin writing fiction, consider yourself a teenager.

Pay attention to the writing.

This sounds like obvious advice, but it's actually brutally difficult for those of us shackled with the demands of survival. You must find a way to carve out space in which to revert to adolescence, come to the craft as a novice, tackle it in all good faith as a beginner.

Forget about queries, synopses, agents, publishers, blogs, and platforms for now. Just write. You're in this for the long haul. And all that stuff is constantly changing.

Beware well-meaning amateur advisors! Especially those who tell you to read everything you can get your hands on. That is standard advice, and it is extremely dangerous to aspiring writers.

Don't read crap!

You will absorb it like a sponge. Find someone who knows good writing and ask them to advise you on what to read. Read the great authors cited here. Read pulp fiction from the first half of the twentieth century (not later!). When in doubt, read Shakespeare.

And don't waste your time forcing yourself to write every day if you find yourself failing and feeling guilty. Why? So you can learn to resent writing's resemblance to work? Think about the very real fact that fiction writers don't typically make much money, and then ask yourself why you'd want to force yourself to do something you have no reason to do but for sheer love and talent, especially if you take the sheer love out of it. So you can be tormentedly talented *and* hardly make anything? Like you're not in that position *already*?

Go ahead and write what you want to write when you want just because you want to write it. There's no law that says you have to publish. Just write. This is your passion, to do with as you see fit.

Of course, if you're hoping to publish someday it doesn't hurt to learn what you can about the publishing industry, so long as you keep in mind that this year—this month, this very minute—the industry is going through upheaval only comparable to the invention of the Gutenberg Press. Nobody has any idea where it's going. By this time next year, the standard way of publishing could be a total mutation of its previous self, taking all of us—particularly the publishing industry—with it.

And whatever else you do, if you want to publish, get used to rejection. That advice is something no publishing writer can hear enough. Literary rejection is not like being turned down for a date. It's not about you. It's about all of us writers as a group. It's like the old joke: "Don't vote. It only encourages them."

Don't submit to someone who might reject you. It only encourages them.

Loving & Hating the Tools of Your Trade

During a period in my early independent editing career, when I was researching online critique groups, I got involved one day in a discussion on semicolons. You wouldn't think there's much to argue about regarding semicolons. I mean, you know, they're. . .semicolons. A dot and a comma.

However, it turns out there are some very strong opinions floating around out there. Not about how to use them—nobody's arguing about how to use them—but about whether or not to use them at all. Are they legitimate? Illegitimate? In common use? Currently illegal?

I made the rash announcement that I love them. Which I do.

I went so far as to say that when I was a teenager I would've been happy to punctuate *entirely* in semicolons. Which I would. This was in contrast to my professional experience that semicolons are no longer in common use in contemporary fiction.

Whoa.

It turns out some aspiring writers really don't want you to 'love' semicolons. They're adamant on this point. They're convinced it's morally wrong. And they are willing to exchange tough words on the subject.

As if it's any of their business.

Writing fiction is not easy work, it's not always productive work, and it has a nasty way of becoming painful rather than soothing work just when we least expect it. As with so many other things in life, writing is hard enough as it is. So whose business is it to try to suck even the smallest vestige of joy out of it for somebody else?

Elizabeth Gilbert gave a talk once on the subject of genius. She was discussing how to approach the book that follows the book that makes your professional name. She was talking about how she's attempting to approach this work that she loves without fear of failure.

I thought that was interesting: "this work that she loves." She didn't say she likes it. She didn't say she likes only those parts it's in good taste to like. She certainly didn't say, "Whatever you do, don't love semicolons, you silly, doomed scribblers." She said, "I love it. I love this work!" She said it a whole bunch of times.

Now, I don't know Elizabeth Gilbert, I've never read her books (no, not even her blockbuster), but I'm willing to say right here that I like her passion for this work about which I, also, feel passionate.

For heaven's sake, you guys, do what you love. If you love to write, then write. If you love aspects of writing—A.A. Milne was particularly fond of writing on clean paper with a brand-new pen nib—go to town with it. Hurrah! You enjoy what you do. It makes you happy. You work with tools you love. Good for *you*.

On the other hand, if there are certain aspects to writing that you hate—I think it was Kurt Vonnegut who said writers are people who hate to write—feel free to hate them. You have my unconditional permission. Hate them with vim. Hate them with vigor. Don't forget to learn how to use them so that you can use them properly when you absolutely can't avoid it, but other than that—be my guest. Do you think Hemingway eschewed character description because he felt neutral about it? He thought it was stupid! He went around telling people so! Do you think happy fiction writers approach their work as though it's washing the dishes: "Don't love it, don't hate it, just got to be done, *ho-hum*"?

What kind of life would that *be*?

Never listen to anybody who tells you not to love or hate anything about your chosen art.

Love your work. Love every little bit of it that you can. Love the paper and pen nibs and keyboard, love the punctuation and vocabulary and syntax, love the alliterations and etymology and *patois* and Great Vowel Shift of the fifteenth through eighteenth centuries. Hate what really burns you up. Throw yourself, like Camille, across the fainting couch of literary aspirations.

Flaubert yelled at the top of his lungs and rolled around on the floor.

We can too.

Writing Sanely in an Insane World

I have a theory about the plethora of children's social disorders cropping up these days. I grew up in the 1960s, when social disorder was the name of the game, and I don't know how many afternoons and evenings I spent in the homes of perfectly nice hippies, sitting on futons covered with Indian cotton bedspreads and trying to make heads or tails out of Ram Dass's *Be Here Now,* while the adults around me tried to decide whether or not it's sane to be at odds with an insane society.

How many of you have ever read *Be Here Now*? I mean, it's *square*. I couldn't even tell when I was holding it upside-down.

Years later, a friend went into my bathroom in the middle of a party and posted a sign over the toilet—*Pee Here Now*—and that made a lot more sense.

I've worked with children for a long time: special kids, privileged kids, alternative-education kids, abused kids, mainstream kids. I was the Director of the Children's Room of the Earthling Bookshop in San Luis Obispo when it first opened (it's gone now), and I've never had such fun as I did going in every morning and switching on the series of lights over the books one by one, like a stage lighting up. Then I spent my day talking to concerned parents and grandparents about why children should read instead of watch TV or play computer games and what books they should be reading. If I died and went to heaven and I was the Director of the Celestial Children's Bookstore, I'd be perfectly happy.

And I've been involved in the secular homeschooling movement since the early 1980s, when I talked my sisters into homeschooling their kids (now grown, gorgeous, brilliant adults whose one glaring fault is they don't come visit me often enough). My husband and I spend twenty-four hours a day with a lunatic twelve-year-old homeschooler who's so comfortable in the *here-&-now* that he couldn't be socially inept if you dropped him in an alligator tank.

But why are increasing numbers of children diagnosed with social disorders requiring prescription medications? Those same children who spend every waking hour from alarm clock to lights-out ferried from one structured event in the charge of strange adults to another, directed, educated, bossed, shuffled, analyzed, and managed, until they don't know which way to turn and can't remember a Sunday afternoon in pajamas just hanging out with their folks. . .

What's happening to our kids?

At odds with an insane society.

So when writers ask what to do about Writer Attention Deficit Disorder—the tendency to wander away from writing projects and get embroiled in the shenanigans of real life—my first thought is, "Is this a disorder? Or is it simply at odds with a formula-driven publishing culture?"

I don't know about you, but I have *boxes* of old manuscripts in my storeroom. That's from my pre-computer era. I also have more folders of writing projects on my computer than I can find or make sense of (the virtual reality of *Be Here Now*), and my idea of a good time is to get the wind up and stroll through those long, rambling virtual corridors reading old fiction. I don't work on it anymore. It's all so ancient and solidified, and my skills have altered so much in the intervening decades, I wouldn't know what to do with it now if I tried. But it's *fun*! All those ideas, all those adventures, all those snappy turns of phrase. There are some things I could say better then than I can now.

Even more fun is to get out the boxes, wrestle them open, breathe the rich, satisfying smell of stacks of old paper (computers don't smell like old paper), lift out pages and folders, let the folders fall open in my lap, read all those antiquated, forgotten, wonderfully-typewritten words with handwritten corrections, like the journals of some unknown nineteenth-century traveler in foreign lands, go back into the mind of the person who wrote them –

What ever happened to those days? Now it's all about product. Write that novel, mail it to a hundred agents, sit by the phone tapping your fingers until they sell the thing to some rich publisher for pots of money. Line up your blog tour, become an expert marketer, build your platform, *push, push, push*. Everywhere you turn, someone's selling you their plans for how to sell yourself.

Remember pyramid schemes?

Anne Lamott suggests giving each of your characters their own acre of land to do with what they will and, in this way, learn who they are.

So take writing as your acre. Give it a wall or a hedge or a mountain range. Install a gate exactly the right size, with exactly the right latch and exactly the right squeak. Give yourself the only key.

And whenever you get the wind up, pull out your key (on a piece of string around your neck) and go in and explore. Heaven only knows what you'll find.

One minute you'll be coming down a mountain path into the yard of characters you left last summer around a kettle of boiling water and garden herbs trying to figure out whether sludge counts as tincture or not, and darned if they won't be having a conversation with someone you've never met before who knows some extraordinary detail about them.

Or you'll be walking along a city street in hot argument with a couple of characters who are *still locking horns*, and you'll say, "But what about—" and suddenly the argument will shift to the real underlying problem that's been waiting to be recognized all along.

Or you'll be lying at dawn watching the curtains blow in on two lovers, and one of them will get up ever-so-carefully, stand by the window for a minute, and silently begin to dress. . .and you'll realize where they're supposed to be and why and what's going to happen when the other wakes up.

If you don't go back and patch in the holes in old stories, that's okay. Maybe that story was practice. Or maybe what you think goes into those holes is boring. Or maybe the story is so old now that it's settled into its shape and is sliding silently backward into the past, where it belongs.

And if you have ideas springing forth like Athena from your brain, leaving previous ideas languishing in their dust, by all means, spring with them!

That's your fountain of youth!

Ponce de León is looking for *you*.

Committing Random Acts of Literature

Editing clients ask me, "Why is it so hard to take good advice? Why am I so attached to my mistakes?"

And the short answer is: because they are your babies.

There is also, naturally, a long answer.

Remember when you were a child, and you'd work for hours on some project by which you were simply fascinated, gluing together popsicle sticks, drawing meticulous illustrations, adding pipe-cleaners and gold stars and googly-eyes, taping together parts the glue kept letting go of or that, in your impatience, you just felt like taping together? You had a vision! It was extraordinary! *You knew where you were going with it.* And when it was done—it was gorgeous. It was beyond gorgeous. It was *exactly* what you wanted it to be.

Oh, the power and the glory.

And years later you find, in the bottom of a box in your parents' closet, a photo of you and your sister with that project, which you've long since forgotten all about. And what is it? It's a bunch of popsicle sticks stuck together with dirty tape and glue.

It takes a minute to figure out what it even *was* or why you both look so pleased. But when you do, it all comes back. And somehow you can see it, the original vision, and the hours of work, the joy, the passion, the sense of overwhelming reward that you got to be you, you got to own this idea, you got to make it come to life. You'd never known, before that project, how extraordinary it is just to be alive.

And then your sister walks into the room behind you and sees the photo and says, "Is that that thing I made in second grade? Man, I loved that thing! Now it just looks like dirty little popsicle sticks stuck together with glue."

And neither one of you knows who made this particular object, after all.

This is why so much of the advice to aspiring writers simply consists of Natalie Goldberg's mimed gesture: "Write." Write and write and write and write. Is it because you need to pile up mountains of work around you, unsteady towers higher than your head threatening to topple at any moment and crush you under their literary weight? So you will have volumes and volumes of badly-written first draft stuff to unload on unsuspecting agents?

No. It is so you will learn to let go.

I wrote my first fiction as a young teen on a big old five-hundred-pound Royal typewriter with a high back and keys you needed a sledgehammer to move. (My mother had the easy typewriter, a big old five-hundred-pound Underwood with a high back and keys only marginally looser. It was the 1970s. She was into antiques.)

I taught myself to poise my fingers over the keys, empty my mind, and then go hell-bent-for-leather, typing like a fiend as fast as I could. I got pretty fast. In spite of the pounding of keystrokes that could be heard in Kentucky, I topped out at about 110 words/minute, not bad if I'd been a typist and actually had a job.

My ideal was to not recognize, when I went back over it, what I'd just written. Instant free reading material! Without leaving the house! (I was a teenager—I hardly left my *room*.)

It's really a very meditative exercise, with the added bonus that you get to think about other things while you do it.

Sit down in front of your keyboard or paper and teach yourself to write without thinking. Produce your own free reading material. Get really fast with those fingers.

Practice lengthening your stride. Write until your fingers slow down enough that you begin to notice the words on the page. Don't re-read them. Give your hands a rest while you go stick your head in a bucket of water, come back later, and do it again with a completely fresh set of characters and scene, on a completely different subject.

Do it again. And again. All disconnected. Rambling. Write about your day ("I am so tired of cornflakes I can't even tell you") or your fight with your stupid sister ("and then *she* said—and then *I* said—") or people who won't leash their dogs in public ("I could rake *my* nails down *their* legs") or any object in your line of sight ("a basket handwoven of palm leaves in 1994 full of mahjongg pieces from two different, battered, old Hawaiian sets, only the green has faded to a browning jade with bits of pale light through the chinks").

If you find yourself rattling on about fictional characters you've rattled on about before, make absolutely no effort to link the two pieces or give them similar plots. Pile up those pages. Lean the towers into corners so they don't fall over and crush you.

Far too much is made of product in this age of heavily-categorized literary genre. Every word is supposed to be saved and sold, or it isn't worth putting down.

Reverse your mental paradigm: *Write everything as if it will never be read.*

Utter and complete freedom: random acts of literature.

In the meantime, study the art of plotting, practice brainstorming simple plots, go out and take copious notes on observing characters, places, things. Jot down exchanges of dialog as they come to you. Make yourself laugh, make yourself cry, make yourself wonder what it's all about. Learn proper grammar and punctuation. Labor away, if you must, at whatever manuscript you're working on, but *do not* attempt to cannibalize your random literature.

Do not.

Go back to your keyboard and write as though you're being chased by pirates with machetes. Don't read it! Don't even listen to yourself! For god's sake, I tell you—*don't listen to yourself.*

Have a life.

Eventually you'll find yourself alone on a cold autumn evening with a fire in the fireplace and a hot toddy by your elbow and a cat on your lap, and you'll feel an overwhelming curiosity to read some of what you wrote. It will feel exactly like the urge to read your favorite book, if you'd never read it before.

So you take a stack of pages and dump them by your most comfortable chair, get the cat again, and sink in. And you read. . .oh, you read. . .like Rabbit running, you read.

Mountains and towers and oceans of this stuff. All so much more vivid and powerful and in-the-moment than the stories you've labored so long and so grievously over. Unimaginable suffering.

And here you produced this without even thinking.

Chapter 28

Writing for Love or Money

Can you support yourself by writing?

I have a friend who does remote-control intervention when she thinks I'm losing it at the keyboard. "Put down the computer. Step away slowly, with your hands in the air."

She does this for my own good because—just like you—I've been writing since I was a fairly young child and have long since incorporated in my brain a direct link between what goes on in the twisted, convoluted, unhealthy recesses of my cerebrum and what happens in my fingers, which gaily record it all in words.

The other night I was writing a scathing email to someone when my laptop battery died, and while I was plugging in the cord my husband came into the room, so I took the opportunity (which I had earlier been too incensed to wait for) to tell him about my outrage before returning to that golden Send key—when I realized during the explanation that I was completely mistaken and on the verge of alienating an innocent friend over nothing.

I'd misread something, that was all.

At times like this it's clear that I need the direct link surgically removed, a sort of authorial frontal lobotomy specifically designed to keep me from writing down things *that don't need to be written down*.

An obsessive compulsion that would reign unchecked in my heart my whole life long, whether anyone ever found out about it or not.

Do I make a lot of money with this obsessive compulsion? Well, I used to make a really solid wage as a technical writer and editor, as do many of my friends and ex-co-workers yet. It was much better than I could have earned as a newspaper or even magazine journalist. But since the economy went down the tubes and took most of the computer documentation industry down with it, I'm no longer employable as a telecommuter. (Unfortunately, even starvation is better than moving back to Silicon Valley.) My husband continues to make decent money as a technical writer, but only because he stuck with it during the ten years' hiatus that I took to raise our young son, so he'd already ensconced himself firmly in a telecommuting job before the economy hit the iceberg. So we still own a house. We don't live in our parents' basements.

Of course, I used to gripe a lot about technical writing. "I hate computers," I whined to my husband. "I hate engineering. I don't *care* about this crap." I wanted to be writing fiction, only with a computer company signing my paychecks.

I learned a lot in my years as a technical writer: solid organization, clarity, tidiness, getting to the point, why easy words are the best words, keeping a reader's attention, and what happens to a writer who thinks they're too smart for their audience. I also became so completely habituated to proper punctuation and grammar that I could probably copy edit now in my sleep.

But I was writing fiction and poetry for decades—that's decades—before I took my college mentor's advice and went into technical documentation.

I wrote fiction and poetry while earning a starving wage as editor-in-chief of the smallest newspapers in the Pacific Northwest, moonlighting as a typesetter and graphic artist to make ends meet. I wrote fiction and poetry as a skrimshander. I wrote fiction and poetry after I broke my arm and spent two years in multiple surgeries, writing for awhile with my left hand (partly to strengthen the muscles and partly to freak my sister out). I wrote fiction and poetry the entire time I was a computer science student at the highly technical Cal Poly San Luis Obispo. I knew that fiction writers usually can't even earn a living. I absolutely had that on my radar. I was going to be a computer scientist because I wanted to be able to pay my bills.

And I wish I had a nickel for everyone who came up to me during that time and said, "You're in the wrong department. Why aren't you in English?"

What could I say? "Why are you in English? Do you believe in fairies?"

Then one fall at the end of three years of computer science I went into a decline. I stopped attending classes. I stopped writing computer programs. I stopped studying for midterms. I started sneaking around in the middle of the day, slipping into Leon's Used Book Store when no one was looking, sidling down the aisles to the back, opening old books and holding them to my face. Breathing deeply.

The smell. The beloved smell of *words*.

I began reading fiction starvingly, obsessively, uncontrollably. Then one evening I got a computer assignment back with just the rudest criticism—really high-handed, fundamentally ignorant nitpicking. I knew my stuff. My mentor was the head of the Computer Science Department. And I knew that this was petty ostracization because I wasn't one of the teenage boys hanging out in this professor's office.

I threw my keyboard in the air over my head.

It was 11:45 on a Tuesday night. One of the happiest days of my life was walking into that professor's midterm — for which I had not studied one word — carrying the paperwork to drop out of the Computer Science Department.

"I hope it wasn't something I said." He snickered.

There is a truth about yourself that you learn from having been around for a long time, and this is which of your dreams fulfill the needs of a phase of your life and which ones fulfill the needs of the whole thing.

Do you ever wonder whether you're writing for love or money?

Quit. For a long time. Try to make it in a better-paying field. I mean, give it your *all*.

If you succeed in a field in which you can make more money, then by all means pursue that career and write fiction on the side. Write when you can, because you can, and because, as O'Connor said, you're good at it. Submit to magazines not because you're desperate for pay (which you won't get until you've been accepted by a lot of magazines that only want to send you contributors' copies, anyway), but because you love this work. And it's fun to see your name in print. And you meet lots of nice people who also love this work. And because rejection doesn't hurt nearly as badly when you're not fooling yourself into thinking — with that gamblers' logic — that you are just about to become financially-independent.

But if you don't make it in a better-paying field, then buckle down and get to work learning the writing business.

If you want a salaried job, get a degree in journalism or study a technical, financial, or medical field — you might very well need a degree in that, too — and learn how to put together a writer's resume and get a job interview in the industry.

If you want to be a freelance contractor, learn to research and write magazine articles and ad copy. Learn lean, clean cover letters, query letters, and spec. Learn about editors' calendars and follow-up and deadlines. Make friends in high places.

If you want to be a book author, learn not only lean, clean query letters, but also synopses and nonfiction book proposals. Research agent lists, contract language, publishing terminology, self-promotion, and how much you can expect to spend on editing, a book tour, and PR. Start building a presence on social media in your nonfiction field. Write a first book and get a really good independent editor.

Study the system by which either a nonfiction book proposal or a novel is submitted to agents, eventually (hopefully) picked up by one, submitted a second time to publishers' acquisitions editors, eventually (hopefully) discussed at length in weekly meetings and benefit-cost analysis sessions, eventually (still hopefully) offered a publishing contract for, and maybe even (if the stars are right) published. Find out what first-time and midlist authors earn. Understand advances, royalties, backlists, returns, and digital, foreign, and subsidiary rights, and research the percentage of new books that actually earn out their advances. Balance your budget. Build up your savings.

Also study the system by which the author of such a book promotes it, builds on its success, and comes back with an even stronger, punchier, more on-target second book that will meet or beat its predecessor. And a third. And a fourth. And a fifth.

Know about Bookscan.

And finally, study the entire contemporary publishing industry meticulously to determine where in it you stand, where you want to stand, and how to get from one place to the other.

Can you write for both love and money? Yes, you can. Is it going to be the way you always dreamed it would be? No, it is not.

Do you have it in you to deal with this?

Well? Do you?

Chapter 29

Career

Can you support yourself while writing?

I've worked with a lot of writers – rank amateurs and fresh-faced hopefuls, struggling perfectionists, soul-searching literati, wildly talented unpublished scribblers, midlist genre names with agents, unsung heroes and reclusive geniuses and award-winning novelists.

Each of these people, in one way or another, woke up one morning and said to themself, "You know what I ought to do? I ought to devote a huge chunk of my life energy and more spare time than I've got telling my fantasies, hopes, dreams, fears, memories, opinions, and sometimes sheer inanity to people who can't interrupt. That would be satisfying!"

Flannery O'Connor said that you can write for a living so long as you're married to someone rich who can type.

John Gardner once wrote a marvelous piece on the best choice of day-job for a fiction writer, assuming (as he was right to assume) that a serious writer needs one. He recommends mail carrier, but he really takes the wind out of the sails of anyone considering fire ranger. He says that doggone radio never shuts up.

Far be it from me to contradict anybody with a track record like Gardner's (although I made my husband sell the motorcycle after we had the baby). But there are one or two other pretty good jobs for writers out there, and you should know about them:

#1: Technical writer

Did someone say professional writer? Yes, I did. With good pay and benefits? Yes. Regular hours, other writers as co-workers, knowledgeable editors at your beck and call, even (if you draw the short straw) someone in the next cube who's an expert on obscure historical grammar points, although he doesn't know the difference between 'that' and 'which' and is willing to come to blows over it? Yes, yes. All this great stuff. Why didn't anybody tell you before?

It's not a secret. It's simply that English Departments, where most writers get their start, don't think of themselves as spawning grounds for technical geeks and therefore don't broadcast geek opportunities the way they do, say, the opportunities to earn teaching credentials and join their own ranks.

Also, the computer documentation bubble burst rather spectacularly in the summer of 2008, when the industry suddenly, *en masse*, decided that it could off-shore its writing departments to countries where the cost of living—and therefore the cost of writers—is considerably less.

But the medical field is booming, and if you have at least a Bachelor's Degree, are an accomplished writer, know your grammar and punctuation inside-out, think logically, make deadlines under pressure, take direction well, are willing to work alongside others, and have some classes in medicine under your belt (or are about to get some) so that you can interact intelligently with your technical colleagues, it's worth looking into.

However.

And this is a big however—please do not attempt to break into any aspect of the technical writing field without *all* (much less any) of these credentials.

Technical writing is a career. The writers and editors who work in the field and their hiring managers are professionals. They've learned their craft in the same way that other professionals learn theirs, through education, experience, and years of dedication—just like doctors, just like lawyers, just like plumbers. They have to. These people earn their paychecks.

#2: Teacher

This one you probably already know about. You probably already *are* a teacher. If you're lucky, you're a professor. If you're really, really lucky, you've got tenure. Nice work if you can get it.

Lots and lots (and lots and lots) of publishing fiction authors are English teachers. English teachers know writing. They know grammar and punctuation. They've studied the literary canon, so they're equipped to recognize the same problems quickly and can often tell how to fix them.

Most of all, they love English. The language. The history. The literature. They love dinking around with things like subjunctives, points of view, themes, premises, post-post-modern literary criticism, and other people's dangling participles.

The downside to teaching is teaching. When you teach, you have scores of people for whose education you're responsible, which means classes, tests, office hours, term papers. Grading term papers takes a lot of hours. Grading poor term papers takes a lot of hours and a lot of *heart*.

Also, public school and many private grammar school teachers earn very little. They get benefits, and they get their long, gorgeous, golden summers off. They also get to grade on their own time, worry over students they care about being shuttled through education like cattle through a chute, and sometimes even buy their own class supplies. And you need a Bachelor's Degree and Teaching Credential to join them.

Community college professors do better, but you need a Master's Degree to teach anyplace accredited.

State college and university professors eat cake, but you need a PhD to teach there.

By all means, if you have the intelligence, passion, and degree it takes, throw yourself into the pool. You'll find yourself rubbing elbows with actual, talented, publishing authors, as well as plenty of accomplished writers just as interested in becoming published as you are.

#3: Journalist

You want to learn to write lean, clean, mean copy fast whenever you want, under deadline, with demons breathing down the back of your neck?

Become a journalist.

Newswriting is heavily structured. It is ruthlessly edited. And it's *constant*. Every morning daily newspaper journalists get up and face the very same deadline they faced the day before. The minute their articles are finished (sometimes before), they're whisked off their desks to the editors' slicing and gutting arena, and—hey, presto!—into print. There's absolutely no better environment to teach you to detach from your work.

Journalists are writing machines. They know how to lead with their best foot forward even when they don't have a best foot (study newswriting to learn to identify your whole point). They know how to follow structure to the letter, even if that means counting the words in a lede sentence and paragraph (study newswriting to learn to line edit). They know how to organize information (study newswriting to learn clarity). They know how to shoot the reader off the end of an article into the next article (study newswriting to learn about cutting resolution and denouement). They get the living daylights edited out of their work (study newswriting to learn how to trim and *cut, cut, cut*).

The only thing they don't do is Hook and Climax—in newswriting, the Hook *is* the Climax. This is because news readers often don't get beyond the first paragraph.

If you're dedicated, smart, fast, not particularly technical and not planning on becoming technical, don't have a degree but are interested in earning a living as a writer, go into journalism. The benefits to your writing skills are enormous.

The pay can be middling, but you sure stay up-to-date on the news.

#4: Librarian, English Department staff, or administrator

Any work in which you are exposed on a daily basis to good writing, among others who share your affection for and interest in it, is good work for a fiction writer. Most of these jobs don't pay much, and if they do you should count yourself very lucky. But they're often pleasant, in nice surroundings, and relatively easy to do with a basic skill set. They're also usually not nearly so rigid about the degree requirement. (Administrative positions are, but they pay a lot better than the others, too.)

Most importantly, you get to make friends with people with degrees in the field of writing who probably know a lot more than you about it, might even be talented and publishing authors themselves, and therefore could be willing to share their expertise and contacts with you for the price of (you) being fun and entertaining. Never underestimate the value of a well-connected personal friend.

If you can't get work somehow associated with writing or literature, take Gardner's advice and look for work that gives you as much time as possible for your writing while keeping you off the streets. Get used to living cheaply.

I'm a fiction writer, but I earn my living as an independent editor.

Gardner was a best seller, but he earned his living as a university professor.

Chapter 30

Professional Habits

Publishing

Handling Rejection

Say you've decided to go for it. You've decided you want to be a traditionally-published writer.

Congratulations! Welcome to the wide, wonderful world of *rejection*.

There's a trick to handling rejection letters: stay in motion. Publishing writers are like the plastic ducks in the shooting gallery at the carnival.

Don't be a sitting duck.

Granted, some rejection letters are quite *encouraging* rejections. The editor thanks you so much for giving them a chance to read your story, says "a lot of good writing crosses our desks that we don't have the right spot for," and asks you to continue submitting. You would do well to get up the next morning and print out another story to send off to them, along with a freshly-edited copy of the first story to send to someone else.

And some rejections letters come with personalized advice. Those get framed and posted over your desk.

And some rejections letters are just bonkers. They're for comic relief. Yes, even agents and magazine editors can be insane.

Stay in motion. This is the publishing writer's mantra.

Muriel Spark has described how she typed and re-typed her stories for years, putting them back in the mail the day after she'd received the latest rejections, scraping and scrounging pennies to pay for postage.

I advise aspiring writers who want to publish to launch into a bout of magazine submissions with three to five stories and send them off one at a time to three to five publications, mark down what was sent where (this is important), and get right to work on new writing.

In a few months, when you hear back, do another editing pass on the pieces that haven't sold yet, rotate them around the list, and send them off again. And again. And again. And again. Five stories times five magazines is twenty-five submissions. Any time you have another five stories ready to go down the pipeline, select another five magazines and start the cycle on them, too.

You know what's very efficient about this system? It eliminates multiple submissions.

Now, some writers *love* multiple submissions. Some can't do without them. Some worry obsessively that they'll grow old and wind up shuffling around in walkers before they ever get published if they do only exclusive submissions. Lots of magazines understand this and accept multiple submissions with grace. All they ask is that you notify them immediately if your story is accepted elsewhere. 'Immediately' is a word that writers who submit multiple submissions should have tattooed on their foreheads. This is professional courtesy.

But I, personally, don't need that tattoo, because I don't have that kind of organizational pizzazz, the kind that allows you to keep track of not one but several submissions of the same piece to a variety of magazines, along with the outcomes of those various submissions. I would like to say I do. But I don't. You know how a fuse looks in a movie right after it's been lit, and it's popping and fizzing and getting brighter and quicker every second while you watch in frozen horror as it inches toward the heroine and hero? That's my brain on multiple submissions.

So keep moving.

And writing. One story does not a writer make. Like you, I love my early works. I would like to have them carved on my headstone after I'm gone, and that's the only way they're ever going to be published, not because they're not full of witty asides and utterly brilliant insights and heart-breaking characterizations, but because they're not professional enough. I edited and edited and edited, and all my favorite parts—the unprofessional parts—are still there.

(I don't have this problem with client manuscripts because line editing is the one aspect of editing that can only be done properly on other writers' work. I simply can't line edit my own manuscripts all the way. I have *tried*.)

The more you write, the better your writing becomes, and that later work is the work that editors want to see. So keep writing. The work will keep getting more professional. And keep sending it out.

It's kind of nice for the obsessive-compulsive part of the writer's brain, the part that would like to spend a few days sorting colored beads into egg cartons.

It might sound like a lot of trouble, however, to someone who just wants to write that breakout novel and begin collecting infusions of bidding-war advances in large, unwieldy chunks.

It *is* a lot of trouble. It's an *insane* amount of trouble. Nobody said that writers are geniuses. We're not. We're obsessive-compulsives who have chosen this particular bone to whittle into toothpicks with our little homemade hunting knives.

Those of us who publish write because we *love* it. Most of us were writing long, long before any editor ever looked in our direction, much less gave us that gold-plated nod of acceptance. We wrote. We wrote. We wrote.

And now we also send out, send out, send out. And we rip open envelopes with our own names written in our own handwriting—stamped with our own stamps—and put those reject/accept check marks next to those magazine names on those lists taped to our desks, polish up, and send out again. When we're not either poring over the lists, or re-editing recent rejections, or making quick friendly little trips to the mailbox for more envelopes we addressed to ourselves. . .we write.

We're busy little obsessive-compulsives. We keep our ducks in a row.

Querying

Generic Agent or Current Resident
Random Literary Agency
New York, NY

Dear Agent,

What if purple aliens that looked just like you and my mother were the only people left after the nuclear holocaust, and they had to repopulate the planet? I wouldn't tell this idea to anyone except you because I think you could really write a great book about it, and we could split the dough. I'd give you half, even though it's my genius, guaranteed blockbuster idea. I'm super generous. Plus, I'm the next Ursula Leguine, only better-looking. And I'll tell you how the story ends when you get to that part!! (hint: it's on the last page!)

Don't try to write back to me, because this is my boyfriend's email account and he'd get jealous (HA HA).

I'll call you in half an hour, just so you know to pick up when you hear it's me, and we can talk about what you're going to get me for the movie. I'll make some kind of noise like a purple alien would make.

Ringy-dingy!
Aspiring Writer

Dear Aspiring Writer:

If you're trying to engage my professional attention, you've failed. If you're pulling my leg, you're freaking me out. And I'm not even going to tell you what the agent said.

Sincerely,
A. Victoria Mixon, Editor
Generic Agent's First Line of Defense

When Wendy Burt-Thomas and I began talking about our interview on query letters, based on her 2009 book *The Writer's Digest Guide to Query Letters*, we discovered that we shared an unusual passion: making up bad examples. She made up all the examples of bad query letters in her book, and I made up the fiction samples I use to demonstrate editing for my website.

"Isn't it the *best*?" Wendy said.

It is! You'd be amazed how much you can learn by practicing something wrong. For one thing, you have to learn what wrong is. And you have to really, truly understand why it's wrong.

1) Why do we not address query letters generically?
2) Why do we not assume personal friendship with professionals we've never met?
3) Why do we not expect agents to be so wowed by our ideas that they're willing to write our books for us?
4) Why do we not tout ourselves as "the next famous author" or our stories as "guaranteed blockbusters"?
5) Why do we have to make absolutely certain that we spell all names correctly? Use impeccable grammar and punctuation? Use exclamation points incredibly sparingly?
6) Why do we not withhold the surprise ending of our stories from agents?
7) Why do we have to make ourselves easily accessible?
8) Why do we not call agents up without an invitation, particularly half an hour after we've sent our queries?
9) Why do we not leap right into discussing big-ticket items like movies?
10) Why do we not make weird noises on agents' answering machines?

Let's take these one at a time:

1) Why do we not address query letters generically?

Do we like getting junk mail? Envelopes that go right through our hands into the trash? And do we get so much mail every day that we have to hire people just to sort out the pertinent letters from the recycling?

Agents don't like junk mail any more than we do, and they get far more mail than they can ever read in comfort—day in and day out, weeks without end. The very least we can do is let them know that we know there's a human being on the other end of our queries, someone whose time and brains and experience matter, someone with an identity, a life, and a name.

2) Why do we not assume personal friendship with professionals we've never met?

Agents work hard. They like to get a little professional respect and courtesy. They don't ask for a lot—not red carpets unrolling before their feet as they walk down the sidewalk, or their personal reserved table at Tavern on the Green, or genuflections from publishers' acquisitions editors every time they come through the door (that's only the first Monday of the month)—but some. Enough for strangers to address them as Ms. or Mr. in a business letter and treat them as though reading queries were work, not dropping by a writer's kitchen to borrow cooking utensils that they're probably never going to return.

3) Why do we not expect agents to be so wowed by our ideas that they're willing to write our books for us?

Agents like to write their books about their own ideas better. They're selfish that way. We just have to get used to it.

4) Why do we not tout ourselves as "the next famous author" or our stories as "guaranteed blockbusters"?

An agent is not easily impressed by hyperbole. Not even really good hyperbole. Not even *ours*. And using it is like throwing ourselves on them across their desk and grabbing them by the lapels.

They don't enjoy it. It feels a little invasive. It disturbs their vibe. It also makes them thankful yet again that they installed that quick-ejector seat in their office, the one they call The Circular File.

5) Why do we have to make absolutely certain that we spell all names correctly? *Can't agents tell whom we mean (especially if*

we mean someone famous)? Why do we have to make absolutely sure that we have impeccable grammar and punctuation and use exclamation points incredibly sparingly? (Don't publishers have editors to fix all that?)

If we're not big enough kids to look up how to spell the names of the people we want to impress an agent with or how to use proper grammar and punctuation, we're not big enough kids to play on the agents' playground. It's that simple.

6) Why do we not withhold the surprise ending of our stories from agents?

They've heard it all. Truly. They're not going to be surprised by anything we think up. Even Woodward and Bernstein had to tell their editor that they were never going to identify Deep Throat.

7) Why do we have to make ourselves easily accessible?

Agents get thousands and thousands of queries, all of them from writers just as hungry as we are. If they have a choice between our brilliant novel and another author's equally-brilliant novel, and they can only get ahold of one of us easily, which one would we like that to be?

8) Why do we not call agents up without an invitation, particularly half an hour after we've sent our queries?

They will not only refuse to take our calls, they will post our query letters to the agents' secret website that serves the same purpose as the bulletin board of bounced checks at the corner liquor store.

9) Why do we not leap right into discussing big-ticket items like movies?

The agent, if they decide to represent us, will deal with that issue when the time comes. They know how to tell when it does—they will let us know.

10) Why do we not make weird noises on agents' answering machines?

Okay, that one I actually do.

Now I'm going to suggest something revolutionary, outside-the-box, inexplicable. Something fun! I'm going to suggest that you give yourself the chance to make up your own Hooks from Hell. Not because you would ever use them—I know you wouldn't—but just to get the hang of it. Here are a few more for you, to prime the pump:

> My mother told me I should write to you because she loves my story and thinks I should turn it into a novel. She thinks if you encourage me, I will.

> I haven't written this yet, but I know it would make a killr book and maybe you could help me with the editting if I really needed some like for grammer and punctuation wich, honestly I could care less about anyway

> I really want to get on Oprah. If you come up with an idea, I promise to try to write about it, and we could both make a million bucks. Just don't go behind my back to get on Oprah before me, that's all.

> You're probably an okay guy, and that's why I'm writing to you. I saw a picture of an agent on a website once, and he looked not completely insane, and I figure all you agents probably look alike, so why not write? Rite? You're probably not a big fat stupid ugly loser, like that last agent I contacted.

Composting Your Writing Skills

Finally—let's talk about downtime. We won't call it writer's block. We'll call it. . ."composting."

How many times has someone told you not to fight the downtime of the writing cycle? And how many times have you listened? Probably about as often as I have, which is never. But that's no reason not to start now. Everybody's got to start sometime.

One of the biggest evils of our consumer society is the blatant lie that if we all kick into the highest gear possible and force ourselves to stay in that gear indefinitely, we'll be able to get more stuff for more money in an even bigger mountain faster than our neighbor before we die.

You can see who benefits from this plan. And it's not us.

But this doesn't seem to stop people from trying. For awhile, marketers were even applying this social model to newborn infants, urging parents to flash math cards in front of the eyes of teeny squishy people who were probably just thinking, "Little flat birds?" I suppose you can't live in the land of insanely-stupid ambition forever. I don't think the Super Baby people are getting much press these days.

Yes, it takes practice to learn to write. Yes, it takes time, patience, and long-term dedication. Yes, if you hope to be a publishing author you will have deadlines to meet, contracts to honor, schedules to keep.

But you will still have your life to live.

I vividly remember being in my peeling blue-painted bathroom in Northwest Washington one morning in the 1980s, looking at the flowering lilac outside the window and thinking that the happiest thing in the world would be knowing that I'd never write another poem again. I quit writing poetry for a long time after that.

It felt *great*.

When I went back to it several years later, I got the surprise of my life. My skills had improved! Without practice! All those years of life experience had made me a much better writer by *osmosis*.

I have a friend who is not only an amazing success as a fiction author, but also a professor of Native American studies, a lawyer, an active human rights advocate, a world traveler, and the mother of three. I'm not suggesting that you run out and try to become her, because you can't. I'm staggered that even *she* can be her. But I am saying that I once received an email from her in Italy, where she and her husband were working that spring, saying that she'd hardly done any writing lately. What I am saying is that even the best and brightest among us is subject to the writing cycle.

Take heart! Being away from your desk is not akin to being Dostoyevsky's brooding, demented narcissist sitting around in the dark thinking of ways to drag innocent passers-by under the floorboards with you. You might be feeling a little down today, maybe not at your best. It happens. But there are no Keyboard Cops.

Maybe you woke up this morning thinking about adding ground oyster shells to your acidic soil before your vegetable starts' tender little eyes pop right out. Or maybe you got into some really ugly subject matter in the piece you were working on last week and need to take a step back and watch some great BBC show like *Jeeves and Wooster* to avoid going into emotional arrest. Or maybe someone you love and want to love your work was less than flattering in a comment recently.

Or maybe (like me) you tried to make popcorn about two hours ago to get yourself motivated for a difficult chapter and spent the next forty-five lively minutes in the backyard shoveling dirt into a saucepan leaping with foot-high flames.

I really didn't want to get started on that chapter, anyway.

We writers have our up days. The stars are aligned, the house is quiet, the weather is perfect, the child is charming and busy in their room. Something has surfaced—some extraordinary plot development or outrageous juxtaposition or brilliant insight, some unforeseen clue to throwing the reader over our shoulders like a captured deer and toting them back to camp amid cheers and applause.

We knew we were going to make it. After all those years of toil. We just *knew* it.

And we writers have our down days. We've used up all the compost in the bin. There's nothing left but coffee grounds, the neighbor's dog poop, and a plastic wrapper that missed the garbage can. We poke around a little, but, come on. We know we're not going to use *that*.

You wouldn't want to push someone into trying to use dog poop and a plastic wrapper, would you? When you already know what can be accomplished with really rich, fruity loam?

Let it rest. Go read a book. Sit on your child's bed and listen to them explain in extraordinary detail why a 4-6-0 HO-scale model train locomotive is far and away superior to a Z-scale cupola caboose (depending upon the manufacturer).

Cook something that makes a lot of messy leftovers. Better yet, get a cup of tea and sit at the kitchen table watching your *beloved* cook something that makes a lot of messy leftovers. Arrange to lick out the bowl.

Wander around looking at your life.

Gaze out the window. Stare in amazement at the same stubborn hummingbird pecking and pecking and pecking at his reflection in the glass in front of your face. Write about being a writer, but not for publication. Go to the thrift store and buy a bunch of cheap second-hand paperbacks with 1950s covers. Don't forget to leaf through the record bins for old boogie-woogie and Dixie jazz. I came home with a stack of 78s six inches high, just this morning.

Stand in the yard and listen. Smell your husband's wool shirt. Pick things up and touch them all over. Hunt down some really good gossip about someone you like a lot, and pay very close attention.

Look at your life. Look at your life. Look at your life.

It's all going in.

Chapter 31

Stepping into History through Literature

A writer's legacy

Fiction is pretend. History is real. Fiction is entertainment. History is the school of hard knocks. Fiction falls from the fingers of its author, willy-nilly, without interference from any outside source. History *is* the outside source.

You'd think history had blessed little to do with it.

If I were Samuel Beckett, I might claim to write in a historical vacuum. Poor Estragon and Vladimir wait and wait for Godot, cut off from the world around them. They could be anyone, from any land, in any human epoch.

But I'd be lying. *Waiting for Godot* clearly owes homage to *King Lear* and just as clearly influenced Tom Stoppard's *Rosencrantz and Guildenstern Are Dead*. History moves on, reflected in the parade of literature, from corrupt Elizabethan politics to the ennui of post-WWII shellshock to the absurdity of anti-establishment psychedelia.

In every era, the little folk face down the powers that be. In every era, the little folk's expectation of failure or success—the expectation of the *manner* of failure or success—alters.

We are the children of our times. When I was a child in the 1960s, dingaling hair-sprayed go-go girls danced in cages alongside idealistic hippies staging peace marches against the war. I grew up in the '70s, amid the cacophony of disco and fear of OPEC. I was a young adult in the '80s, when Reagan's Trickle-Down Economics brought us the tragic, mentally-ill homeless and the adult children of '60s radicals brought political activism into mainstream American culture.

There's *always* been the little folk. There are *always* the powers that be.

And through this we find our fiction, the imaginary universes we dream up, where three-dimensional flesh-&-blood characters grapple with the mocking forces of fate—sometimes gaining ground, sometimes losing it, sometimes on top of the wheel of cosmic fortune, sometimes dragging through the muck and slime at the bottom. They put on their go-go boots and pick up their peace signs and march out there to contend with life to the best of their abilities.

Will they fail?

Of course they will. Life is infinitely bigger, stronger, smarter, and better equipped than a go-go dancer in hair-spray or someone living on nuts and berries. Life is going to *kick their butts.*

Do we want to hear about it?

Of course we do. That's *us* in go-go boots, carting around those towering beehives. That's *us* crying out for peace. We long to be righteous, ethical, innocent, and courageous. Our hearts yearn for meaning. At the same time, we desperately need to belong.

Don't you know how to do the Funky Chicken? Don't you know how to Hustle?

Your fictional characters do. They know all about living heartfelt among the debris of the ridiculous. That's what history does to us.

Write it down. Testify to the real history of the human race.

We long to be remembered.

Conclusion

Tilting at Windmills with Miguel de Cervantes

What kind of person thrives as a writer?

When my husband and I built our house we were told that we could choose any two of three things: time, money, and quality. We could get quality without so much money as long as we had plenty of time. We could get quality without so much time as long as we had plenty of money. If we had neither time nor money. . . well, you can do the math.

How much time do you have? Conversely—how much money?

Of course, I'm pushing the analogy, because an infinite amount of time is not going to teach any of us to produce quality fiction if we don't use that time wisely. There is no point in grinding away in the same old rut year after year, decade after decade. We have to get traction and actually go somewhere.

On the other hand, plenty of money can buy us both perfectly decent ghostwriters *and* independent editors, and the American ant farm of celebrity autobiographies is here to prove it. Unfortunately, it can't buy us the taste and intelligence to pick the best ghostwriters, much less the highest-caliber editors. No, they're not all good. Some of them are *awful*.

It also can't make us authors.

So, what kind of person thrives as a writer?

You'd think the definition would change throughout the ages, as the publishing industry changes, wouldn't you? You'd think the writer who made it big in Elizabethan times wouldn't stand a chance here in the Land of Flash Fiction, or the nineteenth-century author who dished up those endless mountains of literary mashed potatoes would be buried under their own virtuosity long before they ran out of agents' doors on which to knock. But let's look a little closer.

Miguel de Cervantes Saavedra had a vision. Way, way back in 1605, he saw a quirky, motivated, completely unpredictable rascal up against impossible odds. What is the one thing we know about this rascal?

He never knows when he's beat.

On he goes, page after page, chapter after chapter, blundering through the landscape, misunderstanding normal every-day situations, chasing chimaeras, clinging with mind-boggling tenacity to his unique worldview even while his sidekick rolls his eyes and lolls his head in stupefaction.

So riveting is this lunatic that even today, four hundred years after his birth in the first European novel, the apex of his misadventures lends its name to the quintessential dilemma: tilting at windmills.

First—the kind of person who thrives as a writer is the kind who never knows when they're beat. Not only that, their characters don't, either. Year after year, decade after decade, the serious writer continues to get up in the morning, shake the kinks out of their neck, put on their tin-can armor, climb on their threadbare hobby horse, and in all solemn dedication go about the work of bringing down the Windmill of Writing. Are they intimidated by the size of the behemoth, its ferocity, its speed, its deafening roar? Are they daunted by the way the craft flies out of their grasp as soon as they think they've got a grip? Are they trembling even as they lift their quivering quill and launch themself yet again in its general direction?

Damn right they are! But what a *rush* when they've cantered exuberantly under its crushing arms, met in a clash of wood and metal, and come lolloping out the other side still in one piece. Hit me again, Miguelito!

Second—the kind of person who thrives as a writer makes their own dogged way. Granted, they use roads and, in all sincerity, ask and accept whatever good advice they can possibly get. (It can be terribly hard to sort out the good advice from the bad without help. People: *get help*.) But they don't sit down in the middle of a boggy field whining and cursing because the road doesn't go where they think it should. They get where they're going through their own stamina, resourcefulness, and sheer creativity. They do not bicker with the basic rules.

They store a roll of duck tape in the saddle bag and keep patching themself back together, pursuing the course of inventive mania with the respectful mien of a holy fool.

Third—the kind of person who thrives as a writer carries within them a core of sweetness, a pure and fundamental willingness to see life for what it is, in all its complexity and insanity and heartbreak and wildness and glory. Not all great writers are nice people. But all truly great writing has this sweetness as its kernel—this underlying assumption that life is worth immortalizing in art, that something good can come of all this anguish.

Now, you're going to say, "*I* never know when I'm beat! *I'm* basically a sweet person! God only knows, I'm a *fool*." Does this mean you'll make it?

If you take enough time—

If you scrape and save your pennies for the proper education and guidance—

If you cling to what is strongest and most paradoxical inside you, the unique quality at the very core, modeling yourself faithfully on the Man of La Mancha through thick and thin, through trouble and strife, come hell or high water, your whole life through—yes. I think I can safely guarantee that you will create the art you yearn to create.

You will transcend the madness.

And you and Don Quixote and I can clank our tankards over it afterward, in the eternal tavern of literary aspirations.

Appendix

Everything You Need to Know About Writing a Novel, in 1,000 Words

Plot

Plots are myriad, but plot structure is simple: Hook, Development, Climax.

Shakespeare's five-act play, Syd Field's three-act screenplay, Freytag's triangle (although Freytag called Development 'climax' and Climax 'resolution'—causing untold confusion): like a holograph, hook-development-climax works on all levels, from the big picture down through plot parts, chapters, scenes, to actual lines of dialog.

"Where the hell are we?" Kerouac yells.

His driver yells the answer and calls for another drink.

Hook your reader (make them curious), tell your story, throw them off the rainbow when you're done.

The five biggest mistakes in plotting:

1) Starting with backstory. I know, chronology works in life, but not so well in fiction. Chronology did work back when Moll Flanders wanted to tell us all about where she came from before she told us where she wound up. But that was then. This is now. Hook your reader first. You've got to make them curious before they'll listen.

2) Letting the Development sag. The middle of a book is common bogland, and that's why you hear so many people say, "I started that book, but never finished it." F. Scott Fitzgerald spent a lot of energy (and his publisher's patience) on the galleys because *The Great Gatsby* sagged mid-way. It's the writer's job to keep upping the ante on the complications, starting a bigger problem the minute the last one's resolved, keeping the reader turning those pages.

3) Dragging out your Resolution. The Climax is what your reader is reading for, and when they've found it—they're done. If at all possible, end at the instant of Climax, like Henry James in "The Turn of the Screw," when the child's heart just stops. You may grieve to let your characters go, but your reader simply wants to find out what happened. And if you're so talented they can't let go—wow! Even more reason to quit while you're ahead. The best compliment a writer can get is, "I didn't want that book to end." Hello, Constant Reader.

4) Scrambling your plot. It's true, some brilliant works have been written in which the catastrophe is the Hook and the rest of it is exploration of that catastrophe, but this is sleight-of-hand. A story is the process of leading the reader through all joy and anguish to the whole point. The end.

5) Using a trick ending. Never conceal information from the reader so you can slam them with it on the last page. Even mysteries, which appear to be all about trick endings, give the reader clues to see through the trick before they get to the Climax. John Gardner was adamant: if you set the reader up to resent you—they will. Good-bye, Constant Reader.

Character

It might be your Hook that catches the reader's attention, but it's your characters who drag them in and hang onto them for dear life. Know thy characters. They must be real people, not two-dimensional cartoons, with real bodies, real mannerisms and tics, real foibles, dreams, insights, and idiocies to be ashamed of. Know them backward and forward. Then don't tell it all. Hemingway taught us the dignity of an iceberg is due to the weight below the water.

Scenes

You need tension on every single page, according to Donald Maass, and this is about as good as writing advice gets.

Description

Keep the details brief and telling. Raymond Chandler used to be able to burn up a whole first chapter describing a house. We can't do this anymore. Everyone knows what a house looks like. Find those details that make a person, place, or thing significant or unique, mention them, and get back to your characters.

Action

Fitzgerald taught us that action is character. No matter what complications you throw at your characters, no matter what Climax you have in store, each character must act in the only way they know how.

If you've got characters who can act in various ways, you don't know your characters well enough. Learn them. They have reasons for only being able to respond one way. And the different ways different characters deal with pressure is where the tension lies, so it's best to have characters with very different personalities going through this dreadful hell together.

As we all know, action is not always external. Action is very often internal. Conflict is very often internal. Total climactic catastrophe—as we all know—is only too often internal.

Dialog

Leave out most of the words. No kidding. Leave out oh, well, yes, no, um, uh (definitely these last two). Leave out names except for extreme emphasis. Leave out first articles and even subjects of sentences wherever possible. Do you answer a question with, "It's on the table," or with, "On the table"? Try it and see how much snappier your dialog becomes.

For heaven's sake, leave out ellipses. Be like Emily Brontë and use em-dashes instead. Leave off dialog tags. Replace them with brief significant actions or, if you can get away with it, nothing at all. A book filled with characters talking the way we really talk, *with tags*, goes on forever and bores even the writer to tears.

Unless absolutely necessary, make characters talk at cross-purposes. How many of us actually listen to other people? We don't. We're always thinking about what to say next, when they shut up.

Exposition

Exposition seeks not to just inform but to enlighten. Don't waste your reader's time with explanations. They've got brains. Let them use them. Leave out every explanation that can be inferred from the context. When you must cast light upon a scene, do it in context. Either you need to give the reader a breather between bouts of excitement or the tension can be heightened by knowing a little more about what's going on. Take advantage of pacing to interweave backstory and exposition, but always, always keep up with your characters.

Finally...

Never take it too seriously. Just take it seriously enough. You have a life to live.

Index

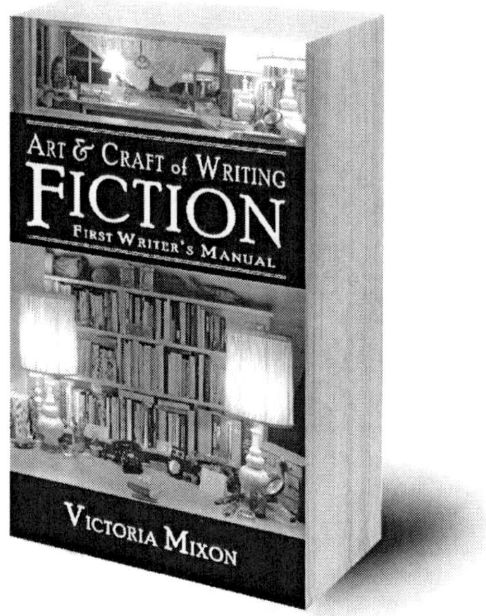

Please take a quick moment to review!

artandcraftofwriting.com/fiction

THANK YOU!

Art & Craft of Writing

Sign up to get your
free books on writing!

artandcraftofwriting.com/freebooks

**"Mixon is brilliant.
These are the lessons
of a writing lifetime."**
—Roz Morris, bestselling ghostwriter
and author of *Nail Your Novel*

artandcraftofwriting.com

About the Author

Mixon has been a professional writer and editor for over thirty years. She is the author of the Art & Craft of Writing series, including *Art & Craft of Writing Fiction: 1st Writer's Manual* and *Art & Craft of Writing Stories: 2nd Writer's Manual*. She is listed in the Who's Who of America and has been covered for her expertise in fiction by the *Huffington Post*. She teaches fiction through *Writer's Digest* and the San Francisco Writers Conference. Mixon is currently writing a forthcoming *noir* mystery series.

victoriamixon.com

@VictoriaMixon

CPSIA information can be obtained at www.ICGtesting.com
Printed in the USA
LVOW11s1507010816

498603LV00004B/432/P